Getting the Most from Broadband

Other Computer Titles

by

Robert Penfold

Getting the Most from Broadband

Robert Penfold

Bernard Babani (publishing) Ltd
The Grampians
Shepherds Bush Road
London W6 7NF
England
www.babanibooks.com

Please note

Although every care has been taken with the production of this book to ensure that any projects, designs, modifications, and/or programs, etc., contained herewith, operate in a correct and safe manner and also that any components specified are normally available in Great Britain, the Publisher and Author do not accept responsibility in any way for the failure (including fault in design) of any projects, design, modification, or program to work correctly or to cause damage to any equipment that it may be connected to or used in conjunction with, or in respect of any other damage or injury that may be caused, nor do the Publishers accept responsibility in any way for the failure to obtain specified components.

Notice is also given that if any equipment that is still under warranty is modified in any way or used or connected with home-built equipment then that warranty may be void.

© 2007 BERNARD BABANI (publishing) LTD

First Published - November 2007

British Library Cataloguing in Publication Data
A catalogue record for this book is available from the British Library

ISBN   978 0 85934 587 3

Cover Design by Gregor Arthur
Printed and bound by J. H. Haynes & Co. Ltd., Sparkford

Preface

Although the number of home broadband Internet connections has grown at a tremendous rate in recent years, the initial take-up was decidedly sluggish. I suppose that the lack of initial interest was not really all that surprising, considering the high installation cost at that time, and the monthly subscription rates were also very high by current standards. All the types of broadband connection available at that time required a visit from an engineer and the installation of some equipment in the user's home, even if the broadband connection was to be carried by the ordinary telephone lines.

Some types of broadband connection still require the services of an engineer and the installation of some extra equipment, but most home users settle for the simpler and cheaper alternative of the so-called "self-installed" broadband connection. With this method there is very little to install, and it is just a matter of using a broadband modem instead of a dial-up type, and fitting a low-cost filter at each telephone socket. The only other installation required is to have the telephone line broadband-enabled at the telephone exchange, and the cost of this is usually absorbed by the service provider. These days, a broadband connection usually costs no more than an unlimited dial-up type.

A broadband connection has two main advantages over a dial-up type, one of which is that it leaves the telephone line free for making and receiving ordinary telephone calls. The other is the increase in speed, which these days is likely to be at least 40 times that of the best dial-up connections. Even using a fairly "run of the mill" broadband connection opens up a range of possibilities that are beyond the capabilities of a dial-up Internet connection. You can listen to high quality stereo music streamed from Internet radio stations, watch streamed television programmes, download CDs, movies, computer programs, and other large files, and do anything that involves downloading large amounts of data. Ordinary web pages load much faster, and with broadband the Internet becomes a much more usable and exciting place.

Sharing an Internet connection between two or three computers in the same house via a simple network also becomes a practical proposition. Sharing an Internet connection is not totally impossible when using a dial-up connection, but a slow connection tends to become a painfully slow connection when shared among two or three computers! Sharing a typical broadband connection still leaves each user with something like ten times the bandwidth of an unshared dial-up connection.

In this book I have concentrated on Internet applications that really benefit from the speed of a broadband connection, which means that those that do not benefit greatly from the extra bandwidth of a broadband connection have not been included. This is not to say that I consider things such as bulletin boards and online auctions to be parts of the Internet that are not worthwhile or "old hat". It just means that they can be used very successfully using an ordinary dial-up connection and are not therefore fully germane to this publication. I have concentrated on aspects such as audio and video streaming, VoIP, and uploading/downloading large files, which are difficult or impossible without the speed of a broadband Internet connection. One obvious omission from this book is online gaming in its various forms, which is now too vast a subject to fit into a book of this type.

Robert Penfold

Trademarks

Contents

5

Blogging 117

Broadband
basics

Dial-up difficulties

There was only one way of connecting your home or small business to the Internet in the early days, and that was to use a dial-up connection. Your PC connected to the ordinary telephone socket via a device called a modem (modulator – demodulator), and the signal sent down the telephone line was a sort of warbling sound. Although a great deal of ingenuity went into getting the highest possible speed from this system, the limited bandwidth of an ordinary telephone line meant that the maximum achievable speed was quite modest.

In fact the highest speed achieved using the UK telephone system is 56 kilobits per second when receiving (downloading), and 33 kilobits per second when sending data (uploading). Actually, these speeds are the theoretical maximums, and in a practice it is unusual for anything close to these speeds to be achieved. A download speed of about 46 to 48 kilobits per second is more typical, and with a poor telephone connection a much lower speed would be likely.

Although the speed of a dial-up connection is not very high, it is actually adequate for most Internet surfing. New pages will not appear particularly fast, but in most cases any substantial lack of speed is due to the server being overloaded and causing long waits. The lack of speed tends to become more obvious if the Internet connection is used for anything beyond simple surfing.

Suppose you wish to download a music or program file that contains about 100 megabytes (100,000 kilobytes) of data. With a dial-up connection the actual download speed is unlikely to work out at much more than about 5 kilobytes per second. At this rate is would take over five and a half hours to download a 100 megabyte file. Something like a copy of a CD-ROM containing around 650 megabytes would take in the region of one and a half days.

Despite the low transfer rate, downloading large amounts of data using a dial-up connection is possible, provided you have the determination and patience of course. A lack of reliability can be a problem with dial-up connections, so the chances of downloading a file for many hours without interruption are probably quite small. There is a way around this in the form of a program called a download manager, which enables an interrupted download to be continued from where it left off. At least, it does provided the server at the other end of the system supports this facility.

For many users the main drawback of a dial-up connection is that long periods on-line mean that the telephone can not be used for other purposes. The telephone can not be used to make or receive telephone calls for the whole time that the Internet is being accessed. This contrasts with a broadband connection where the Internet connection is available whenever the computer is operating, and it does not restrict the use of the telephone in any way. There is no need to go through a dialling and connecting each time that Internet access is required. You just launch your browser program and start surfing the Internet.

ADSL broadband

The speed of a broadband connection depends on the type you obtain, plus technical considerations that might result in reduced rates. The type of broadband connection provided via an ordinary telephone line in the UK is the ADSL variety. ADSL stands for Asynchronous Digital Subscriber Line, and it is sometimes referred to as just DSL. The basic scheme of things is to have two signals carried by one pair of wires. One signal is the ordinary audio (voice) signal while the other is at a very high frequency that is well beyond the limits of human hearing. Filters are used to make sure that ordinary telephones only receive the audio signal, and that broadband computer equipment only receives the high frequency type.

While this arrangement is fine in theory, there are significant practical problems. These stem from the fact that the ordinary telephone lines are only designed to handle the low frequency signals from ordinary telephone handsets. They do not work well when carrying high frequency signals, and they tend to radiate the signal which can then cause radio interference. This system could potentially blight radio reception throughout the country, particularly on the medium and long wavebands. The high frequency signal has to be kept at a very low strength in order to reduce the problem with radio interference. This limits the speed that an ADSL broadband link can have for a given range from the telephone exchange.

In practice it is not quite as simple as that, since some telephone wires provide a higher quality connection than others. The fact that you live a few hundred metres from the local telephone exchange does not guarantee that a very high speed connection will be possible, although it certainly increases the chances. Another point to bear in mind is that the equipment in your local exchange might not be able to handle a very high connection speed.

The early ADSL services operated at relatively low rates, with a download speed or 512 kilobytes per second being typical. The upload rate was usually much lower, with a typical rate of 256 kilobytes per second. Evolving technology has resulted in generally higher download rates, with most ADSL broadband providers having one megabit (1024 kilobit) or two megabit (2048 kilobit) connections as standard. Higher rates of up to eight megabits (8192 kilobits) per second are offered by many providers, but bear in mind that this is the maximum rate and not a guaranteed minimum. In order to achieve this sort of speed you have to live within range of a suitably equipped telephone exchange, and have a connection of suitably high quality.

Unlike a dial-up connection, the quoted ADSL connection rate should be genuine rather than theoretical. If a broadband Internet provider states that you will be provided with a two megabit connection, then downloading at two megabits from a suitable server should certainly be possible. You will only get a lower rate if you live too far from the exchange for the full rate to be achieved, or if the quality of the connection is too low for some other reason. However, the broadband supplier should explain any reduction in the connection rate before you sign up to the deal, or give the option of cancelling the contract if a full-speed connection can not be provided.

With real-world broadband there are a few factors that can result in download rates that are slower than expected, but most of these are due to limitations elsewhere in the system, and not due to what could reasonably be considered problems with the Internet connection. There are one or two considerations that could result in a slight reduction in the download speed. However, these will mostly produce reductions of no more than a few percent, and are unlikely to be of any great practical significance.

An important point to keep in mind with ADSL broadband connections is that a super-fast download speed does not mean that the upload rate will be fast as well. It seems to be quite normal for the upload rate to be relatively slow at (typically) 256 kilobits per second even when very high download rates are used. In other words, the upload rate remains much the same as it was in the days when a 512 kilobit connection was the norm. This can limit the usefulness of the connection in some applications.

ADSL speed

Even a basic 512 kilobit per second broadband connection offers a download rate that is about ten times faster than the true rate of a 56 kilobit dial-up connection. The increase I obtained when changing from a dial-up connection to a 512 kilobit ADSL connection was actually about a twelve-fold increase. This clearly makes it much quicker and easier when downloading large files. In the earlier example of it taking a day and a half to download the contents of a CD-ROM, the download time would be reduced to about three hours or so using a 512 kilobit broadband connection. While this is still far from being instant, it represents a far more practical proposition.

A broadband connection opens up possibilities that are not available to dial-up users. It is possible to listen to streamed audio via a dial-up connection, and the audio quality can compare well with that of normal telephone quality. However, the bit rate is not high enough for true hi-fi quality even with a mono signal, and the quality with a stereo signal is likely to sound decidedly ropy at times. A broadband connection at a rate of 256 kilobits per second or more is more than adequate to provide high quality streamed audio in mono or stereo.

It is becoming increasingly common for the Internet to be used for streamed video, which usually comes complete with a streamed audio track as well. Although there are systems for sending audio and video over an ordinary dial-up connection, these provide only very limited resolution and overall quality. The reliability of these systems tends to be quite poor, which is presumably due to the problems with the quality of the Internet connection rather than limitations in the video encoding/decoding systems. A 512 kilobyte broadband connection can provide much better results, but do not expect DVD quality from what is, by video standards, quite a low bit rate. A download rate of one megabit a second or more is better for streamed video.

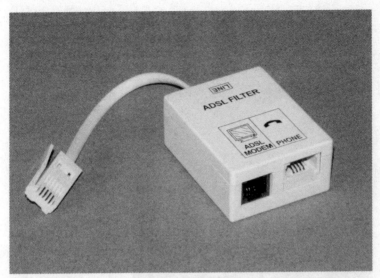

Fig.1.1 The most common form of microfilter

Installation

Having a broadband connection used to require an engineer to call and install some electronic equipment. This would typically leave the existing telephone wiring and equipment largely unchanged, but there would be an additional box having a networking socket, and this was the one used for the broadband connection. While having its advantages, an obvious problem with this method is that it involves the cost of having the engineer install and set up everything. This would often be a few hundred pounds.

The more popular method these days is to use a so-called "self installed" broadband connection. This does not involve any changes to the existing wiring, and requires only a minimal amount of additional equipment. Each telephone socket is fitted with a device called a "microfilter". A microfilter usually has a short lead that plugs into the telephone socket, and a couple of sockets on the main unit (Figure 1.1). One socket is for a telephone and the other is for the broadband modem. You can also obtain microfilters that look rather like a two-way telephone adapter (Figure 1.2), but one of the sockets is for a broadband modem. Remember, it is normally necessary to have one microfilter per telephone socket, and not just one filter at whichever socket happens to be used with the modem.

It is possible to use an ordinary modem with a telephone line that is broadband enabled, but the modem must be used via the ordinary telephone socket of a microfilter. It is possible that the filter will produce some loss of performance, although no problems were evident when I tried using a modem with two different microfilters. Although it is unlikely that you would need to use a dial-up connection when a broadband type is available, an ordinary modem might still be needed for sending and receiving faxes. Also, it is a good idea to have a dial-up connection available as a backup in case the broadband connection fails for some reason. Obviously the backup will be no use either if the lines goes "dead", but it does sometimes happen that the broadband connection is inaccessible while the line works fine in other respects.

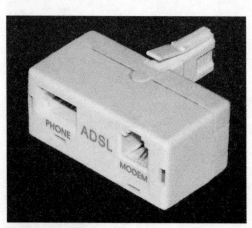

Fig.1.2 An alternative form of microfilter

All change

Of course, some changes have to be made at the telephone exchange in order to permit a telephone line to be used for a broadband Internet connection. This slightly complicates matters if you should decide to switch from one broadband provider to another. With a dial-up connection there is no need to have a period in which there is no Internet connection when you switch from one provider to another. It is perfectly possible to be signed up with two or more ISPs at once, so there can be an overlap between the end of one contract and the beginning of the next.

It is not currently possible to avoid at least a small gap in service when switching from one broadband supplier to another. The break in service is necessary because your telephone line is connected to the equipment of your ISP at the telephone exchange. When switching to another supplier it is necessary for the line to be disconnected from the equipment of your original supplier and then connected to the equipment of your new ISP. It is not possible to have a period during which your telephone line is connected to the equipment of both ISPs.

Most ISPs now co-operate when a switch in broadband supplier is required, and the break in service can be as little as an hour or two, but it will still occur. In order to obtain this fast switch from one supplier to another it is necessary to get a MAC (migration authorisation code) from your existing supplier. You then supply this code to the new broadband supplier when signing up with them. Of course, it is only possible to have the fast switch from one supplier to another if they both support this method. If one or both do not support it, there is no option other than letting your existing contract expire, and then signing up with another supplier "from scratch". Unfortunately, this can result of a gap of several weeks in duration while you are waiting for the new supplier to go through the process of connecting your line to their equipment.

Contentious point

With an ADSL broadband connection your computer is connected to the Internet via a pair of ordinary copper wires that were originally designed to carry voice signals. Modern technology manages to make very good use of what is really an old-fashioned system, but there are some compromises. One of these is that an ordinary ADSL connection is contended. In other words, some the connecting wires and equipment at the telephone exchange are used by more than one broadband connection. The number of broadband connections that share a single resource is called the contention ratio.

The contention ratio for a broadband connection intended for business use is relatively low, but is still likely to be 10:1 or 20:1. The figure for a home broadband Internet connection is usually more like 30:1 or 50:1. In theory, the actual connection speed of each line could be quite low at times of peak demand, since the overall bandwidth is shared by many users. The speed of each line would still be comfortably higher than a dial-up connection, and in practice there is little likelihood of even half the users using the system simultaneously. At least, I suppose it could happen occasionally for a fleeting moment, but it is unlikely that a large number of users would simultaneously download large amounts of data.

Contention ratios have not been a major issue in the past, since the actual ratios were far lower than the guaranteed maximum figures. Also, few people were using the Internet for applications that required vast amounts of data to be downloaded. This situation is obviously changing somewhat, with ADSL broadband now being used by relatively large numbers of people, and high bandwidth applications such as downloading television programs becoming very popular. This greatly increases the chances of the actual connection speed being significantly less than the connection speed quoted by your ISP. There could be a real advantage in using an ADSL broadband connection that has a relatively low contention ratio.

Cable

Note that there are no problems with contention ratios when using a cable broadband connection. The cable in this case is of the fibre-optic variety, which avoids some of the problems associated with an ADSL connection. The two cable operators in the UK have merged into a single company, and are now part of Virgin Media. Unfortunately, the cable network falls well short of covering the entire country, and in many areas it is simply not an option. Unless the cable network runs past your house it will not be possible to use this type of Internet connection. You can check whether the cable network is available at your postcode by going to the Virgin Media website and using their online checking service. This is the web address:

http://allyours.virginmedia.com/websales/ service.do?id=2&buspart=search

Points to remember

For most users there are two main advantages of a broadband connection, one of which is that it does not prevent the telephone line from being used to send and receive ordinary calls. Although a common set of connecting wires are used, you effectively have separate Internet and telephone lines.

The other main advantage is the relatively high rate at which data can be downloaded. A modern broadband Internet connection is typically about 40 times faster than a dial-up connection. Ordinary web pages download much faster when using a broadband connection, but the extra speed opens up new possibilities such as listening to high quality streamed audio, and large files such as complete movies can be downloaded in a reasonably short space of time.

It is no longer necessary to have an engineer install equipment in your home in order to use an ADSL broadband connection. With the self-install version of broadband it is just a matter of using the appropriate type of modem and plugging a microfilter into each telephone socket. A microfilter is normally used at every telephone socket in the house, and not just the one that is used with the modem.

An ordinary dial-up modem should work well with a telephone socket that is fitted with a microfilter. This is useful if you wish to have an ordinary dial-up Internet connection available as a standby, or if you still need to use an ordinary modem to send and receive faxes.

A high contention ratio means that your ADSL broadband connection is sharing resources with many other users. This could result in the connection speed being greatly reduced at times of high demand. Although the contention ratio has not been a major issue in the past, this could change in the future due to increased and more intensive use of the Internet.

Cable broadband is carried by fibre-optic cables which do not suffer from some of the problems associated with ADSL broadband and its simple copper connecting wires. However, the cable network is far less extensive than the ordinary telephone system, and it is simply not an option for people in many parts of the country.

Security matters

First line of defence

While a broadband Internet connection has massive advantages over a dial-up type, it also has one major drawback. It is obviously very convenient to have an Internet connection that is always available whenever the computer is switched on. There is no delay if you wish to go online to check your e-mail, do some research, or whatever. It also brings new possibilities, such as instant messaging and voice over Internet telephone systems. The Internet connection is always active, and is instantly available to any program that requires it.

The big drawback of a permanently-on Internet connection is that it makes your computer vulnerable to attack from hackers for long periods of time. More than this, the relatively high speed of the connection makes it possible for a successful attack to do a great deal of damage in a fairly short space of time. Malicious software can be downloaded by your PC in a matter of seconds. With a broadband connection you still have all the security issues associated with a dial-up connection, but the permanently-on the nature of the connection plus its high speed tends to multiply the problems. It is important to take security matters seriously with any Internet connection, but it is especially important with any form of broadband connection.

Choosing the right equipment can help to minimise the risk of attack from hackers. It is common for new users of broadband connections to use a basic broadband modem that typically connected to a USB port. This is all that is required in order to use the connection with a single PC, but from a security point of view it leaves something to be desired. The problem with this method is simply that there is no hardware barrier between the Internet and your PC. It gives hackers the opportunity to hack direct into your computer.

One of the big advantages of a broadband connection is that it is easily shared between two or more computers. This is achieved by using a device that is a combined modem and router. The router is the device that enables the computers to share a common Internet connection, and it ensures that the right data is fed to each PC in the system. When hackers try to gain access to the system via the Internet, they are initially trying to access the router, rather than one of the PCs in the system. The router therefore acts as a barrier between the computers in the system and the outside world. Most practical routers include a firewall facility that makes it very difficult for hackers to bypass the router and gain access to one of the PCs in the network.

Of course, using a router may seem to be an extravagance if you will never have any need to use more than one PC with your Internet connection. The cost of a combined modem and router is certain to be more than that of a simple broadband modem. On the other hand, with the current low asking prices for computer hardware it need not cost a great deal more. It is probably worthwhile paying a little extra for the added security that the router provides. Also, if you should wish to add another PC into the system at some future date, you will probably need nothing more than a network cable in order to accommodate it.

Malware

A hacker is a person who tries to gain access to your PC or network and take control of it. They are then able to take information from your computer, change files, or do practically anything they desire. Although many computer users seem to regard this as the most common form of attack, it is actually relatively rare for a home or small business computer to be hacked. It is certainly a threat that has to be taken seriously, but there are other security issues that are at least as important.

Most attacks on computer systems are in the form of attempts to make the user download software that will have a detrimental effect on the system. There are numerous types of malicious software currently in circulation, and the generic name for any software of this type is "malware". Viruses were the most common form of malicious software in the early days of computing, and this type of software initially attaches itself to suitable files on the hard disc drive of the computer. It then tries to spread itself to as many files as possible, spreading to other files or even to other computers if it can find a suitable route.

A virus can have various purposes, and in some cases no significant damage will occur to the data on the computer. There will probably be an on-screen message, or some sort of joke effect on the screen to let you know that the computer has been infected, but apart from that everything will function as normal. Unfortunately, the vast majority of viruses are much more sinister than this. Many will try to do as much damage as possible to the file system on the hard disc drive, causing the loss of valuable data and probably rendering the computer inoperative. The boot sector of the hard disc drive is a popular target, and damage to this will make it impossible to boot the computer into the operating system.

Strictly speaking, a virus is something less than a complete computer program, and it can only operate properly once it has attached itself to a suitable file that is already present in the system. This is supposedly analogous to a real virus, which only becomes active once it has attached itself to a living cell. Many attacks on computer systems are in the form of programs that are put forward as something useful and harmless, but which actually have a malicious purpose. Programs of this general type are normally called Trojan horses or just Trojans.

There are various ways in which a Trojan can attack a computer system, and some will simply try to damage to the file system on the hard disc drive. However, attacks that are simply designed to damage the computer in some way are relatively rare these days. Unfortunately, most computer attacks are now much more sinister in nature, and will try to make some form of unlawful use of the PC. A common form of attack is one that tries to use the hacked PC as a robot that sends out spam e-mails. Many Trojans will try to download and install other malicious programs on the PC, such as diallers or software that makes it easy for hackers to enter and gain control of the computer.

The so-called backdoor Trojan is a particularly sinister form of software that attempts to steal information from the PC and send it to a hacker via the Internet. In other words, a backdoor Trojan is used to steal information such as passwords, bank details, or anything that could be used by a thief to obtain money or goods at your expense. Many backdoor Trojan programs operate in conjunction with a type of program called a key logger. This type of program records all the characters typed onto the keyboard, perhaps together with other information such as a list of all the web pages that you visit. The recorded data is stored on the hard disc in a file which the backdoor Trojan then sends to the hacker via the Internet. A backdoor Trojan is clearly a serious threat on any computer, but especially so on one that is used for things such as online banking, or share dealing.

Another sinister form of attack is where your computer is made ready so that it can be taken over whenever the hacker desires, and then used to attack other computer systems. Probably the most common way in which criminals make use of this approach is the denial of service (Dos) attack. This is a form of blackmail where a company is asked to pay a substantial sum of money in order to avoid having their Internet site bombarded with a huge number of users. The idea is to have so many people trying to access the site that the server can not cope, and legitimate users are prevented from using it. This causes a large loss of business to the company concerned, and what is likely to be a large loss of income as well. Of course, the abnormally large number of hits on the site is generated by numerous robot computers operating under the control of the criminals.

Script virus

These days you have to be suspicious of practically all types of file. Many applications programs such as word processors and spreadsheets have the ability to automate tasks using scripts or macros as they are also known. The application effectively has a built-in programming language and the script or macro is a form of program. This makes it possible for viruses or other harmful programs to be present in many types of data file. Scripts are also used in some web pages, and viruses can be hidden in these JavaScript programs, Java applets, etc. There are other potential sources of infection such as Email attachments.

I would not wish to give the impression that all files, web pages, and Emails are potential sources of script or macro viruses. There are some types of file where there is no obvious way for them to carry a virus or other harmful program. A simple text file for example, should be completely harmless. Even in cases where a harmful program is disguised as a text file with a "txt" extension, the file should be harmless. The system will treat it as a text file and it can not be run provided no one alters the file extension. Similarly, an Email that contains a plain text message can not contain a script virus. Do not get caught by files that have a double extension such as file.txt.exe. A file such as this is an executable program (exe) type and not a basic text (txt) file.

It is probably best to regard all files and Emails with a degree of suspicion. Even though simple text can not carry a true virus, it can carry a virus of sorts. Hoax viruses are quite common, and are typically in the form of an Email stating that an earlier Email might have contained a virus. You are then given instructions that will supposedly remove the virus. Of course, the virus is a hoax and does not exist. The instructions for the removal of the nonexistent virus may do nothing much at all, but will often be designed to make it impossible to boot the computer into the operating system.

Worm

A worm is a program that replicates itself, usually from one disc to another, or from one system to another via a local network or the Internet. Like a virus, a worm is not necessarily harmful. In recent times many of the worldwide virus scares have actually been caused by worms transmitted via Email, and not by what would normally be accepted as a virus. The usual ploy is for the worm to send a copy of itself to every address in the Email address book of the infected system. A worm spread in this way, even if it is not intrinsically harmful, can have serious consequences. There can be a sudden upsurge in the amount of Email traffic, possibly causing parts of the Email system to seriously slow down or even crash. Some worms compromise the security of the infected system, perhaps enabling it to be used by a hacker for sending spam for example. This can obviously cause a major reduction in the speed at which programs run.

Adware

This is a form of spyware, but it is not designed to steal important information such as passwords. In common with normal spyware, it gathers information and sends it to another computer via the Internet. Its purpose is usually to gather information for marketing purposes, and this typically means gathering and sending details of the web sites you have visited. Some free programs are supported by banner advertising, and the adware is used to select advertisements that are likely to be of interest to you.

Programs that are supported by adware have not always made this fact clear during the installation process. Sometimes the use of adware was pointed out in the End User License Agreement, but probably few people bother to read the "fine print". These days the more respectable software companies that use this method of raising advertising revenues make it clear that the adware will be installed together with the main program. There is often the option of buying a "clean" copy of the program. Others try to con you into installing the adware by using the normal tricks.

Provided you know that it is being installed and are happy to have it on your PC, adware is not a major security risk. It is sending information about your surfing habits, but you have given permission for it to do so.

If you feel that this is an invasion of privacy, then do not consent to it being installed. The situation is different if you are tricked into installing adware. Then it does clearly become an invasion of your privacy and you should remove any software of this type from your PC. Note that if you consent to adware being installed on your PC and then change your mind, removing it will probably result in the free software it supports being disabled or uninstalled.

Diallers

In many ways it does not make any difference whether your computer connects to the Internet via some form of broadband connection or via a simple dial-up type. The security threats are much the same either way, but the risks are much greater with broadband due to its permanently-on nature and much faster connection speed. On the face of it, diallers are an exception to the rule in that they are not a problem when using any form of broadband Internet connection.

A dialler is a program that uses the computer's ordinary modem and dial up connection to access an expensive premium number. This is done in the hope that the user of the computer will not notice that anything is awry until they receive a telephone bill with a few hundred pounds of unexplained telephone calls to pay for. Dialler programs do not pose a threat provided the computer does not have an ordinary modem that is connected to a telephone socket. In practice it is quite common for this connection to be present even where a computer uses some form of broadband connection. In some cases the dial-up connection is retained as a backup to the broadband type, and in others it is still needed so that faxes can be sent or received.

Where appropriate, broadband users must still regard diallers as a significant security threat, and one that could prove expensive. Ideally, the connection from the ordinary modem to the telephone socket should only be present when the modem is actually in use. This virtually eliminates potential problems with diallers, and should ensure that nothing untoward happens even if a program of this type does become installed on your PC.

Common sense approach

The first line of defence against malware is to use your common sense. When dealing with the Internet it is not advisable to take anything at face value. In fact just the opposite is true, and everything should be treated with a degree of suspicion. In particular, be very suspicious when any software tries to download and install itself on your PC. The situation is complicated by the fact that many application programs as well as the operating system itself are often set by default to automatically download updates. You therefore have to differentiate between software that is trying to download and install itself legitimately, and software that has some malicious purpose.

The safest approach is to disable any form of automatic update, and then manually search for updates from time to time, and install any that are found. Many users consider this to be taking things a bit too far and make use of automatic updates, but block the installation of any software unless they are absolutely certain that they know what it is, and that it is safe. With a modern version of the Windows operating system you should always be warned before any software is downloaded and installed on the computer. The pop-up dialog box provides an opportunity to prevent the software from being installed. In the case of Windows Vista it is also likely that there will be a warning if any programme tries to run itself. This again provides an opportunity to block the operation, and prevent any problems that might otherwise be caused by malicious programs installing and running themselves.

Pirated software is illegal, but surveys suggest that it is to be found on a high percentage of the world's PCs. Software of this type has always represented as a security threat, and the situation is certainly no different today. Much pirated software will actually run perfectly well and seem to be perfectly all right, but the reality of the situation is often very different. This type of software is frequently what I suppose constitutes a form of Trojan horse. In other words, it seems to run perfectly well, and in a sense it is, but installing it also introduces all sorts of malware into your computer system. Never install any software unless it is fully legitimate and obtained from a reliable source.

Some PC users leave their computers running continuously in the belief that it gives better reliability. It did in the days when computers were based on valves, but there is no evidence that it significantly improves reliability with modern computers. It will increase your electricity bills, and it also increases the vulnerability of your PC if it has some form of always-on Internet connection. No one can hack into your computer system if it is switched off.

Anti-virus software

The old adage about "prevention is better than cure" certainly applies to computer viruses. In addition to some basic security precautions, equip your PC with antivirus software and keep it up-to-date. No antivirus software can guarantee one hundred percent protection, but the popular programs of this type will usually detect and deal with viruses before they have a chance to spread the infection or do any damage to your files. An up-to-date antivirus has to be considered essential if you have some form of broadband connection.

Do not fall into the trap that seems to snare many computer users. They take the view that they do not need antivirus software until and unless a virus attacks their PC. This is a rather short-sighted attitude and one that is asking for trouble. By the time that you know a virus has infected your PC it is likely that a substantial amount of damage will have already been done to the system files and (or) your own data files. Using antivirus software to help sort out the mess after a virus has struck is "shutting the stable door after the horse has bolted". The virus may indeed be removed by the antivirus software, but there may be no way of correcting all the damage that has been done.

Another point to bear in mind is that your PC could be rendered unbootable by the virus. Many viruses attack the operating system and will try to make the system unbootable. If the system is not bootable, you can not install antivirus software. Most antivirus programs do some basic checks as part of the installation process. The program will not be installed if any hint of a virus is detected. The reason for this is that the installation process involves copying numerous files onto the hard disc and making changes to some of the Windows system files. This can provide an opportunity for the virus to spread and do further damage.

Real world programs

There are a number of "big name" antivirus programs, and any of these should provide your PC with excellent protection against viruses and other harmful files. These programs provide broadly the same functions but are different in points of detail. We will consider a representative example here. It is worth emphasising the point that it is not a good idea to have more than one of these programs installed on your PC at any one time. Antivirus programs are less intrusive than they used to be, but they still operate continuously in the background monitoring the PC's activity.

Having two of the programs operating simultaneously can produce conflicts that can easily result in the PC crashing. With many of the older antivirus programs you never actually managed to get that far. Having two of them installed on a PC usually resulted in it failing to boot into Windows. It might seem reasonable to have two or three antivirus programs installed, since this gives a better chance of a virus being detected. In practice it does not work very well when applied to real-time monitoring. It can be useful to have the ability to scan using two or three antivirus programs in succession, but having more than one operating at a time is definitely something to be avoided.

Many PCs are supplied with security software already installed. This "free" bundled software is usually more costly than it seems at first, since the updates are only provided for what is typically about three months. It is unlikely that updates will be provided for more than a year even if you buy a retail version of an antivirus program. It is not so much the updates to the program itself that are of importance, as the updates to its database of malicious software. The program will stand little chance of detecting and removing new viruses, etc., unless it has an up-to-date database that includes details of these malicious programs.

Security programs usually have quite low subscription rates, so continuing with the updates for pre-installed antivirus software would probably be money well spent. Something that is definitely not a good idea is to carry on using an antivirus program which has a database that is out of date. A program of this type will provide some protection, but it is only fully effective against malicious programs that were produced months ago. Eventually it will only deal with viruses, etc., that were released years earlier. It is probably relatively new viruses that pose the greatest threat.

Free protection

There are better ways of handling things than continuing to use a commercial antivirus program that is relying on out-of-date virus definitions. There are online virus checking facilities that can be used to periodically scan your PC, but the drawback of this method is that there is no real-time protection for your PC. By the time you do a virus scan it is possible that a virus could have been spreading across your files for some time. By the time it is detected and removed it is likely that a significant amount of damage would already have been done.

An antivirus program running on your PC will usually provide real-time protection. In other words, it monitors disc drive activity, Internet activity,

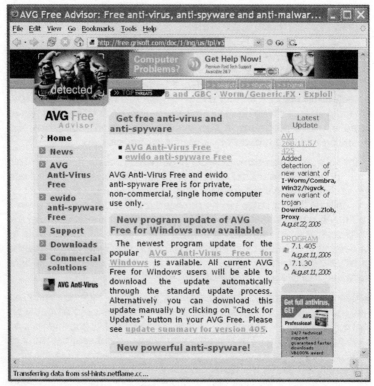

Fig.2.1 The homepage for AVG's free software

or anything that might involve a virus or other malicious program. If any suspicious files are detected, there is an attempt to alter system files, or any dubious activity is detected, the user is warned. In most cases the virus or other malicious program is blocked or removed from the system before it has a chance to do any harm.

The alternative to using online virus scanning is to download and install a free antivirus program. There are one or two totally free antivirus programs available on the Internet, where you do not even have to pay for any online updates to the database. The free version of AVG 7.0 from Grisoft is one that is certainly worth trying. The Grisoft site is at:

www.grisoft.com

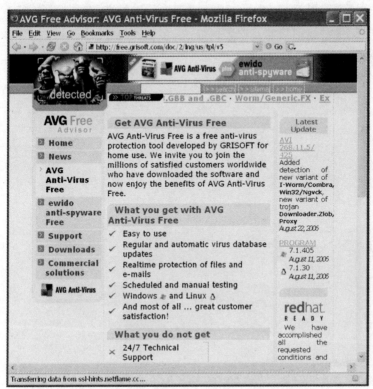

Fig.2.2 This is the page that deals specifically with AVG Free

On the home page there might be a link to the free version of the program, but it does not seem to feature quite as prominently in the home page as it did in the past. At the time of writing this, the web address for Grisoft's free software is:

http://free.grisoft.com/doc/1/lng/us/tpl/v5

If there is any difficulty in finding the home page for the free edition, try using "AVG", "free", and "edition" in any good search engine. Having found the right page, it will look something like the web page of Figure 2.1. This gives some information about the free software available from

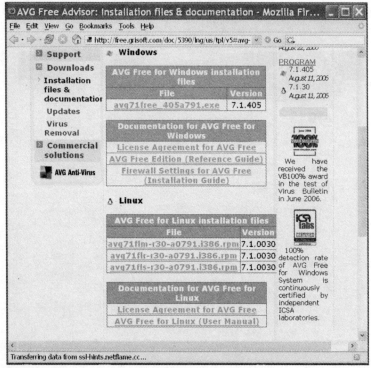

Fig.2.3 A number of files are available for download

Grisoft, including their antivirus program. Operating the AVG Anti-Virus Free link in the left-hand column brings up the page that deals specifically with this software (Figure 2.2). This page includes a link that enables the program file to be downloaded. In fact there are a number of links (Figure 2.3), but it is the one for the Windows installation files that is needed in this case. It is actually just a single file that is downloaded, but this is an archive that contains all the installation files.

There are also some documentation files available, and it is possible to read these online (Figure 2.4) provided your PC has the Adobe Acrobat Reader program installed. However, it is definitely a good idea to download them and store them on the hard disc drive in case they are needed for future reference. It is a good idea to at least take a quick look through the Reference Guide which, amongst other things, provides installation instructions.

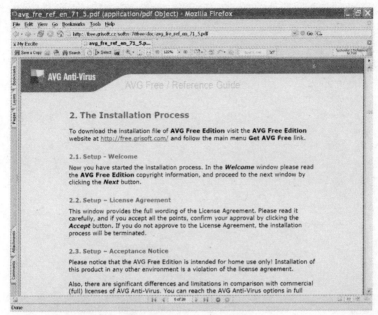

Fig.2.4 The documentation can be read online

Daily updates to AVG are available free of charge, so although free, it should always be reasonably up-to-date. This program has a reputation for being very efficient, and it did once detect a couple of backdoor Trojan programs on my system that a certain well-known commercial program had failed to detect. It is certainly one of the best freebies on the Internet, and it generally performs very well in comparison to commercial equivalents.

Earlier versions of the free AVG program had one major limitation, which was the lack of a rescue mode of the type provided by Norton Antivirus and some other programs. In the current version there is a basic facility that enables a rescue disc to be produced. This can be used to backup important system files so that they can be restored if the originals become damaged by a virus. There is still no facility to boot from a floppy disc or a CD-ROM drive and then run virus checks.

Note that the rescue disc only works with hard disc drives that use the FAT 32 format. Windows XP can operate under this format, but it is normally used with the NTFS format. If in doubt about the file system

2 **Security matters**

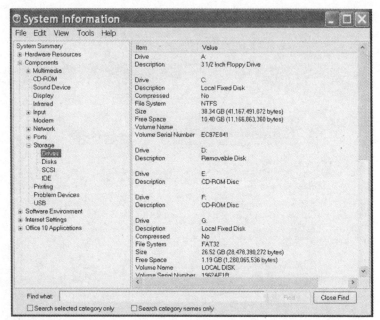

Fig.2.5 The System Information shows the format used for each drive

used on your PC, launch the System Information program and the select Components, Storage, and Drives in the left-hand column. Details of the drives will then be displayed in the main panel (Figure 2.5). Drive C is normally the boot drive, and in this example it is formatted using the NTFS system.

Anyway, the program works effectively in the background detecting the vast majority of viruses, Trojans, etc., so there is little likelihood of a rescue mode being required. However, if you should get unlucky it might be necessary to resort to another antivirus program in order to clear an infection.

In use

AVG does have a useful range of facilities and in other respects it is a very capable program. In common with most antivirus programs you can set it to scan the system on a regular basis, and it also has an automatic update facility. Manual scanning is also available, and this is

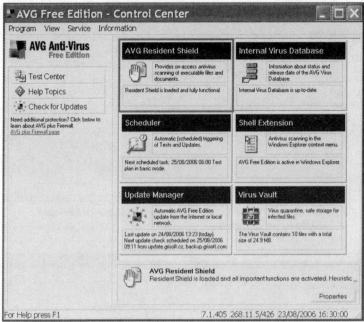

Fig.2.6 The AVG Control Center

another standard feature for this type of software. If you suspect that there might be a virus infection somewhere in the PC you can get the program to do a complete scan of the entire system. Another standard option is to scan one or more of the interchangeable disc drives such as a floppy or CD-ROM drive. This is useful in cases where you suspect that a disc someone has given you might contain a virus.

AVG normally runs automatically at start-up and then runs in the background until the PC is shut down, but it can be started in the normal way from the Start menu. It then appears in a window like the one shown in Figure 2.6. Operating the Test Center button launches a new window that looks like Figure 2.7, which has three large buttons in the main panel. The top button is used when you wish to scan the entire for viruses (Figure 2.8). A window like the one of Figure 2.9 is produced when the process has been completed.

In this case no viruses have been found. The test results will show what action was taken if one or more viruses were detected. The action taken

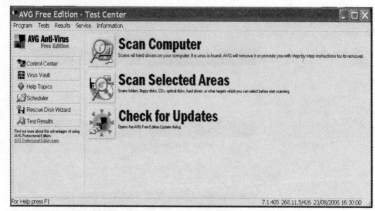

Fig.2.7 The Test Center enables the whole computer or selected drives to be scanned

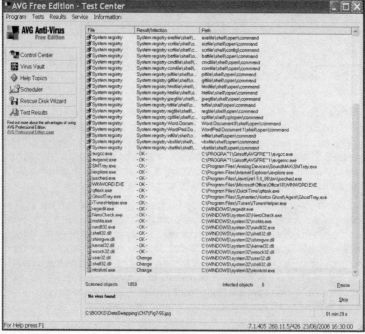

Fig.2.8 The whole system is being scanned for viruses

Fig.2.9 *The scan has been completed and nothing has been detected*

depends on how the program is set up and precisely what it finds. It will leave the infected file unchanged, delete it, or quarantine the file by moving it to the secure folder that is called the "Virus Vault" in AVG terminology. Alternatively, it will do nothing and ask the user to select the required option.

The middle button in the main panel of the Test Center is used when you wish to scan only selected parts of the system. You are provided with a window that shows the parts of the system that can be scanned (Figure 2.10). Simply tick the checkbox for any part that you would like the program to check, and then operate the Scan Selected Areas button. Note that it is not possible to expand the entries for drives and select individual files and (or) folders. The entire contents of a selected drive have to be scanned.

In general, it is not a good idea to scan part of the system. For example, it is tempting to save time by only scanning the boot drive, but this is

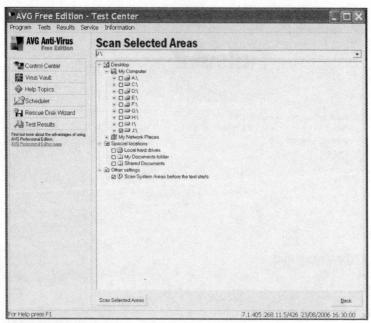

Fig.2.10 This window shows the parts of the system that can be scanned

leaving the system open to infections.   Viruses and other malicious software often have the ability to spread across a system, or to hide themselves on something other than the boot drive. Therefore, it is good to avoid shortcuts and to scan the entire system.

The ability to scan a selected drive or drives can still be useful though. If someone sends you a disc, it is a good idea to scan it for viruses, but you will probably not wish to scan the rest of the system at the same time.   Using this facility of the free AVG antivirus program it is easy to select and quickly scan the CD-ROM, DVD, Flash card, or whatever.

Non-virus

Antivirus programs, as their name suggests, are primarily concerned with the detection and removal of viruses. Most will actually detect a wider range of threats, including most Trojans, spyware, and backdoor Trojans. How well these types of threat are detected varies somewhat from one program to another. These days, most antivirus programs will

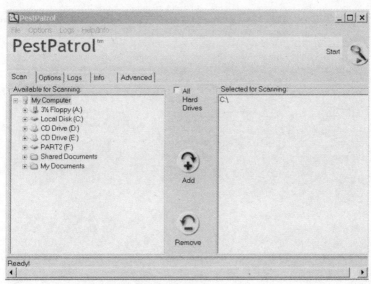

Fig.2.11 The initial screen of Pest Patrol

do a good job of detecting any attacks that pose a serious threat to the security of the computer system.

Antivirus programs are not usually designed to detect what could be termed nuisance programs, such as adware programs and their related files. Many of these programs do not present a real danger to the security of the computer, but their nuisance value can be immense. There are programs that are designed to deal with this type of thing, and they will mostly detect some of the more serious threats such as spyware. A new laptop computer is unlikely to be supplied with any preinstalled software of this type, so it is a good idea to install one of these programs yourself.

Pest Patrol is one of the best known programs for removing adware and other nuisance programs, and it is the one that will be used as the basis of this example. The initial screen of Pest Patrol is shown in Figure 2.11, and the first task is to select the drives that will be scanned. This is just a matter of selecting the required drives in the panel on the left using the standard Windows methods. The Add button is then left-clicked in order to add the drives to the list in the right panel. A drive can be removed from the list by selecting its entry and operating the Remove button. Simply tick the checkbox if you wish to check all the hard drives.

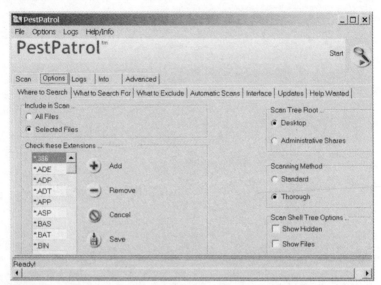

Fig.2.12 Available options include thorough and standard checking

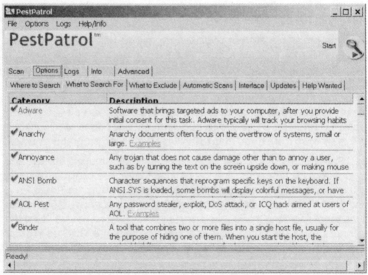

Fig.2.13 Testing can be restricted to certain types of pest

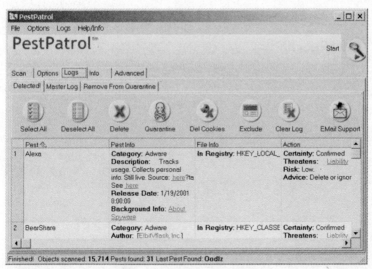

Fig.2.14 A list of scrollable test results is provided

Operating the Options tab produces a further row of tabs, and these give access to a range of options that control the way Pest Patrol scans the disc. There are standard and thorough options for example (Figure 2.12), and you can also set the program to only look for certain types of "pest" (Figure 2.13). It is by no means essential to do any "fine tuning" though, and the program should work well enough if it scans the discs using the default settings. To go ahead with a scan it is just a matter of operating the Start button in the top right-hand corner of the window.

You are presented with a scrollable list of results once Pest Patrol has finished the scan (Figure 2.14). It is essential to look down the list, item by item, even in cases where there are a large number of entries. What you and Pest Patrol consider to be "pests" could be rather different. Remember that removing adware files could result in any programs supported by that adware becoming inoperative. You are unlikely to get away with installing supported software, disabling the associated adware, and then continuing to use the supported software. Blocking adware with a firewall does sometimes leave the supported application fully operational, but this is a morally dubious practice.

Having decided the fate of the various entries, it is just a matter of selecting each batch and then operating the appropriate button. In this example

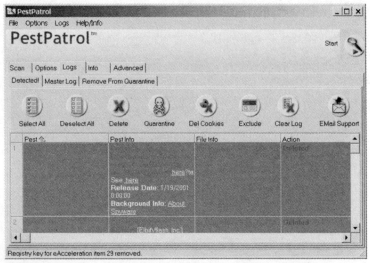

Fig.2.15 The list now shows what has been done to each file

none of the detected files were required, so they were all deleted. The
list changes to show what has been done to each file (Figure 2.15). Note
that the program may be unable to delete some files and folders. It will
then show the location of the relevant files or folders and recommend
manual deletion.

Firewalls

A considerable amount of protection can be provided by using antivirus
software, installing a program to deal with nuisance software, and more
basic measures such as ensuring that the Browser program has sensible
security settings. Even so, the computer could still be vulnerable to
certain types of attack. Further protection can be provided by using a
firewall, which can be either a piece of hardware or a program. A firewall's
basic function is much the same whether it is implemented in software
or hardware.

Although some people seem to think that a firewall and antivirus programs
are the same, there are major differences. There is often some overlap
between real world antivirus and firewall programs, but their primary aims
are different. An antivirus program is designed to scan files on discs

and the contents of the computer's memory in search of viruses and other potentially harmful files. Having found any suspect files, the program will usually deal with them. A firewall is used to block access to your PC, and in most cases it is access to your PC via the Internet that is blocked. Bear in mind though, that a software firewall will usually block access via a local area network (LAN) as well.

Of course, a firewall is of no practical value if it blocks communication from one PC to another and access via the Internet. What it is actually doing is preventing unauthorised access to the protected PC. When you access an Internet site your PC sends messages to the server hosting that site, and these messages request the pages you wish to view. Having requested information, the PC expects information to be sent from the appropriate server, and it accepts that information when it is received. A firewall does not interfere with this type of Internet activity provided it is set up correctly.

It is a different matter when another system tries to access your PC when you have not instigated the initial contact. The firewall will treat this attempted entry as an attack and will block it. Of course, the attempt at accessing your PC might not be an attack, and a firewall can result in legitimate access being blocked. Something like P2P file swapping is likely to fail or operate in a limited fashion. The sharing of files and resources on a local area network could also be blocked. A practical firewall enables the user to permit certain types of access so that the computer can work normally while most unauthorised access is still blocked. However, doing so does reduce the degree of protection provided by the firewall.

Windows firewall

There is a firewall program built into the original version of Windows XP, but it is not activated by default. A rather more advanced firewall program is installed as part of SP2 (Service Pack 2), and it is switched on by default, as is the Vista firewall. New PCs are supplied with Vista or a version of Windows XP that already has SP2. Accordingly, there is no need to install SP2, and the firewall will be switched on by default.

The Windows XP/Vista firewall program can confuse users, as it sometimes causes warning messages to appear on the screen when programs are run. This occurs when a program tries to access the Internet and its activity is detected by the firewall. In most cases the program will be something like a media player or web browser that is quite legitimately trying to use the Internet connection.

When asked if you would like to go on blocking the program's Internet access or unblock it, choose to remove the blocking only if you are sure that the program is one that you are using, and that it has good reason to use the Internet connection. Backdoor Trojans, spyware, etc., gather information from a PC and try to send it to hackers via the Internet. The built-in firewall should detect and block most programs of this type provided you do not override it.

The new Windows XP/Vista firewall is certainly better than the original, but it is not as good as most third-party firewall programs. Consequently, if you have an alternative firewall program, in most cases it will be best if this is used and the built-in program is switched off. The built-in firewall will probably not offer any facility that is not available from the third-party alternative.

Ports

When dealing with firewalls you are almost certain to encounter the term "ports". In a computer context this normally means a socket on the PC where a peripheral of some kind is connected. In an Internet context a port is not in the form of any hardware, and it is more of a software concept. Programs communicate over the Internet via these notional ports that are numbered from 0 to 65535. It enables several programs to utilise the Internet without the data for one program getting directed to another program.

Firewalls usually have the ability to block activity on certain ports. The idea is to block ports that are likely to be used by programs such as backdoor Trojans but are not normally used for legitimate Internet traffic. A Trojan could be set to "listen" on (say) port 80, and send the data it has collected once it receives a message from a hacker. By blocking any activity on port 80, the firewall ensures that the Trojan can not send any data, and that it will not be contacted in the first place.

Note that most software firewall programs will block this type of activity anyway, because the firewall will detect that an unauthorised program is trying to use the Internet. It will alert the user and only permit the data to be sent if the user authorises it. Presumably the user would "smell a rat" and deny permission for the Trojan to access the Internet. Most hardware firewalls would prevent the message from the hacker from reaching the Trojan, and would also prevent the attack from succeeding. Even so, it is useful to block ports that are likely to be used for hacking the system. Doing so makes it that much harder for someone to "crack" your system, which is what Internet security is all about.

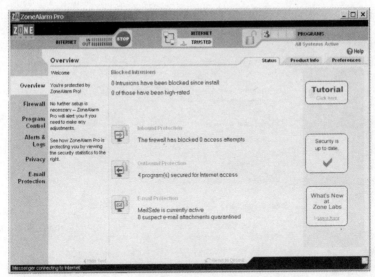

Fig.2.16 The Zone Alarm Pro firewall program in operation

False alarms

Many of the early firewall programs had a major problem in that they were a bit overzealous. While you were trying the surf the Internet there were constant interruptions from the firewall as it warned you of supposed attacks on the system. In reality these attacks were wholly or largely nonexistent. What the programs were actually detecting was normal Internet activity, and many of the false alarms could be prevented by setting up the program to ignore certain programs accessing the Internet. Some of these programs were virtually unusable though.

Modern firewall programs mostly operate in a rather less "in your face" fashion, and produce fewer interruptions. Even so, it is usually necessary to go through a setting up process in order to keep down the number of false alarms, and further tweaking may be needed in order to get things working really well. Of course, if you would like to be informed about every possible attack on the system, most firewalls will duly oblige provided the appropriate settings are used. This certainly gives the ultimate in security, but it could make surfing the Internet a very slow and tedious process.

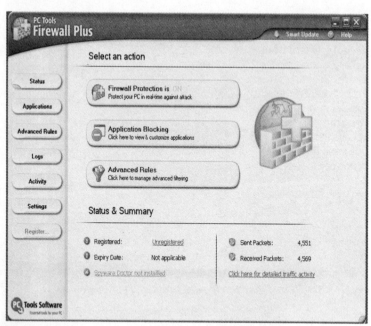

Fig.2.17 Firewall Plus is another free firewall program

Free firewall

There are plenty of software firewalls to choose from, and most of them are capable of providing your PC with a higher degree of security than the built-in firewall. Some firewall software is quite costly and can be difficult to set up. Fortunately, there are several good firewall programs that cost little or nothing. Zone Alarm (www.zonealarm.com) is a popular firewall, and it exists in free, trial, and full commercial versions. Figure 2.16 shows Zone alarm Pro in operation. It is quite easy to set up and use, and the free version represents a good starting point for private users wishing to try a good quality firewall at minimum cost.

Firewall Plus from PC Tools (www.pctools.com) is another popular firewall program that can be downloaded and used free of charge. Figure 2.17 shows the main window of this program, but for most purposes the default settings will suffice and no setting up is required in order to get this program running properly. Of course, programs such as Zone Alarm and Firewall Plus normally operate unseen in the background. A pop-up message appears when the program detects suspicious activity, such as in the example of Figure 2.18, where Firewall Plus has detected a program trying to access the Internet. In this case it was just a browser program that has been detected, and the Allow button was therefore operated so that the program could access the Internet.

Fig.2.18 A program has tried to access the Internet

Points to remember

Prevention is better than cure. A good antivirus program can cost little or nothing and will immediately spot most viruses. New viruses are appearing all the time, so remember to keep the antivirus program up-to-date. The antivirus programs bundled with many PCs are fully operational, but mostly have update subscriptions that only last for a very limited period. The subscription must be extended in order to keep the program up to date and working well.

If you do not intend to subscribe to an antivirus program you should certainly install one of the free programs such as AVG Free. Although they cost nothing initially and have free updates, some of these programs do an excellent job. Do not rely on a commercial antivirus program with an out-of-date database. Such a combination is unlikely to detect recent viruses.

It is a good idea to scan discs, including Flash cards, when they are first installed in one of your computer's drives. Most antivirus programs can be set to scan a selected drive, and many will automatically scan any new disc that is introduced into the system.

Some antivirus suites include a set of bootable floppy discs or a bootable CD-ROM so that antivirus checks can be made on a PC that does not have antivirus software installed. Using this type of software, checks can be made on a PC even if it can not be booted into Windows. One drawback of this method is that the antivirus software will not be fully up-to-date.

Antivirus software usually scans for more than viruses, and other harmful files such as Trojans and spyware will usually be found. Things such as adware will not be detected though, as they are often installed legitimately. Programs such as Pest Patrol will scan for adware and the like, and will remove them if required.

Antivirus programs are of limited use against hackers. In order to keep hackers at bay it is essential to use either a software or hardware firewall. Ideally, both should be used if you have some form of broadband connection, especially if it is of the "always on" variety. Windows XP and Vista have a built-in firewall program, but there are third-party firewall programs that provide a greater degree of protection.

3

Downloading
and sharing

Speed

Downloading large files is an application where the speed of a broadband Internet connection is certainly a great asset. Downloading a few hundred megabytes of data using a real-world dial-up connection would take many hours, and might never be completed successfully. Even using a relatively slow broadband connection it would take only two or three hours to download the same amount of data, and with the fastest of broadband connections it would require a matter of minutes rather than hours.

Of course, in real-world computing matters are never as straightforward as that, and downloading large files using a fast Internet connection will not always be "plain sailing". The download speed is governed by the slowest part of the system, which will almost invariably be your Internet connection when using a dial-up type, but this is by no means a foregone conclusion when using some form of broadband connection. As the speed of broadband connections has steadily increased over the years, the rest of the Internet has not always kept up with developments. The practical result of this is that file servers and the Internet infrastructure may not always be able to equal the download speed of your Internet connection. The faster your Internet service, the less likely it is that the other parts of the system will be able to keep up with it.

Are you being served?

While there can be problems with the equipment between your PC and the server, in practice it seems to be problems with the servers that give most problems when trying to download at high speed. The server is the computer system that stores the Internet pages you visit, or files that you download. There is a limit to the workload that the server can handle efficiently, and there is also a limit on the speed at which it can upload data to the Internet.

Some servers are highly sophisticated and can easily accommodate a large number of users simultaneously, while others are just ordinary PCs that are quite old. Similarly, some servers connect to the Internet via what is essentially just an ordinary broadband connection of some type, while others have hi-tech connections with massive bandwidths. Unfortunately, the fact that you are dealing with an up-market server that has a super-fast link to the Internet does not mean that it will always be able to supply data to your PC at a high rate. Neither does it follow that a primitive server with a more modest link to the Internet will always be slow at providing data.

An important factor is the number of users accessing the server. You may well get quick service if you are the only person accessing a relatively slow server, but only a slow download rate if you are one of several thousand people using the latest hi-tech server. At times when a server is busy you may therefore find that the maximum download rate is far less than the highest rate that your Internet connection can accommodate. In fact some servers limit the number of users to a figure that enables each user to receive a fairly high download rate, so some download services simply become unavailable at times of high demand.

This is a bit inconvenient from the user's point of view, but in most cases it is possible to go ahead with the download if you try again later. There can be a more serious problem with sites that utilise low-cost or free web hosting services. The hosts of some web sites place limits on the total amount of data that can be downloaded per month. Sites that make use of this form of economy hosting can therefore be unavailable for several days if they suddenly become very popular and the month's download allocation is reached before the end of the month. With this type of thing you just have to keep checking the web site so that you can access the file you require as soon as it goes back online.

Optimising speed

One way of avoiding problems with overloaded servers is to download files at times when demand is likely to be low. Judging when demand will be low can be a bit problematic though. There should be no difficulty if the site is one that is only likely to be of interest to people living in your own country. Demand is likely to be very low from late in the evening through to early the next morning. Depending on whether it is a business or leisure oriented site, the peak demand is likely to be in the afternoon or evenings.

There may be no real slack period with a site that has users all over the world, since there will always be plenty of users in one part of the world or another. Practical experience suggests that in the UK, many sites seem to be at their best in the early morning, before 9-00 AM. However, it might be necessary to try awkward sites at various times of the day in order to find a time when the required files can be downloaded efficiently.

Download managers

There are programs that designed to manage and in some cases speed up downloads. Programs of this type are generally called download managers. One advantage of these programs is that they will usually be able to resume a broken download, carrying on from the point at which the download stopped. The built-in download facility of a browser often lacks this facility, making it necessary to start again from the beginning if the connection to the server is lost.

Broken downloads are not a major problem with broadband connections, since the reliability is generally much higher than that obtained when using a typical dial-up connection. Also, the time taken to download a given amount of data is much less, giving less time for things to go wrong. However, things can still go awry from time-to-time, and some servers operate with something well short of one hundred percent reliability. The ability to resume broken downloads is certainly a very worthwhile facility. Note though, that it is a facility that can only work if it is supported by the equipment at both ends of the link. Therefore, the fact that you are using a download manager does not mean that it will always be possible to resume broken downloads. Fortunately, these days the vast majority of servers support this feature.

Most download managers try to ensure that files are always downloaded at the highest possible rate, and there are two main approaches to this problem. One of these is to test the various sources of the file so that the fastest server or servers can be used. A download manager is normally set to popup automatically when a download is about to commence. Figure 3.1 shows Accelerator Plus in operation, and in this case it has not been able to find any information about alternative download sites, or "mirror" sites as they are termed. This gives no option but to download the file from the original site. The chances of finding mirror sites depend on the popularity of the file you are trying to download. With a very

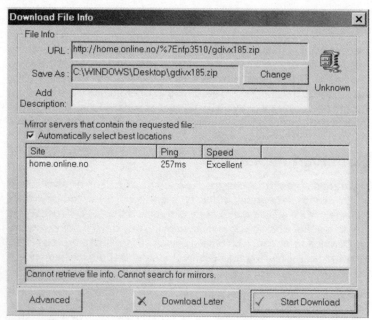

*Fig.3.1 Accelerator Plus in action. In this case only one download site
has been found*

popular download there could be dozens of alternative sites available.
Figure 3.2 shows the result when trying to download the popular Winzip
program. In this case there are so many mirror sites that the list has
gained a scrollbar.

Pinging

The list includes a ping time for each site and a rating of that ping time.
Pinging is sending a small packet of data to a server and back again.
The shorter the time this takes the faster the download is likely to be. It
tends to be assumed that the rate at which data can be downloaded is
purely dependent on the speed of the connection to the Internet service
provider and the speed at which the server can send data. However,
data is not downloaded from the server in the form of one continuous
stream of data. It is sent in smaller chunks called "packets", and a
dialogue is needed between your PC and the server in order to ensure
that everything works smoothly. Time is lost each time your PC and the

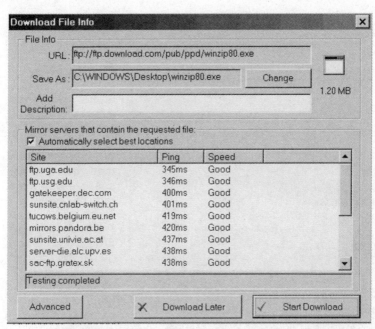

Fig.3.2 In this example Accelerator Plus has found about 20 sources for the file

server try to establish contact. Pinging is used to measure how quickly (or otherwise) your PC and the server can establish contact, rather than just measuring the rate at which data can be transferred between the two. With a short ping time there is relatively little time wasted trying to establish contact so that messages or packets of data can be exchanged efficiently. Of course, if the rate of data flow is very low, this will also produce a long ping time.

The obvious approach is to use whichever site gives the shortest response time, but many download managers take things a step further. The fastest site is used initially, but if this site fails to live up to expectations another fast site will be tried instead. There may be an option to manually select the sites to use, but automatic selection is easier and likely to yield the best results. Operating the Start Download button gets things under way, and a small window then appears. This shows how things are progressing (Figure 3.3) and also indicates if it is possible to resume a broken download, which it normally is. Where appropriate, the bottom section gives details of how the data is being downloaded using simultaneous connection to several sites.

Fig.3.3 The program has selected and is using four download sites

Optimising

Some download manager programs have facilities to optimise various Windows settings so that the fastest possible download rate is achieved. There are also special optimiser programs and numerous Internet sites that give advice on this subject. In general, there is probably no point in most broadband users bothering with this type of thing.

Provided a suitably high download rate is achieved when using a fast server there is not really a lot to be gained by experimenting with some of the Windows settings. Altering settings in the Windows Registry has to be regarded as a little risky, and it is possible to do serious damage to the operating system if you make a major error.

I suppose the situation is rather different if you consistently obtain download rates that are well short of the maximum theoretical rate for your Internet connection. When this occurs it is probably best to contact your Internet service provider first in order to check that you are connected at the correct speed and that there is no problem with their hardware. They should be able to suggest some checks that can be made at your end of the system to determine what is wrong. It is perhaps worth resorting to optimising techniques if the download rates still seem rather low. Bear in mind that most broadband connections rely on equipment that is shared with a number of other users. Download rates can be significantly reduced at times when several users are downloading files or engaging in other activities that require a large amount of bandwidth.

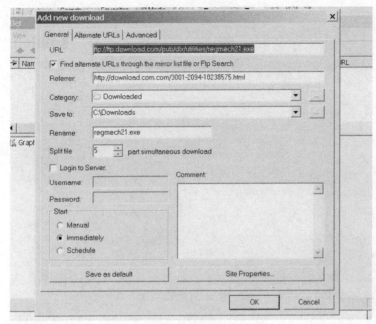

Fig.3.4 Anything from one to ten threads can be used

Multiple threads

Probably the most effective method of accelerating a download is to use the multiple thread approach. Suppose that you have an Internet connection that can handle a maximum download rate of one megabit per second, but a server will only supply 150 kilobits (0.15 megabits) per second. With the multiple thread approach to things the download manager divides the file into five equal parts which it then downloads separately from the server. Having downloaded all five sections it then joins them to produce the complete file.

The point of using five separate downloads is that, with luck, each part of the file will download at 150 kilobits per second. This gives an effective download rate of 750 kilobits per second (5 x 150 kilobits = 750 kilobits). In practice it is unlikely that the download rate would be accelerated to quite this degree, since there are minor inefficiencies in the system, and using five threads increases the loading on the server. Even so, the download rate would typically be increased by a factor of about four, which provides a large reduction in download times.

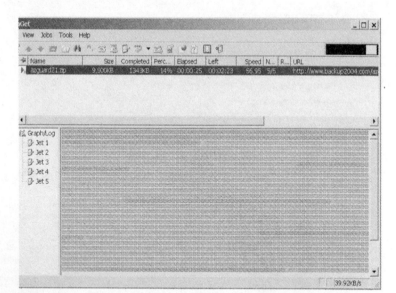

Fig.3.5 The progress made by each thread is shown here

Of course, the multiple-thread method of downloading is of little help in cases where the server is providing data at a high rate. In fact it might reduce efficiency and produce a slight reduction in the download rate when used with a fast server. Not all servers will permit more than one connection per IP address, so it will not always be an option. Some servers permit multiple connections, but with a limit of two or three per IP address. Many FTP servers only permit one or two connections per user, but the more usual HTTP types are generally more accommodating. Where the server is a bit slow, even one extra connection still permits a very worthwhile increase in download speed.

The popular FlashGet download manager program is one that can handle multiple threads. Figure 3.4 shows FlashGet 1.6 in operation, and a pop-up window offers a number of options. The one of interest here is the Split parts field, where a value of one to ten can be used. This controls the number of threads used for the download, and the default value is five. Figure 3.5 shows a download in progress, and the lower section of the window shows the amount of data downloaded by each of five threads.

Peer-to-peer

Vast amounts of data are swapped over the Internet using peer-to-peer (P2P) networks. The MP3 format and using a computer to play music first became big news when the original Napster site was launched. This enabled users to look at the music available on the hard disc drives of other users and download anything that took their fancy. The problem with this system, or any similar system, is that there is no reliable way of preventing users from illegally swapping material that is protected by copyright. After a number of legal wrangles the original Napster was taken over and eventually turned into a site providing legal music downloads. Note that the original site at www.napster.com is only for US residents. However, there is a UK version at www.napster.co.uk.

Napster was an early example of a peer-to-peer network, which is a term used to describe any system that enables users to share each others' data via the Internet. Although the original Napster no longer exists, there are plenty of peer-to-peer file sharing programs available, and some of them are available as free downloads. The companies behind some of these programs are embroiled in ongoing legal disputes with the recording companies and organisations that represent them. Some peer-to-peer programs have been discontinued as a result of these legal wrangles. A peer-to-peer program can be used for legitimate file swapping, but it can also be used for illegally swapping material that is still in copyright. This has made peer-to-peer systems something of a "grey area", since they are legal or illegal depending on how they are used.

If you use a peer-to-peer file sharing system it is important to bear in mind that there are potential problems. A substantial amount of the material available on the popular systems seems to be within copyright and downloading it is illegal. Perhaps of greater importance, making this type of thing available for others to download from your computer is also illegal and has resulted in prosecutions in the US and the UK. When using peer-to-peer systems it is important to make sure that you do not download or make available anything that can not be swapped legitimately.

Downloading files via a peer-to-peer network can be problematic. It is very easy to end up with an incomplete file that can never be fully downloaded, or a complete but badly corrupted and useless file. There are plenty of jokers operating on these systems, and one of their tricks is to put files on the system that are not what they are purported to be. Sometimes this is relatively innocent, with the downloaded file actually

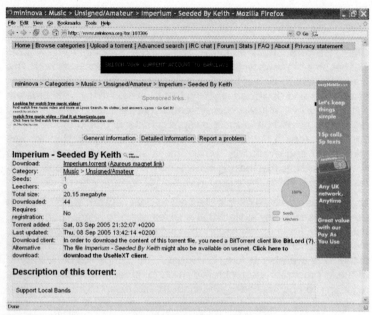

Fig.3.6 In order to download a file using a program such as Bit-Torrent you must first locate its Torrent file

being a piece of music, a picture, or whatever kind of file you were trying to download, but the wrong one. In other cases the downloaded file is pornography, a file that is infected with a virus, a backdoor Trojan, or something of this general type. You need to be on your guard if you use one of these systems, and they are probably not something that newcomers to computing should get involved in. Many experienced computer users refuse to have anything to do with peer-to-peer systems.

Torrents

Should you decide to try peer-to-peer systems there are plenty of programs to choose from. Probably the most popular peer-to-peer system at the time of writing this is the Torrent method of file sharing. The original Torrent file sharing program is Bit-Torrent, but there are now others such as Bit-Comet, u-Torrent, and Bit-Lord. The popular download sites such as www.download.com should have Bit-Torrent and a fair selection of alternatives. Note that the free versions of some peer-to-

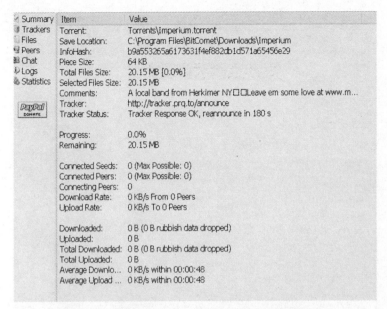

	Item	Value
✔ Summary	Torrent:	Torrents\Imperium.torrent
🔲 Trackers	Save Location:	C:\Program Files\BitComet\Downloads\Imperium
🔲 Files	InfoHash:	b9a553265a6173631f4ef882db1d571a65456e29
🔲 Peers	Piece Size:	64 KB
🔲 Chat	Total Files Size:	20.15 MB [0.0%]
🔲 Logs	Selected Files Size:	20.15 MB
🔲 Statistics	Comments:	A local band from Herkimer NY☐☐Leave em some love at www.m...
	Tracker:	http://tracker.prq.to/announce
PayPal DONATE	Tracker Status:	Tracker Response OK, reannounce in 180 s
	Progress:	0.0%
	Remaining:	20.15 MB
	Connected Seeds:	0 (Max Possible: 0)
	Connected Peers:	0 (Max Possible: 0)
	Connecting Peers:	0
	Download Rate:	0 KB/s From 0 Peers
	Upload Rate:	0 KB/s To 0 Peers
	Downloaded:	0 B (0 B rubbish data dropped)
	Uploaded:	0 B
	Total Downloaded:	0 B (0 B rubbish data dropped)
	Total Uploaded:	0 B
	Average Downlo...	0 KB/s within 00:00:48
	Average Upload ...	0 KB/s within 00:00:48

Fig.3.7 The Torrent file has been run and Bit-Comet has been launched. Unfortunately, on this occasion there are no sources for the file

peer programs are supported by adware. It is therefore advisable to check this point before downloading any of these programs if you are not happy with adware that might, for example, produce pop-ups when you use your web browser or the peer-to-peer client itself.

The Torrent way of doing things is a bit different to most other peer-to-peer systems. It is generally regarded as being more efficient at sharing large files and at avoiding corruption of files. In a music context the files will often be relatively small, but a system that maintains the integrity of the data is clearly advantageous with any type of file. For users, the most obvious difference between a Torrent system and traditional peer-to-peer systems is that there is no built-in search facility. In order to download something using this system you require a Torrent file. This gives the peer-to-peer program the information it needs in order to contact sources of the required material and download it. There are various web sites that have databases of Torrent files, and some of the Torrent programs can access a range of these sites, effectively giving them a built-in search facility.

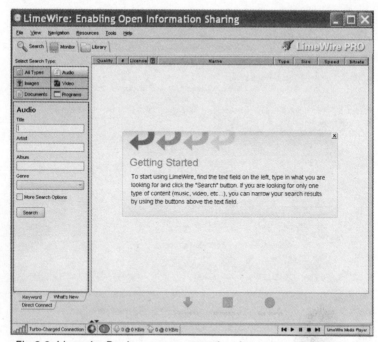

Fig.3.8 Limewire Pro is a more conventional peer-to-peer program that has a built-in search facility

Having located a Torrent file that looks interesting it is just a matter of running it. The operating system will then launch the default Torrent application which will then set about downloading the file. In Figure 3.6 I have located a likely looking Torrent file, and left-clicking its link on the web page resulted in it being run in Bit-Comet (Figure 3.7). Unfortunately, the selected Torrent file was quite old, and the requested file failed to download because there were no sources available.

Out of date

This is another way in which the Torrent system differs from some other peer-to-peer systems. With most other methods of file sharing it is only possible to find a file if at least a fragment of it is available on the system. Without all or part of the file in the system there is nothing for the search engine to find. With the Torrent method, the fact that you have located a Torrent file does not mean that the target file is still present on the system

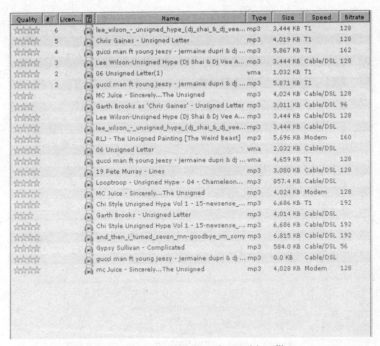

Quality	#	Licen...	🔲	Name	Type	Size	Speed	Bitrate
☆☆☆☆	6	📄		lee_wilson_-_unsigned_hype_(dj_shai_&_dj_vee...	mp3	3,444 KB	T1	128
☆☆☆☆	5	📄		Chris Gaines - Unsigned Letter	mp3	4,019 KB	T1	128
☆☆☆☆	4	📄		gucci man ft young jeezy - jermaine dupri & dj ...	mp3	5,867 KB	T1	162
☆☆☆☆	3	📄		Lee Wilson-Unsigned Hype (Dj Shai & Dj Vee A...	mp3	3,444 KB	Cable/DSL	128
☆☆☆☆	2			06 Unsigned Letter(1)	wma	1,032 KB	T1	
☆☆☆☆	2	📄		gucci man ft young jeezy - jermaine dupri & dj ...	mp3	5,871 KB	T1	
☆☆☆		📄		MC Juice - Sincerely...The Unsigned	mp3	4,024 KB	Cable/DSL	128
☆☆☆		📄		Garth Brooks as 'Chris Gaines' - Unsigned Letter	mp3	3,011 KB	Cable/DSL	96
☆☆☆☆		📄		Lee Wilson-Unsigned Hype (Dj Shai & Dj Vee A...	mp3	3,444 KB	Cable/DSL	128
☆☆☆☆		📄		lee_wilson_-_unsigned_hype_(dj_shai_&_dj_vee...	mp3	3,444 KB	Cable/DSL	
☆☆☆☆		📄		RLJ - The Unsigned Painting [The Weird Beast]	mp3	5,696 KB	Modem	160
☆☆☆☆		📄		06 Unsigned Letter	wma	2,032 KB	Modem	
☆☆☆☆		📄		gucci man ft young jeezy - jermaine dupri & dj ...	wma	4,659 KB	T1	128
☆☆☆☆		📄		19 Pete Murray - Lines	mp3	3,080 KB	Cable/DSL	128
☆☆☆☆		📄		Looptroop - Unsigned Hype - 04 - Chameleon...	mp3	857.4 KB	Cable/DSL	
☆☆☆☆		📄		MC Juice - Sincerely...The Unsigned	mp3	4,024 KB	Modem	128
☆☆☆☆		📄		Chi Style Unsigned Hype Vol 1 - 15-newsense_...	mp3	6,686 KB	T1	192
☆☆☆		📄		Garth Brooks - Unsigned Letter	mp3	4,014 KB	Cable/DSL	
☆☆☆☆		📄		Chi Style Unsigned Hype Vol 1 - 15-newsense_...	mp3	6,686 KB	Cable/DSL	192
☆☆☆☆		📄		and_then_i_turned_seven_mn-goodbye_im_sorry	mp3	6,815 KB	Cable/DSL	192
☆☆☆☆		📄		Gypsy Sullivan - Complicated	mp3	584.0 KB	Cable/DSL	56
☆☆☆☆		📄		gucci man ft young jeezy - jermaine dupri & dj ...	mp3	0.0 KB	Cable/DSL	
☆☆☆☆		📄		mc Juice - Sincerely...The Unsigned	mp3	4,028 KB	Modem	128

Fig.3.9 The search has produced a list of matching files

and downloadable. Most Torrent sites do their best to remove out of date files, but there will inevitably be a significant percentage of files that are "past their use-by dates".

With any peer-to-peer system it might be worthwhile trying again later if a file either fails to start downloading, or it partially downloads and then stops. A blockage in the distribution system might have been corrected by the time you try again, or someone with the missing part of the file might have joined the system. However, it is a fact of peer-to-peer life that some files prove to be impossible to download. It is another fact of peer-to-peer life that many files download only very slowly and intermittently. It is up to you to decide whether the more awkward files are worth the time and effort involved in downloading them.

Limewire Pro (Figure 3.8) is a more typical peer-to-peer client that has a search facility in the left-hand section of the window. Here you can select the type of file required (audio, video, software, etc.) and add search

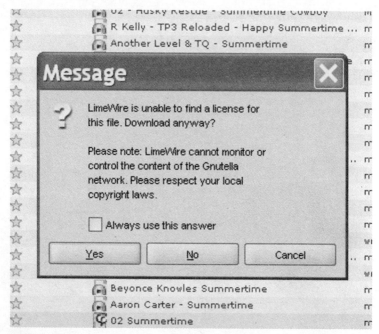

Fig.3.10 The warning message indicates that no licence has been found for this file

strings to help the search engine find suitable files. Any suitable matches are then listed in the main panel to the right of the search facility (Figure 3.9). To download a file it is just a matter of selecting its entry, operating the Download button, and hoping.

A warning message (Figure 3.10) will be issued if the program can not verify that the file can be downloaded legitimately. This does not necessarily mean that it is not legitimate, and there is the option of continuing with the download anyway. The decision is yours. The bottom section of the window is used for monitoring downloads. It shows the number of sources, the percentage that has been downloaded, the download speed, and so on. With luck, before too long it will show that one hundred percent of the file has been downloaded (Figure 3.11).

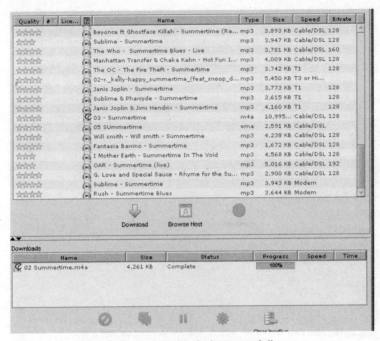

Quality	#	Lice...		Name	Type	Size	Speed	Bitrate
★★★★				Beyonce ft Ghostface Killah - Summertime (Re...	mp3	3,893 KB	Cable/DSL	128
★★★				Sublime - Summertime	mp3	3,947 KB	Cable/DSL	128
★★★★				The Who - Summertime Blues - Live	mp3	3,781 KB	Cable/DSL	160
★★★★				Manhattan Transfer & Chaka Kahn - Hot Fun I...	mp3	4,009 KB	Cable/DSL	128
★★★★				The OC - The Fire Theft - Summertime	mp3	3,742 KB	T1	128
★★★★				02-r._kelly-happy_summertime_(feat_snoop_d...	mp3	5,450 KB	T3 or Hi...	
★★★★				Janis Joplin - Summertime	mp3	3,773 KB	T1	128
★★★★				Sublime & Pharcyde - Summertime	mp3	3,615 KB	T1	128
★★★★				Janis Joplin & Jimi Hendrix - Summertime	mp3	4,160 KB	T1	128
★★★★				03 - Summertime	m4a	10,995...	Cable/DSL	128
★★★★				05 SUmmertime	wma	2,591 KB	Cable/DSL	
★★★★				Will smith - Will smith - Summertime	mp3	4,238 KB	Cable/DSL	128
★★★★				Fantasia Barrino - Summertime	mp3	1,672 KB	Cable/DSL	128
★★★				I Mother Earth - Summertime In The Void	mp3	4,568 KB	Cable/DSL	128
★★★				OAR - Summertime (live)	mp3	5,016 KB	Cable/DSL	192
★★★★				G. Love and Special Sauce - Rhyme for the Su...	mp3	2,900 KB	Cable/DSL	128
★★★★				Sublime - Summertime	mp3	3,943 KB	Modem	
★★★★				Rush - Summertime Blues	mp3	3,644 KB	Modem	

Download　Browse Host

Downloads

Name	Size	Status	Progress	Speed	Time
02 Summertime.m4a	4,261 KB	Complete	100%		

Fig.3.11 The file has been downloaded successfully

Speed test

Should you feel that your Internet connection is falling "short of the mark", there are plenty of websites that will help you to test its speed. However, with anything of this type you have to remember that it is not, strictly speaking, the speed of your Internet connection that is being tested. It is actually the speed of your Internet connection, the server that hosts the test website, and the Internet infrastructure that connects the two. Consequently, you might get significantly different results if you try a range of speed testing sites. In fact it is highly likely that significant differences will be found.

For an initial test I tried the test site a www.speedguide.net (Figure 3.12), which produced the results of Figure 3.13. The nominal download and upload speeds of the Internet connection used for this test were respectively 1024 kilobits per second and 256 kilobits per second. The results produced by the test were a download speed of 858 kilobits per

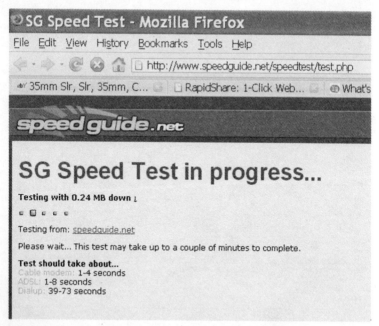

Fig.3.12 The test is under way at the spreedguide.net site

second and an upload rate of 236 kilobits per second, which are both a bit disappointing.

An alternative speed checking site at www.speedtest.net enables a site close to your location to be selected. The point of doing this is that, in general, faster results are obtained using a server that is reasonably close. This should result in the data taking a reasonably direct route rather than doing a tour of the world's Internet hubs. However, there is no absolute guarantee that using a server that is close to your location will ensure a relatively direct link between the two ends of the system. It is still possible that the connection will be made via Internet hubs thousands of miles away, but this is highly unlikely.

In this example (Figure 3.14) it seems to have produced the desired result, with reported download and upload speeds of 947 kilobits per second and 246 kilobits per second respectively. These are still slightly short of the maximum possible download and upload rates, but are perfectly acceptable. If you try a few speed tests you should get a good idea of the sort of download rate you can expect from real-world sites.

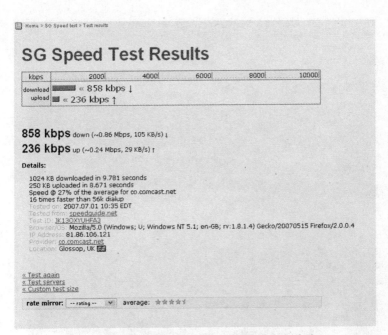

Fig.3.13 The results are not bad, but are a little disappointing

File swapping

The speed of a broadband connection makes it possible to use the Internet as a means of sending large data files to other people. One slight snag is that the maximum upload speed of most broadband connections is far lower than the highest achievable download rate. It is often just 256 kilobits per second, and is unlikely to be more than 512 kilobits per second. The practical consequence of this is that it will usually take far longer for the sender to upload data than it does for the recipient to download it. However, unless hundreds of megabytes or more of data is involved, upload times should still be reasonable.

Email transfer

There are numerous ways of exchanging data over the Internet, and the best option depends on the amount of data involved, how often data will have to be transferred, and the number of recipients. Email is becoming

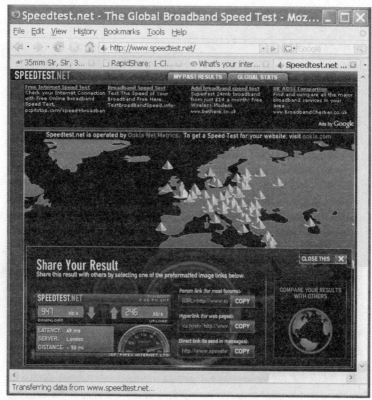

Fig.3.14 Improved results are obtained using a server that is closer

a very popular means of swapping data, but it can be difficult to exchange large amounts of data using this method. The Emails themselves are of little use for swapping anything other than simple text files. However, practically any Email service should be able handle attachments. These are simply files that are sent with an Email, and they can be opened or downloaded by the recipient. This way of working has obvious attractions, but the main advantage is the ease with which it can be implemented.

Most people already have at least one Email address, making it possible to exchange files over the Internet with a minimum of fuss. There is no need to find any web space or to use any special software. You just use your existing Email account and software. Even if you would prefer not to use your main Email account for file swapping, there is no major problem. There are plenty of free Email services, and signing up to one of these takes very little time.

Of course, there are some drawbacks to using Emails as a means of file swapping. One potential problem is that some Email servers are not particularly fast, especially at times of high demand. This means that transfer rates can occasionally be quite slow even when using a broadband connection. As pointed out previously, with many Email services it can be difficult to swap large amounts of data. The restriction on the number and size of attached files used to be a major drawback, but recent competition amongst the providers has resulted in much more generous allowances.

In the past, some providers only permitted one or two files to be attached to each Email, with a total file size of only one or two megabytes. Sending multiple Emails seemed to permit larger amounts of data to be sent, but in practice there was a problem with this method. The capacity of many Email inboxes was often in the region of two to five megabytes, and some of this would usually be occupied by stored Emails. It was therefore necessary to download and delete one lot of attachments before the next lot could be received. Doing things this way was possible, but decidedly cumbersome.

Many Email service providers gave users the option of paying for a larger inbox, but these days it should not be necessary to opt for one of these premium services. Free accounts now seem to come complete with inboxes having capacities of between about 100 megabytes and a few gigabytes. Even the lower figure should be adequate for most users, but you can seek out one of the more generous providers if you need to transfer and store large amounts of data online.

When transferring data via Email attachments you have to bear in mind that the number and size of attachments permitted by most providers has not kept pace with the increased sizes of inboxes. In general, it is possible to send more and larger files than in the past, but there is likely to be a limit of something like six files and a total of ten megabytes.

The restrictions seem to be different for each service provider, so you have to check on the limits imposed by your particular provider prior to sending large amounts of data. Bear in mind that there might also be restrictions on what can be received by the system used by the recipient. If your Emails fail to meet any restrictions imposed by the receiving system, it is certain that some of the attachments will be filtered. It is possible that all the attachments will be filtered.

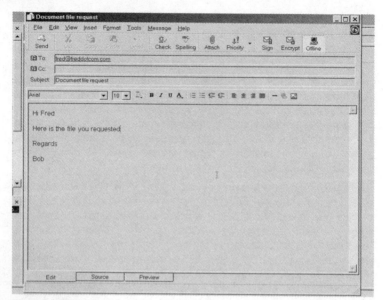

Fig.3.15 The first step is to compose the Email in the normal way

A limit on the number of files is not really a major drawback. It is possible to combine a number of files into a single archive file using programs such as WinZip and WinRAR. The recipient can split each archive back into its constituent parts using the same program that was used to create it. The main purpose of programs such as WinZip and WinRAR is to compress the data so that files are made as small as possible. With some types of file this can greatly reduce the amount of data, which makes it far easier to keep within the service provider's restrictions. It also helps to speed up the uploading and downloading processes. Unfortunately, many types of file already incorporate data compression. Trying to "squeeze" these files using data compression is unlikely to provide a significant reduction in their size.

Filtering

Internet security is now a major issue for users and providers of Internet services. One practical outcome of increased Email security is that some service providers do not permit certain types of file to be included as attachments. At the other end of the system, some providers will not

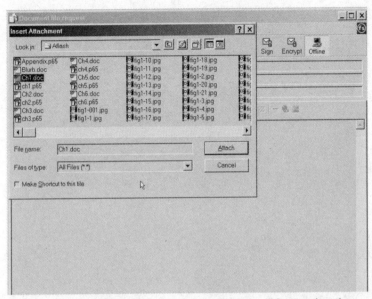

Fig.3.16 Use the file browser to load the file that will be used as the attachment

accept attachments containing certain file types. Trying to send a file of a proscribed type will usually result in an error message. Sometimes a certain file type might be acceptable to your Email provider, but not to the recipient's provider. This will usually result in the attachment being filtered, and the recipient's service provider will then send you an Email explaining why the attachment has been filtered.

The file types that are most likely to be filtered are executable program files, such as those having EXE and COM extensions. Extensions to program files such as DLL types might also be prohibited. It is quite likely that you will never need to send any of the proscribed file types, but compressed files can sometimes cause problems. Most types of compressed files should be permissible, including those having the common filename extensions such as ZIP and RAR. It is the self-extracting files that are likely to cause problems. This type of file is a program file that usually has an EXE extension.

The file is actually a simple decompression utility plus the compressed data. Running the program results in the data being decompressed, and then it is stored in the folder specified by the user. This type of

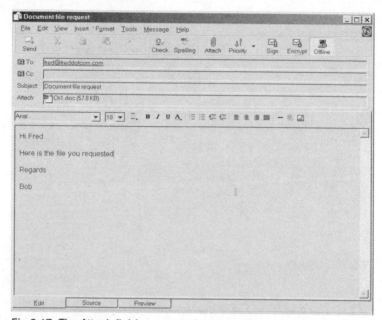

Fig.3.17 The Attach field now contains an entry

compressed file has the advantage of not requiring the recipient to have a decompression program of the appropriate type. There is a slight drawback in that including the decompression program with the data results in a larger file. When sending compressed files via Email it is

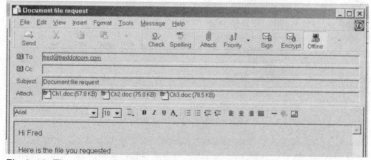

Fig.3.18 There are now three attachments listed in the Attach field

better to use an ordinary type that does not include the decompression program. This should avoid problems with the file being filtered, and ensures that the amount of data sent is kept to a minimum.

Sending

Sending an attachment is usually pretty straightforward. In Outlook Express the first step is to compose the Email in the normal way (Figure 3.15). Next operate the Attach button near the top of the window in which the Email has been composed. This produces a standard Windows file browser (Figure 3.16) where you can select the file for attachment to the Email. Operate the Attach button when the correct file has been located and selected.

This takes the program back to the document window where the Attach field near the top should show the name of the attached file and its size (Figure 3.17). To attach more files to the Email just repeat this process as many times as necessary. The Attach field in the document window will show the names and sizes of all the attached files (Figure 3.18). The Email is sent in the normal way once all the files have been attached. Web based Email services such as Yahoo! and Hotmail have similar facilities. Normally it is just a matter of operating the Attachments button when composing the Email, and then using a simple file browser to select the required files. There will be a warning message if you try to use too many attachments or the total size of the files is greater than allowed.

Archiving

If you need to archive files in order to reduce the number of attachments, using an archiving and compression program such as WinZip is very straightforward. When using an unregistered version of WinZip you must first agree to the

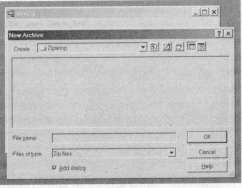

Fig.3.19 Selecting a filename and folder for the new archive file

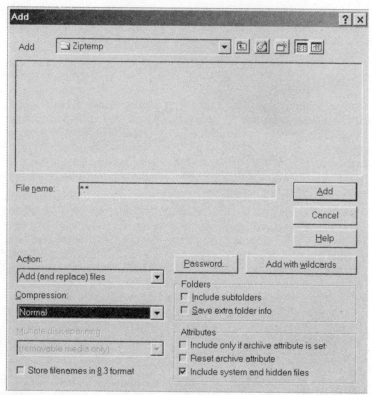

Fig.3.20 Another file browser is used to select the files for the archive

licensing conditions by operating the appropriate button, and then the main window will appear (Figure 3.19). It is assumed here that the "classic" interface was specified during the installation process. You can opt for the wizard approach if preferred. However, as the standard Winzip "classic" interface is not difficult to use and it is generally quicker than using the wizard, I would recommend using the standard interface.

The first task is to tell Winzip where you wish to deposit the archive file, and to provide a name for the file. Select the New Archive option from the file menu (Figure 3.20) to bring up the usual file browser (figure 3.21). If necessary, use the menu at the top of the window to alter the folder to be used for the archive file. A name for the file is entered in the File

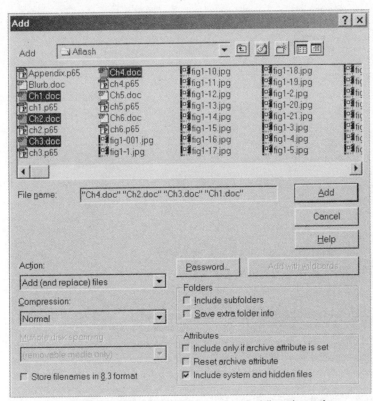

Fig.3.21 A number of files can be selected by holding down the Control key

Name text box, and there is no need to add the Zip extension. This will be added automatically by the program.

Operate the OK button to move on to the next window (Figure 3.22), where the files to be archived are selected. This is done using the top section of the window, which is a standard file browser. It is advisable to have all the files for the archive in a single folder as they can then be selected in one operation. Use the browser to locate the right folder and left-click on the first file to select it. Select the other files by holding down the Control key and left-clicking on their entries in the file browser. There are various options available in the bottom section of the window, but for most purposes the defaults will suffice. With all the required files selected (Figure 3.23), operate the Add button to create the archive file.

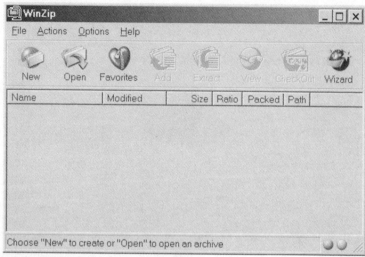

Fig.3.22 The main screen of WinZip 8

The main window then returns, and it displays the contents of the newly created archive (Figure 3.24). It shows the original size of each file together with its compressed size and the degree of compression. In this case the Word DOC format files have been compressed by impressive ratios of around 74 to 77 percent. Some 279k of data has been compressed to a mere 69k. This shows the effectiveness of this method with the right types of file. A ten-megabyte limit could effectively be increased to nearly 80 megabytes with suitable files.

File splitting

A compression program such as WinZip is a possible solution where a file is only slightly too large for your Email service. As pointed out previously, some types of file compress very well while others remain virtually the same size after compression. The only way to tell how small or otherwise a file will be after compression is to try the "suck it and see" method. Where compression will make a file small enough to pass through the system, this almost certainly represents the best way of handling things.

With some types of file there is no major problem in breaking them into small pieces and reconstructing them again. With something like a large

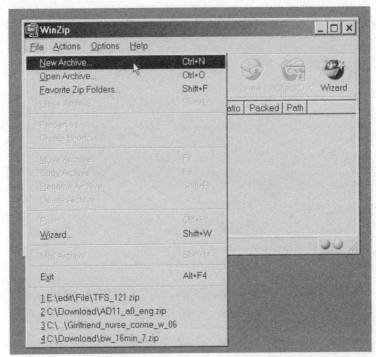

Fig.3.23 The first step is to select the New Archive option

word processor file for example, there should be no difficulty in breaking the document into several chunks and then recombining them again using the word processor. This type of thing is clearly not applicable to all types of file, and it can not be used with a program file for instance. However, there are programs that can take any file, slice it into several pieces, and then combine the pieces again to produce the original file without a byte out of place. In fact the search engine of a major software download site will probably come up with about 50 or more programs of this general type.

Alternative methods

There are plenty of alternatives to using Email as a means of exchanging files, although these are probably only worthwhile where very large files

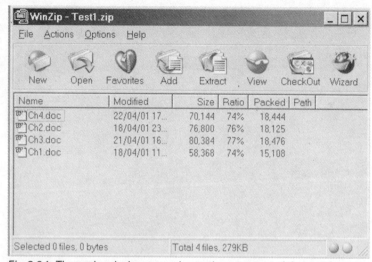

Fig.3.24 The main window now shows the contents of the archive

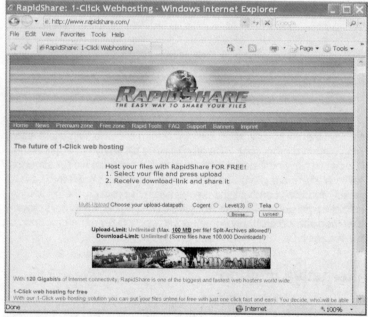

Fig.3.25 The full path and filename are entered in the textbox

Fig.3.26 If preferred, the file can be located and opened using the file browser

are involved. Most ISPs provide their broadband customers with a certain amount of free web space as part of the package. The amount of space varies considerably from one company to another, and it is not always included as standard. Where some free web space is provided, there is usually a size limit of between five and one hundred megabytes.

A fairly small web space allocation is unlikely to be of much practical value when swapping files with others, since it requires more expertise than using the Email method, but does not provide any increase in the maximum file size that can be accommodated. The situation is different with a limit of around fifty or one hundred megabytes, which is far higher than can be handled easily using Email attachments. However, you are effectively making your own miniature website when using this method, which makes life easy for those downloading the files, but requires more expertise on the part of the person producing the website. A simple site of this type is not difficult to set up, and some ISPs even provide helpful

Fig.3.27 A bargraph shows how the upload is progressing

utilities that aid the building of your own website. However, initially it will still require a bit more time and effort than using Email attachments.

An advantage of this system is that, where necessary, files can be distributed to a number of people with a minimum of effort. You only have to upload the files to the website once, and they can then be downloaded by each person that requires them. It is not necessarily true to say that there is no limit on the number of people that can download the files once they have been uploaded to your site, because ISPs often impose download or bandwidth caps, but this should only be a problem if you need to supply large files to dozens of people.

There is a drawback in using your own website, which is that the files are not secure, and can be downloaded by anyone who knows where they are, or just happens to stumble across them. The Email method is not totally secure, but the website approach is not secure at all. Either it

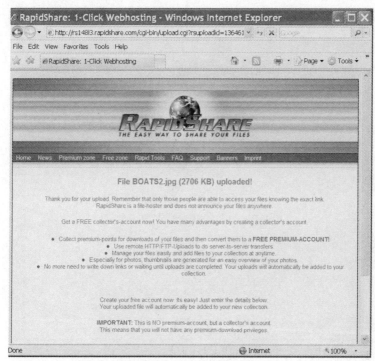

Fig.3.28 The file has been uploaded successfully

should not be used with files that are in any way of a sensitive nature, or the files should be encrypted.

It is possible to use file hosting services if your ISP does not provide plenty of free web space, or you do not feel that making your own website is a practical proposition. The cost of most file hosting services is quite low, and in some cases there is a free service that will suffice for most purposes. Probably the most popular of these services is Rapidshare (www.rapidshare.com), which allows files of up to one hundred megabytes to be uploaded. Larger files can be accommodated by splitting and recombining files using a program such as Winrar.

Even with the free service, there is no limit on the number of files that can be uploaded. However, there are download limits for users who do not have a paid-for account. This works on the basis of having an enforced wait between the downloading of one file and the next. It is still possible

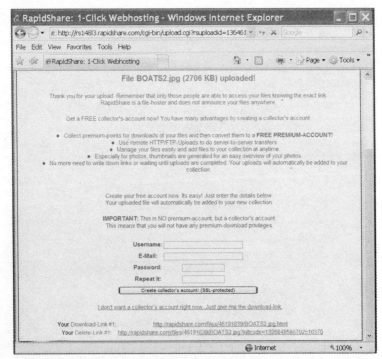

*Fig.3.29 Two links are provided, one of which is used for downloading
the file. The other can be used to delete it*

to download a few hundred megabytes during the course of a day, which
is perfectly adequate for most users.

Rapid uploading

Uploading to a free file hosting site is usually very straightforward, with
no special software being required. An ordinary browser program such
as Internet Explorer together with the built-in features of the host site is
all that should be needed. In the case of Rapidshare it is a matter of first
going to the homepage (Figure 3.25), and then entering the path and
filename of the file you wish to upload, or using the file browser to select
the required file (Figure 3.26). Left-clicking the Upload button starts the
transfer of the file to the server, and there is the usual bargraph to show
how things are progressing (Figure 3.27). Eventually the upload process

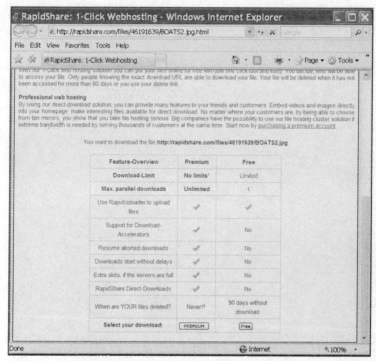

Fig.3.30 Users without an account must operate the Free button

will be completed, and the window will change to indicate that server has received the file (Figure 3.28).

Rapid downloading

Assuming that you do not have and do not wish to create a Rapidshare account, it is then a matter of scrolling down to the bottom of the page and operating the link that produces the download address for your file. The bottom section of the window then changes to look something like Figure 3.29, where there are actually two web addresses. One of these is used to download your file, while the other is used to delete it.

With free accounts your files are automatically deleted after 90 days with no download activity, so it is not absolutely necessary to remove files once you have finished with them. However, doing so might be desirable

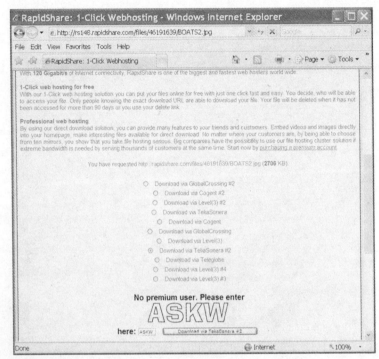

Fig.3.31 The security code must be entered in the textbox

from the security point of view, and it is good practice to delete files from websites once they are not needed any more. This avoids unnecessarily occupying space on the server, and is the "good manners" thing to do when using free web space.

Make a note of the download address and the file to which it applies. It is obviously not possible to download a file without its download address, and this address must be supplied to everyone who will need to download the file. Note that the address provided is not a direct link to the file, but is one that takes users to the file via the Rapidshare system. Using a Rapidshare link produces a window like the one shown in Figure 3.30, and non-account holders can access the file by operating the Free button near the bottom of the window.

This moves things on to a page where a four-character code must be entered into the textbox (Figure 3.31). Free web services often have a

*Fig.3.32   The image file has been downloaded and is displayed in a
             browser*

simple security system of this type where you have to read and then
enter a code, and this is done to prevent inappropriate use of the service
using robot computer systems. Provided the correct code is entered,
the normal download procedure will start. This varies according to the
type of file involved and the particular browser in use. In this case the file
was a Jpg image type, and it was opened in a new browser window
(Figure 3.32).

Instant messaging

Some instant messaging services now provide a file swapping feature,
but it does not normally work in a fashion that is analogous to an Email
attachment. It operates in a way that is more like networking, with shared
folders being used to permit users to upload and download files. This is
a subject that is covered in chapter 6, and it will not be considered further
here.

Points to remember

Some download managers try to obtain fast downloads by using mirror sites. Data is downloaded from whichever site provides the fastest download rate at the time.

Probably the most useful facility of a download manager is its ability to continue where it left off in the event that the connection is lost. This is especially important when trying to download from a server that is not very reliable.

In theory, it is possible to optimise download speeds by making changes to some of the Windows Registry settings. In practice this method is unlikely to make a significant difference to broadband users, since the default settings usually give excellent results. Do not alter any of the Registry settings unless you are sure you know what you are doing. When editing the Registry it is easy to end up doing more harm than good.

Some download managers try to speed up downloads by using several simultaneous connections to the server. This can be very effective where the server otherwise provides data at a rate that is much slower than the highest rate your Internet connection can handle. However, it will not help when accessing a fast server, and not all servers permit multiple connections from a single IP address.

Although peer-to-peer systems can be used as a legitimate means of swapping files, systems of this type tend to contain a large percentage of files that can not be downloaded legally. Unless you can be reasonably sure that downloading files will not involve any copyright infringement, do not download them.

Downloading files other than from sites of well-established and respected companies has to be regarded as a slightly risky business. Downloading files via peer-to-peer services has to be regarded as very risky, since a significant percentage of the files on offer contain viruses, Trojans, etc. Only download material in this way if your PC is fully protected by antivirus software, a firewall, and a program specifically for dealing with spyware, adware, etc.

Speed test sites can be useful for checking the sort of download and upload rates you can expect from real-world websites. The Internet infrastructure can have a small but significant effect on download and upload speeds, so expect slightly different results from different speed testing sites.

Most Email services now provide users with large inboxes having capacities of a few hundred megabytes. This makes it easier to transfer large files as Email attachments. Note though, that there are often fairly modest limits on the number and size of Email attachments. A size limit of five or ten megabytes per Email is typical.

Some Email services have security measures that remove certain types of file. In particular, any form of executable (program) file is likely to be filtered, so it is best to avoid using self-extracting archives.

File hosting sites provide a convenient means of exchanging large files, and some of these provide free services that are adequate for most users. This method makes it easy for numerous users to download the files, but bear in mind that any system that places your files on a website lacks security. Any file swapping of this general type should not be used for files that contain any sensitive information unless they have been encrypted.

Free file hosting websites can be useful for file swapping. The maximum file size is often quite generous at around 100 megabytes or more, and larger files can be accommodated using splitting and joining techniques.

Audio and Internet radio

Streaming

Downloading media files and listening to streamed media via the Internet has been a growth industry in recent years, and has already resulted in large changes to the way in which many people listen to music, the news and weather, etc. Streamed media is where you go to a web site and listen to radio programmes that are either supplied on demand, or are streamed "live". The "live" streams are the Internet equivalent to an ordinary radio station, and the term "Internet radio" is sometimes used to describe a service of this type.

An on-demand service has an archive of audio recordings that are streamed to the user as and when requested. Downloading audio files is similar to this, but you do not normally listen to the file as it is downloaded. You download the complete file and then play it whenever you happen to feel like it. With any form of streamed audio you listen to it as it is fed to your PC, but there is not normally any facility for storing the audio as a file so that it can be played again later. In order to listen to the material again you have to go back to the web site and stream it to your PC again. This may seem like an unnecessary restriction, but it is often a stipulation of the copyright holder that the programme material can only be streamed and not stored on recipient's computers for use at later dates.

In this chapter we will only consider audio files and streaming. With a broadband connection it is also possible to download and stream videos as well, and this is an increasingly popular application for a broadband Internet connection. However this subject is covered in a separate chapter (see chapter 7) and it will not be discussed any further here.

Quality issues

Strictly speaking, you do not need a broadband Internet connection in order to download sound files or to listen to streamed audio via the Internet. On the other hand, and being realistic about things, audio via the Internet is an application that will often be slow or even impractical when using a dial-up connection. The situation is very different with even a relatively slow broadband connection. Large audio files can be downloaded quite quickly, and high-quality streamed audio is no problem.

It is with streamed audio that the limitations of a dial-up connection are most likely to be noticed. A minimum connection speed of about 128 kilobits per second is needed in order to provide a reasonably good quality stereo output. The maximum of 56 kilobits per second provided by a dial-up connection is barely sufficient for high quality mono audio. In practice, due to the limitations of real-world dial-up connections a bit rate of significantly less the 56 kilobits per second has to be used. There are systems that are designed to stream stereo audio over a dial-up connection, and at times the technical quality of these systems is reasonable. However, much of the time the limitations of the low bit rate are all too apparent, and some very odd sounding results are produced!

Technical quality is not an issue when downloading files that will be stored on the computer's hard disc drive and then played using a media player, or when downloading files that will be used to produce audio CDs. It is more a matter of time, since it will take several hours to download a complete CD, and this is assuming that the files are in some highly compressed form. Downloading the 600 to 700 megabytes of data on an audio CD could take a day or two!

Another problem with a dial-up connection is that the connection tends to be lost every so often. This can be a major problem if you live well away from the telephone exchange, or the cables that connect your telephone system to the exchange are "not as young as they used to be". It is a problem that seems to affect all dial-up Internet connections to some extent. While broadband connections are not totally immune to these drop-outs, unless you are very unlucky they will be extremely rare.

It is usually possible to resume an interrupted download provided it is handled by some form of download manager program. Interruptions with streamed audio are obviously more problematic. In most cases the problem is not that the connection with the source is lost, but is rather that the link can not maintain the data flow at an adequate rate.

Practical streaming systems always use a system of buffering, where a certain amount of data is downloaded before you start listening to the audio. This means that you are actually listening to a slightly delayed version of the programme. Although a "live" stream is genuinely sent to your PC "live" as it happens, you are not actually listening to the material "live" as it happens. Of course, the short delay is usually of no consequence.

The point of the buffering is that the audio stored in the memory buffer can fill in any gaps that would otherwise occur when the data can not be streamed at an adequate rate. While buffering is reasonably effective at glossing over a few small gaps, it is of no use if the link to the source can not maintain an adequate flow of data. The buffering will work well at first, but then the audio will go for a few seconds, stop, go for a few more seconds, and then stop again, and so on.

Intermittent operation tends to be a major problem when using a dial-up connection, but it can also occur with a broadband type. The stated transfer rate of a broadband connection is genuinely achieved most of the time, but bear in mind that the rate can be lower during periods of peak activity due to contention rate issues. In practice this is unlikely to be a major problem, since the speed of most broadband connections is much higher than the bit rate used for high quality stereo audio. Your broadband Internet connection is likely to be more than adequate for most audio streaming even if it does slow down slightly from time to time.

An important point to bear in mind when trying to maintain quite high data transfer rates is that the speed of the system is limited by its slowest constituent part. The Internet can sometimes slow down due to a bottleneck somewhere between your PC and the server. The more normal cause of problems is simply that the server is overloaded, and can not supply all users with data at an adequate rate. Some systems are designed to limit the number of users to a manageable level so that this type of thing is avoided. However, with a server of this type you will find that the service is sometimes fully utilized by the existing users and is unavailable to new users for a while.

Audio formats

As anyone familiar with the world of computing would expect, a number of music file formats have been produced over the years. Some of these use no compression, while others use lossless compression, and in either case there is no loss of audio quality. With lossless compression there is a reduction in the file size so that download times are reduced. Several types of audio file use compression that does involve a loss of quality, but the loss of quality is usually minimal and the reduction in file sizes can be very significant. A 650 megabyte audio CD would typically be reduced to less than 100 megabytes of compressed data using one of these formats. Many audio formats are of little or no interest to users of portable players or to those using a computer to play digital music files. These are the formats that are of most interest in the current context.

MP3

This is the format that has become synonymous with digital music and portable music players. It is known by a variety of names such as MPEG 3 and MPEG 1 level 3, but these days it is most commonly referred to as MP3. It is apparently based on the same fractal mathematics that is used for the JPEG image format. Like the JPEG image format, it achieves a fairly high degree of compression, but it can also give a noticeable reduction in quality.

With MP3, and some other digital music formats, you will encounter the term "bit rate". This is the total number of bits per second used when encoding and playing back the file. The 16-bit audio on a CD is at a sampling rate of 44,100 per second. This works out at 705,600 bits per second, but there are another 705,600 bits per second in the other stereo channel. This gives a total rate of 1,411,200 bits per second for the full stereo signal. A thousand bits is a kilobit, and a million bits is a megabit, so this rate would more normally be given as 1,411.2 kilobits per second or 1.4112 megabits per second.

The MP3 format supports a wide range of bit rates, but the lowest ones are only suitable for low quality signals. Most people find that 128 kilobits per second represents the lowest rate that gives acceptable results with stereo music. However, not everyone is happy with a rate as low as this, which is well under one tenth of the rate used for CDs. Higher rates of 160, 192, 256, and 320 kilobits per second are quite common, and provide superior sound quality. Bear in mind though, that higher bit rates do not provide a massive increase in sound quality, but do give a massive increase in file sizes. For example, a file encoded at 256 kilobits per second is twice the size of one encoded at 128 kilobits per second.

MP3 VBR

Some MP3 files are now encoded using a variable bit rate (VBR). As the name suggests, this method does not use a constant bit rate, but instead varies the bit rate to suit the program material. The rate is speeded up for complex material and slowed down if it is deemed that this will not noticeably impair the sound quality. The idea of this is to give a high perceived sound quality while keeping file sizes as small as possible.

Variable bit rate encoding can produce some impressive results, but bear in mind that not all portable players and media player programs support this type of MP3 file. Note also that portable players do not always support files that are encoded using a high constant bit rate such as 320 kilobits per second. Consequently, the fact that you have downloaded an MP3 file does not mean that it is certain to play properly on your portable MP3 player. The chances of problems occurring are relatively small if you have a modern and fairly upmarket player. They are quite high if you are using an older or budget MP3 player. Most modern PC media players can handle high bit rates.

MP3 is not a format that is free of licensing restrictions. It is owned by the Moving Picture Experts Group (MPEG), as are the various Mpeg video encoding formats. This is largely of academic importance to most users, since they will not use MP3 in a fashion that incurs any royalty payments.

WMA

This is the Windows Media Audio format, which should not be confused with its video counterpart (WMV). WMA was designed to be the standard audio format for use with Windows and the software that runs under this operating system. With many other music file formats in use on Windows PCs, including the ever popular MP3 format, it is has not really achieved this status. It is in widespread use though, and some portable music players will happily work with most WMA files.

Like MP3, the WMA format uses compression techniques that produce some loss of sound quality. WMA is generally regarded as being more efficient than MP3, and it can therefore be used at lower bit rates while still maintaining acceptable sound quality. Some users find a rate as low as 64 kilobits per second gives what they deem to be acceptable sound quality, but most people find that 96 kilobits per second is a more realistic minimum rate.

There are now two forms of the WMA format in addition to the standard (constant bit rate) type. One of the extra versions is a lossless format, but as one would expect, this does not provide a great deal of compression and it is not supported by most portable players. There is also a variable bit-rate version. This is well suited to use with portable

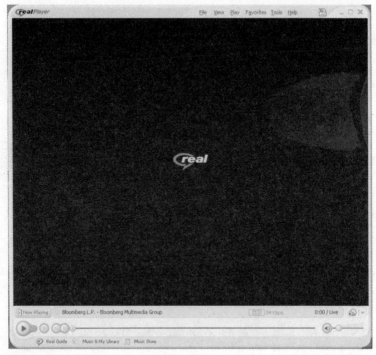

Fig.4.1 The free version of the Real Player is adequate for most users

music players, but at the moment there are relatively few portable players that can handle WMA variable bit rate files.

Many of the files sold by legitimate download sites are in a protected WMA format. This subject is dealt with in more detail later in this chapter, but a protected WMA is one that has "strings attached". In general, this means that you can only burn a protected file to an audio CD a certain number of times, and that the file can only be played on certain computers. You are unlikely to be able to play a protected WMA file on a portable player, or legally convert it to a more amenable format. Consequently, you have to make quite sure that a file of this type will be of real use to you before buying and downloading it.

Real thing

The Real Audio format is another one that uses large amounts of compression, but can incur a significant loss of quality as a result. It

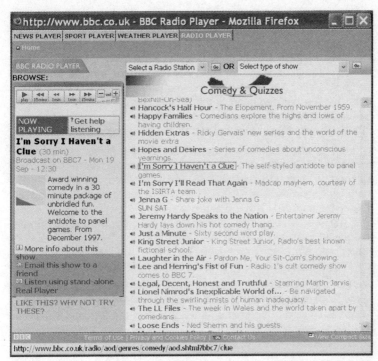

Fig.4.2   The BBC Radio Player is based on the Real Player and will only work if the latter is installed on your PC

can, of course, provide very high quality results provided the bit rate is not made too low. The Real Audio format can be used to produce compressed music files, but it is not used in this way to any great extent. It is a format that is often used in applications that require streamed audio. The video version (Real Video) is used a great deal for streamed video.

It is quite common for very low bit rates to be used with the audio and video versions, giving what are often extremely rough results. This seems to have resulted in some users gaining the impression that the Real formats are only suitable for low quality applications. They are capable of high quality results though, provided a suitably high bit rate is used. Sometimes streamed audio sources provide an option for broadband users to use a higher bit rate, and this should provide greatly improved results.

The Real Audio format is not widely supported by portable players or media player programs. The normal way of playing a Real Audio file or material streamed in this format is to download the free version of the Real Player (Figure 4.1) from the Real web site (www.real.com). There are commercial versions of the Real Player that provide additional features, but for most purposes the free version is perfectly adequate. Note that the basic version of the Real Player is not only suitable for playing Real Audio files and streamed material. It is capable of playing CDs and media files in a variety of formats, including some video types.

In order to play streamed material via the Real Player program it is normally just a matter of left-clicking the appropriate link. The program will then be launched automatically and will start to play the streamed material. In some cases it will not be obvious that it is the Real Player is playing the material. This is where the supplier of the streamed material uses the Real Player with their own skin for the program. In other words, the player you see on the screen does not look like the normal Real Player program, and it might even have one or two features that are not found on the normal version of the Real Player program.

The BBC Radio Player is a good example of this (Figure 4.2). This does not look anything like the normal version of the Real Player, and it has additional facilities that enable users to select the required station or recorded material. However, the standard Real Player program is there under the add-on skin that is downloaded when the BBC Radio Player is launched. Unless the Real Player program is properly installed on the PC, the BBC Radio Player program can not function.

Files that are in the Real Audio format usually have an "ra" file extension. Those in the Real Video format generally have an "rv" or "rm" (Real Movie) file extension. Some Real Audio files now have an "rm" file extension. The idea seems to be that all Real files should have the same "rm" (Real Media) extension, and that the player can still sort out which type of file it is playing. Matters are not always as clear-cut for users though.

Files that are in a Real format can be downloaded in the normal way, and played on the Real Player program. Can you save streamed audio or video to disc so that you can watch it or listen to it at some later time? This is a question that tends to be asked by practically everyone that uses streamed media, and it seems reasonable. After all, you can easily record ordinary radio and television programs. Unfortunately, the ordinary Real Player program does not have a facility for recording streamed programs.

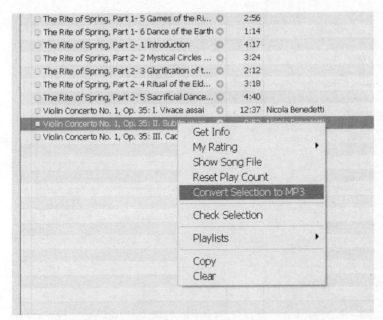

Fig.4.3 The iTunes program can convert files to the MP3 format

It is possible to obtain programs that will store streamed signals on the hard disc of a computer, and the data is usually converted into a normal (non-streamed) audio or video format. Whether it is possible to use such programs legally is another matter. Recording most streamed media seems to be prohibited, which is a pity, but you should always stay within any licensing restrictions.

AAC/MP4/M4a

This is the Advanced Audio Coding system, which is also known as MP4 and M4a. It enables high degrees of compression to be achieved while retaining excellent audio quality. It is in widespread use because it was adopted by Apple as the normal format for their iTunes program and music download service, and their iPod players. All the iPods can be used with MP3 files as well incidentally. Unfortunately, few MP3 players can handle AAC files, although it does seem to have much more widespread support amongst media player programs. There is more than one version of AAC, and it is the LC (low complexity) version that is widely supported by hardware players.

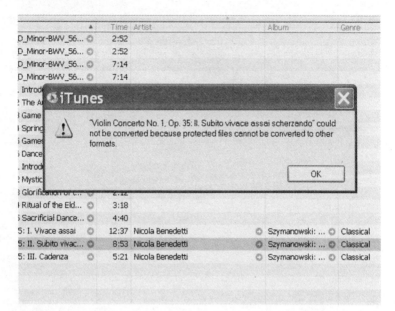

	Time	Artist	Album	Genre
D_Minor-BWV_56...	2:52			
D_Minor-BWV_56...	2:52			
D_Minor-BWV_56...	7:14			
D_Minor-BWV_56...	7:14			
. Introd				
? The A				
3 Game				
I Spring				
5 Games				
5 Dance				
. Introd				
? Mystic				
3 Glorification of t...	2:12			
I Ritual of the Eld...	3:18			
5 Sacrificial Dance...	4:40			
5: I. Vivace assai	12:37	Nicola Benedetti	Szymanowski: ...	Classical
5: II. Subito vivac...	8:53	Nicola Benedetti	Szymanowski: ...	Classical
5: III. Cadenza	5:21	Nicola Benedetti	Szymanowski: ...	Classical

iTunes

"Violin Concerto No. 1, Op. 35: II. Subito vivace assai scherzando" could not be converted because protected files cannot be converted to other formats.

OK

Fig.4.4 An error message is produced if you try to convert a protected AAC file

Note that files downloaded from the iTunes store are in a protected AAC format. Protected AAC files usually have an M4p file extension, with the "p" presumably standing for protected. The restrictions on these files are such that it is not possible to legitimately convert them to another format such as MP3. This means that they can not be played on most portable players other than iPods, and can not be converted to a format that is compatible with players other than iPods. Perhaps not surprisingly, you can play the downloaded files on as many iPods as you like.

You may sometimes find helpful web sites or bulletin boards which explain that it is actually possible to convert protected AAC files into MP3 format using the free Apple iTunes program. The usual suggestion is that you load the file into the iTunes Library, right-click its entry, and then choose the Convert Selection to MP3 option from the pop-up menu (Figure 4.3). This will give the desired result with a non-protected AAC file, but with a protected file it will simply produce an error message (Figure 4.4). Bear in mind that even if you did find a method of converting protected AAC files to another format such as MP3, actually doing so would be outside the licensing restrictions.

MPC

This format is most commonly called MPC, but it is also known as the Musepack format. It seems to be aimed primarily at producing very high quality results rather than the highest possible amount of compression for a given audio quality. This is probably the reason for its relative lack of popularity. MPC is not supported by hardware players, but MPC files can be handled by some media player programs. However, this usually requires a plug-in to be installed. It is a format that does not seem to be used a great deal these days.

OGG

The OGG format, which is also known as the OGG Vorbis format, was designed to be an open source alternative to the proprietary systems such MP3 and WMA. In other words, it is largely free from any licensing restrictions and for most purposes this format can be used free of charge. In fact, OGG Vorbis would appear to be fully open source, which means that anyone can use it in any way they like, with no royalty payments or other charges being incurred. This has obvious attractions for small scale commercial or amateur distribution of music in a highly compressed form.

While the use of OGG is nothing like as widespread as MP3 or WMA, its good performance and cost-free use make it attractive to many users. Consequently, it is a format that you are quite likely to encounter if you download free and legitimate music files. The OGG format is supported by a reasonable number of media player programs. It is not supported by WMP 10 or 11, but it is not too difficult to find a free plug-in on the Internet that enables WMP 10 or 11 to play OGG files. A few portable music players can handle OGG files, but this feature is still something of a rarity. It produces good results at quite low bit rates, so technically it is a good choice for portable music players.

WAV/Wave

The Wave format is more popularly known as the WAV format, and files of this type normally have a WAV extension. It is a very basic format that is lossless because it does not use any form of compression. This limits its usefulness, because it tends to produce very large file sizes. It is best suited to small sound clips and sound effects where the lack of compression will not result in huge files. It is a standard Windows format, and as such it has quite widespread support. Many portable players and media player programs can handle WAV files. It is often used as a "halfway house" when converting from one format to another or ripping CDs.

FLAC

FLAC stands for "free lossless audio codec". Codec is a term that you will often encounter with digital music and video, and it is a contraction of coder/decoder. This is simply the software or hardware device used to generate a compressed audio or video file, and to turn it back into a decompressed stream of data. FLAC is a lossless format that achieves a moderate amount of compression. It is closely associated with the OGG format and I suppose it could be regarded as a sort of lossless version of OGG. At the moment anyway, it is less widely supported than OGG, and its relatively small compression ratios are unlikely to make it popular for use with hardware players. It is supported by some media player programs, and it can be played by WMP 10 and 11 with the aid of a free plug-in program from the Internet.

Like the OGG format, its free status makes it attractive to users on a tight budget. Therefore, it is a format that is likely to be encountered if you download free and legitimate music files. The fact that it provides no loss of quality makes it well suited to applications where the file will be decompressed and burned to an ordinary CD. OGG is a better choice in applications where the ultimate in sound quality is not essential.

APE

Believe it or not, this is a lossless format from Monkey's Audio, and it is sometimes known by the Monkey's Audio (or just Monkey Audio) name. It has probably been the most popular lossless audio format, and might still be. However, it is under pressure from alternatives such as FLAC. Relatively few players can handle this format, but there is a free plug-in for the Winamp player program. There is also a free compression and decompression program for use with Wave files. The free software and more details of the APE format are available from the Monkey's Audio web site at www.monkeysaudio.com.

ALE

ALE stands for "Apple lossless encoder", and this format was produced for users that require maximum quality rather than small file sizes. With a 40 gigabyte iPod it is possible to store large amounts of music using this format, but it has less appeal to those using iPods with much lower storage capacities. This format is little used by those that do not have Apple audio products.

ATRAC

These days this format is often called ATRAC3 rather than just ATRAC. It was originally devised as a compressed format to permit Sony to get a usable amount of music onto each of their MiniDiscs, as used in their MiniDisc (MD) players. It is now used for other Sony portable music players, and also for their Connect music download service. ATRAC files can be played on a PC using the player program that can be obtained from one of Sony's Connect sites (www.connect-europe.com/GB/en/website/static/node23.html for the UK version of the site).

MIDI

MIDI stands for "musical instruments digital interface". There are vast numbers of MIDI files on the Internet, and they can be played by many media players including WMP 10. However, this is a music format and not what could accurately be described as an audio format. The purpose of MIDI is to enable suitably equipped electronic musical instruments to communicate with each other, and (usually) with a computer. A number or instruments can be connected together to effectively form one huge instrument that can be controlled by a computer. A MIDI file consists of a series of instructions, such as turn on this note on channel 12, and switch off that note on channel 14. The file contains no sounds as such. It is up to the instruments in the system to turn the instructions into the corresponding sounds.

As pointed out previously, many media player programs can handle MIDI files, including WMP 10. You do not need a set of musical instruments connected to your PC in order to play these files. All you need is a sound card that has a suitable built-in synthesiser, or a basic soundcard plus some software that can give it this facility. In practice, most PC soundcards are able to handle MIDI files, and in some cases there are two or three types of synthesis available. Unfortunately, the sound quality varies considerably from one soundcard to another. Where two or more types of synthesis are available, there can be considerable differences in quality from one method to another. Some MIDI files and soundcards produce very good results, while others are mediocre at best.

MIDI has huge limitations as a general means of distributing music. Since it can not handle recorded sounds it can not accommodate vocalists at all, and it only handles instruments after a fashion. MIDI is not compatible with hardware players since they lack any form of built-in synthesis. It is a file format that is really only of use to those involved in music-making using electronic instruments and computers.

Changing formats

As far as possible, it is best to avoid the need to convert music from one file format to another. Where a large number of files are involved, converting them all to a different format would be very time consuming, and could be impractically so. Another point to bear in mind is that the result of a conversion is something of an unknown quantity, or perhaps that should be an unknown quality. It will certainly not give an improvement in quality, and is unlikely to fully maintain the quality of the original. It would be reasonable to expect a slight reduction in quality, although the loss of fidelity will often be insignificant in practice.

Note that it is perfectly all right to decompress a file in a lossless format and then convert it to a highly compressed format. Decompression is not really a conversion, and it restores a perfect copy of the original. The only loss of fidelity will be the normal loss caused by converting the music to a highly compressed format.

When using a media player on a PC it is not usually necessary to convert a file to a format that the player can accommodate. Most players can handle a wide variety of file formats, and in some cases even more formats can be handled with the aid of plug-ins. Many of these plug-in programs are available as free downloads from the Internet. For example, there are plug-ins that enable WMP 10 and 11 to play files in the FLAC and OGG formats, and there is an APE plug-in for the popular Winamp player program. Where you have files in a format that is totally incompatible with your normal player it would probably be more practical to switch to a different player program for those files instead of trying to convert them to a compatible format.

If you download music files with the intention of burning them onto audio CDs, try to avoid using file conversions prior to the burning process. These can make a fairly slow process even slower. Few file formats can be handled by WMP 10 and 11 when burning CDs, but alternatives such as the popular Nero range can accommodate a wider range of formats. Yet more formats can be accommodated with the aid of plug-ins. Some formats seem to evolve slightly over a period of time, so it is advisable to do some searching on the Internet to ensure that any plug-ins you use are the most up-to-date versions available. If you get error messages when using a plug-in it is likely that it is an older version than the one used to create the source files. Installing the latest version of the plug-in should cure the problem. If not, it is likely that the source files have been corrupted and are unusable.

File conversions are most likely to be needed because files are downloaded from the Internet in a format that is not compatible with your hardware player. Most portable players are only compatible with a very limited range of file formats. In fact many MP3 players are strictly that, and can not play any other format. There will probably be restrictions on the types of MP3 file that can be played, with those having high bit rates or variable bit rate files being unplayable. If you play an MP3 file and it is too fast and (or) intermittent, it is a fair bet that it has a bit rate that is too high for the player.

Copy protection

If you are paying for downloaded files it is important to make sure that they are in a file format that is fully compatible with your player. Many of the files that these sites provide are in some form of protected format. This means that it would probably not be possible to convert them to another format, and that it would almost certainly be outside the licensing conditions if you did find a way of making the conversion.

Sometimes files are offered in two formats, one of which is protected and one that can be burned to a CD, used on an MP3 player, or whatever. The version with fewer restrictions will usually cost more, and might only be available as a complete CD with the individual tracks not being sold separately. Unfortunately, unrestricted files tend to cost a lot more than the protected versions, and in some cases it is actually cheaper to buy the CD. It is important to understand exactly what you are getting before paying for any music downloads. The chances of getting a refund are not good if you successfully download files that you can not use.

If in doubt, it is probably better to buy the CD. Unless the CD has some form of copy protection, which is also known as Digital Rights Management (DRM), it should be easy to rip the tracks into files of practically any format. Ripping them to a format that is suitable for a hardware player should certainly pose no real problems. CDs that are protected by DRM are something of a rarity at the time of writing, but are likely to prove totally useless if you wish to rip their contents. In some cases they can not even be played on a computer.

Files made available for no charge might be in a form that most players can handle such as MP3 or WMA, but many are not. The free downloads are mostly provided by bands, individual artists, and even full symphony orchestras trying to obtain some cheap publicity. They will probably wish to avoid the hassle and costs associated with proprietary file formats, and often opt for APE, FLAC, or OGG files. Apart from OGG, there is little chance of a portable player being able to handle these formats, and you are quite likely to be out of luck with OGG.

Many media player programs can use plug-ins that expand their repertoire of compatible file formats, but there is no equivalent to this for hardware players. It is possible that there will be a firmware upgrade available for your player, and that this will expand its capabilities. Unfortunately, it is unlikely to give an increase in the supported file formats. In order to play these formats, or any of the other less common ones, it is usually necessary to convert them to something more suitable such as MP3 files.

It has to be pointed out here that the fact that you can download something free of charge does not necessarily mean that you can use it in any way that takes your fancy. The copyright in the recording is usually retained by the artist or artists who produced the recording. There will usually be a ban on selling copies of it in any form, and making non-commercial copies might not be permitted either. There could also be restrictions on copying that effectively make it illegal to convert the file into a suitable format for a hardware player and upload it to the player. In effect, you can download the file to your PC and play it using a suitable media player program, but anything beyond this is not permitted. If the licensing conditions are too restrictive you have to give serious thought as to whether it is worthwhile downloading the file.

Converting

In general, media player programs do not have much ability to convert files from one format to another. Plug-ins that enable them to play a greater range of file formats do not necessarily enable them to do anything else with those formats. In fact it is unusual for these plug-ins to permit anything other than the files to be played. You might even find that some of the more advanced facilities of the program do not function when using some plug-ins. Actually, the more advanced features often work with only one or two types of file, and the chances of them working with the less common file types via a plug-in are practically zero.

CD burning programs do not offer file conversion as such, but by burning the file to a CD it is converted into a form that is easily turned into MP3 files and files of other formats. This is a rather slow and cumbersome way of handling things though, and it involves burning a CD that will probably be of no further use once the conversion has been made. This

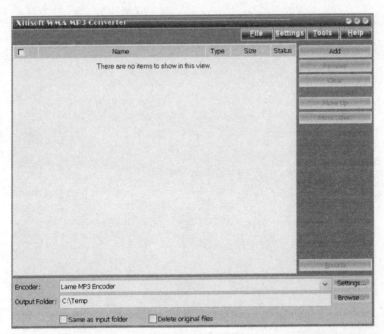

Fig.4.5 The opening screen of the Xilisoft WMA MP3 Converter

method is something that is best avoided unless desperation sets in, which it may well do from time to time!

The easy way to convert files from one format to another is to use a special audio file conversion program, and plenty of these are available on the Internet. Unfortunately, there seems to be a lack of free programs of this type that are easy to use and work well. Many of these programs are shareware though, so you can try them and ascertain that they work properly before handing over any money. I would definitely advise testing any form of file conversion program before buying it, since this type of software is not really known for its technical excellence and reliability. It is not aided in this respect by the occasional tweaking of some file formats.

The Xilisoft WMA MP3 Converter (www.xilisoft.com) is one of the better known file conversion programs, and despite its name it does actually handle a wide range of file formats including MP4, APE, FLAC, and OGG. Figure 4.5 shows the opening screen of this program. There are some options available at the bottom of the screen where you can choose the

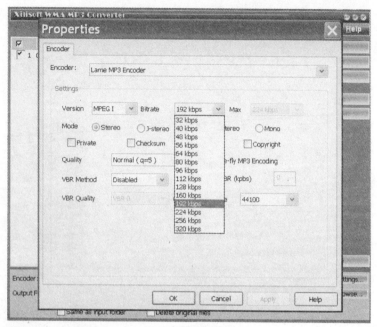

Fig.4.6 A full range of bit rates is available

encoder that will be used, the destination folder for the converted files, and whether the original file should be deleted.

In theory it should not matter which encoder you use when there is a choice of two or more for the same file type. In practice you might find that one gives more reliable results than the others, so it might be worth experimenting a little. It is not a good idea to delete the original file until you are sure that the converted version fully meets your requirements. You might not have selected the correct settings, or the computer could glitch during the conversion. Therefore, it is not advisable to accept the option that deletes the original file unless you have a backup copy.

Keeping an archive copy the original version of the file is probably a good idea. At some later time you might need to convert it to yet another format. Results are likely to be best if you make the conversion from the original file rather than one that has already undergone a conversion.

You have the option of changing the output folder from its default setting. Even if you do not change the destination folder for the converted file,

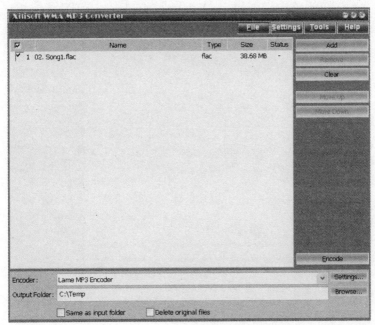

Fig.4.7 A FLAC file is loaded and ready for conversion

make a note of the folder that the program is using. This avoids the embarrassment of converting the file and then being unable to find the converted version on the computer's hard disc drive!

Selecting Encoder Properties from the Settings menu produces the Properties window of Figure 4.6. Here you can select various options, but in most cases the defaults will be suitable. However, you will have to set the required bit rate and type (constant or variable). Operating the File button produces the usual file browser so that the required source file or files can be selected. In Figure 4.7 a single FLAC format file has been selected and the program is ready to start. Operating the Encode button gets the conversion under way (Figure 4.8), and the process usually takes a matter of seconds for each track.

Changing bit rates

It is not always a change to a totally different format that is required. Media player programs can mostly handle any version of a supported

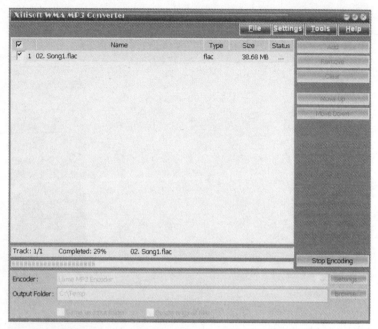

Fig.4.8 A bargraph shows how the conversion is progressing

format, and they are not usually fazed by high or variable bit rates. The same is not true of hardware players, many of which can not handle bit rates of more than about 160 kilobits per second. Even where the specification sheet for a player indicates that high rates can be accommodated, in reality there are often problems when using rates that are close to the upper limit. I have a "cheap and cheerful" MP3 player that can supposedly handle MP3 files with bit rates of up to 256 kilobits per second, but in practice it produces garbled results with most files recorded at this rate.

Breaks in the audio, odd noises and effects, playback that is too fast, and generally erratic operation could indicate that the file has become corrupted. However, it is a good idea to check a suspect file by playing it using a computer and a media player program. There is clearly nothing wrong with the file if it plays perfectly using a media player program. Assuming the hardware player is not faulty, it is simply that the player is not able to operate continuously at high bit rates. Files that use a variable bit rate also tend to be problematic when used with hardware players.

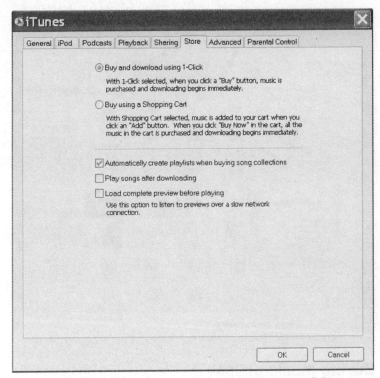

Fig.4.9 The radio buttons give a choice of normal or one-click ordering

There can be problems with erratic operation, or the player might simply refuse to make any attempt to play the file.

Although the software manufacturers do not usually make it a selling point, and sometimes make no mention of it in their advertising literature, most audio conversion programs can be used to make conversions to a lower bit rate. In general, the process for making this type of conversion is the same as usual, but the output format is the same as the input type. The output bit rate must be set at the required new rate, and any other output parameters must be set at the desired settings. The Xilisoft WMA MP3 Converter is a program that is able to make a conversion to a lower bit rate.

Fig.4.10 The iTunes home page

Buying music online

There are numerous stores selling music downloads, and for this example the Apple iTunes store has been selected simply because it is probably the biggest and best-known. Note that this source provides protected AAC files and not the MP3 variety. The downloaded files should play perfectly well using a computer plus a suitable player, such as the iTunes type. They will also play on iPods, but not other MP3 players. In order to use the iTunes shop it is first necessary to download and install the iTunes software from the Apple site at:

http://www.apple.com/itunes/download/

Before trying the iTunes download service it is a good idea to check that the iTunes program is set to use the store in the way that best suits your requirements. Select Preferences from the Edit menu and then operate the Store tab of the preferences window. The Store section of this window is shown in Figure 4.9, and it is the two radio buttons at the top of the window that are of most importance. These give the option of one-click

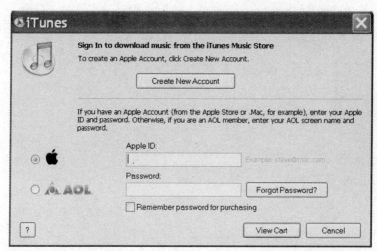

Fig.4.11 An Apple ID and password are needed to place an order

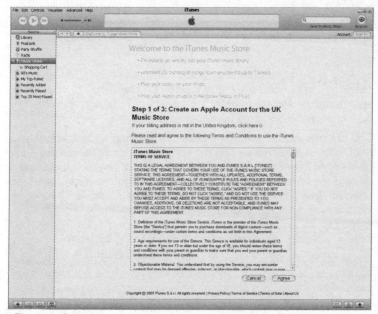

Fig.4.12 A new account can be created from within the iTunes
          program

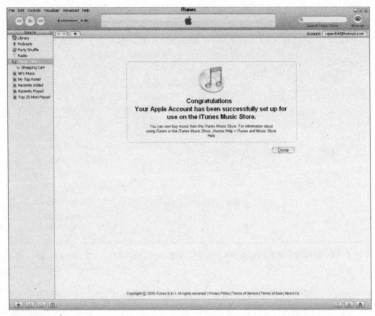

Fig.4.13 The account has been created and an order can be placed

ordering or the conventional method of using a shopping basket and a checkout. With one-click ordering you can literally order downloads with a single click of the mouse. This gives the ultimate in convenience, but it is not necessarily the best approach.

One obvious problem with any one-click ordering system is that you have to be careful that you do not accidentally order something. It is probably not a good choice for those who are not very expert at using a mouse. Perhaps of greater importance, with the one-click option the selected track starts to download as soon as you order it. This can be inconvenient, particularly with a slow dial-up connection. Ordering more music can be virtually impossible until the download has finished and there is sufficient free bandwidth to continue using the Internet.

The shopping basket method is relatively slow and cumbersome, but it provides an opportunity for you to check that you have not accidentally ordered the wrong track before committing yourself to the sale. You can also choose everything you require and then download it. The shopping basket method is the safer option until you have gained some experience

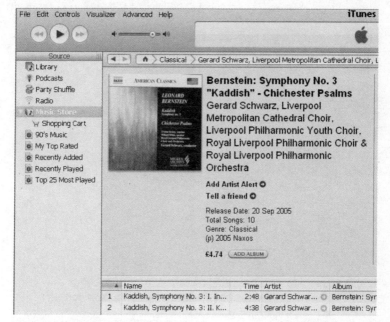

Fig.4.14 The CD's details are shown in the upper section of the window

with the iTunes service. As with any music download service, bear in mind that downloading more than a few tracks can take a very long time when using a dial-up Internet connection. Try not to get carried away.

In order to enter the iTunes store it is just a matter of left-clicking the Music Store entry in the left-hand column of the iTunes program. Of course, there must be an active Internet connection so that the program can connect to the iTunes site. There will be a short delay while the program makes the connection to the Internet, contacts the iTunes site, and downloads the home page, but the latter should soon appear in the main panel (Figure 4.10). If the shopping basket method of ordering has been selected, there will be a Shopping Cart entry in the right-hand column of the window. Left-clicking this entry will usually show the contents of the shopping cart, if any. However, initially it will produce the pop-up window of Figure 4.11.

In order to use the Apple iTunes store it is necessary to first register with this service. Once registered, you can sign on to the iTunes site using your Apple ID and password. You can sign up with iTunes by operating

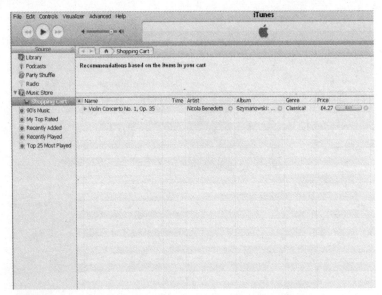

Fig.4.15 Here one item has been added to the shopping cart

the Create New Account button and going through the usual Internet sign-up process. This is all done from within the iTunes program (Figure 4.12), which effectively becomes a web browser when using the iTunes store. Note that you have to provide credit or debit card details in order to register with the iTunes store even if you will be using the shopping cart method of ordering. Assuming all goes well you should end up with the page shown in Figure 4.13, and you are then ready to proceed.

The iTunes store has the usual range of music categories plus a search facility. Having found a likely CD, its details will be provided in the upper part of the main panel (Figure 4.14). There is a button here so that you can order the entire CD. The individual tracks are listed in the lower section of the main panel, with a button for each one so that individual tracks can be ordered. All the individual tracks are not available for some CDs. Note that there are three buttons in the top left-hand corner of the main panel, and these provide the usual browser function of going back one page, forward one page, and going to the home page. Of course, in this case the home page is the iTunes home page and not the one used for your normal web browser.

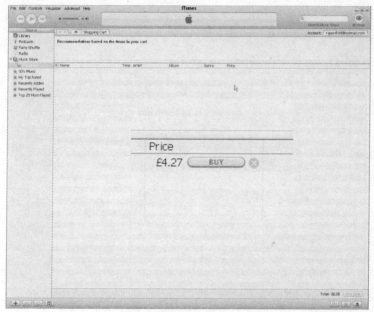

Fig.4.16 Operating the "X" button (see inset) removes an item from the basket

Having ordered something, it should be shown in the shopping cart (Figure 4.15). You did not operate the ordering button or something has gone wrong with the system if it does not appear here. If you change your mind and decide not to go ahead and buy something, just operate the tiny button marked with an "X" that is just to the right of the item's Buy button. It will then be removed from the list (Figure 4.16) and you will not have been charged anything.

In order to go ahead and buy something from the shopping cart it is just a matter of operating the Buy button. This will produce the message of Figure 4.17, which is your last chance to back out before committing yourself to buying the track or CD. Assuming you wish to go ahead with the transaction, operate the Buy button. The iTunes program then starts to download the track and the item disappears from the shopping cart. The banner at the top of the window keeps you informed about the progress made with the download (Figure 4.18). If the item you have ordered consists of several tracks, these will be downloaded as separate items. However, this is all handled automatically by the program, so you just sit back and wait for the download process to be completed.

Fig.4.17 *You are asked to confirm the purchase of an item*

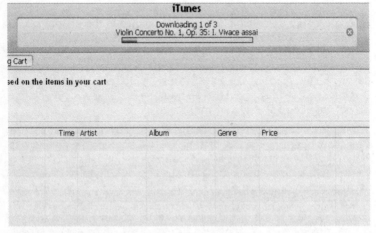

Fig.4.18 *The information banner shows how the download is progressing*

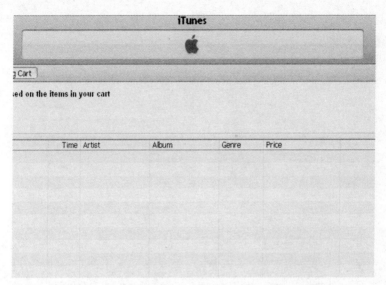

*Fig.4.19 The return of the Apple logo to the information banner
indicates a successful download*

The banner at the top of the window will return to its normal state with
the Apple logo once the downloading has been completed (Figure 4.19).
The downloaded track or tracks should have been automatically loaded
into the library. If you go to the library view it should be possible to
locate the new entry or entries. In this example the three newly
downloaded Nicola Benedetti tracks are present and correct at the bottom
of the track list (Figure 4.20). Delving into the file structure of my hard
disc drive located the actual files that were downloaded (Figure 4.21).
Note that these have an M4p extension, with the "p" presumably being
used to indicate that these are in protected AAC/MP4 format.

Artwork

The Artwork section of the iTunes Info window shows any artwork that is
associated with the selected track. This will probably be blank for any
tracks that were not purchased from the iTunes store. In the example of
Figure 4.22 the selected track is one that was downloaded from the iTunes
store in the demonstration provided previously. It therefore shows the

Fig.4.20 The tracks have been added to the library

cover design for the CD that the tracks were taken from. If the selected track was not obtained from the iTunes store it is still possible to associate some artwork with it, provided you have the necessary image or images. There is an Add button that launches a file browser, and this can be used to associate an image file with the selected track.

It is possible to display the artwork associated with the current track in the main iTunes window. In the bottom left-hand corner of the window there are four buttons, and the one at the right end of the row toggles this feature on and off. In Figure 4.23 this feature has been activated, and the artwork is displayed near the bottom left-hand corner of the screen.

There is a facility to print out the artwork, which is very useful if you burn a collection of tracks to a CD. It can be used to print a CD insert, but as yet it is not possible to print a label for the CD itself. Artwork is printed by selecting a track that is associated with the artwork and then choosing Print from the File menu. The Print window (Figure 4.24) has a range of options. For a CD insert it is normally the "CD jewel case insert" radio

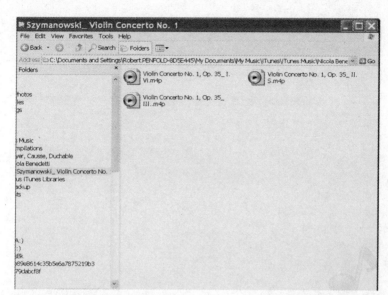

Fig.4.21 The files are present and correct on the hard disc drive

Fig.4.22 The artwork for the track, if any, will be displayed here

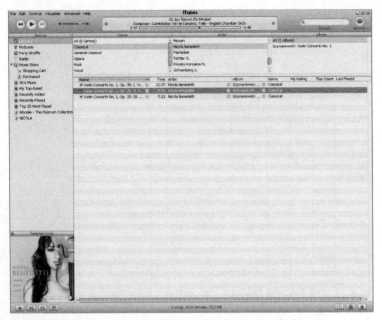

Fig.4.23 The artwork can be displayed in the main window

button that must be selected, together with "Single cover" from the Theme
menu. A track listing is included on the rear of the cover, and this will
include any tracks that are associated with the artwork.

Music hire

There is a recent trend towards what is effectively the hiring of music via
downloads. The basic idea is that you have access to a huge library of
music tracks that you can download and play. Rather than paying a
certain amount per track, you pay a monthly fee. With some sites that
charge a monthly fee you can only download a certain number of tracks
per month, but the new idea is to permit unlimited downloads per month.
This sounds too good to be true, and it is. The music tracks you download
are protected and are only usable if you have valid licence to use them.
The licences will remain valid provided you keep paying the monthly
subscription fee. If your subscription lapses, so do your licences, and
the downloaded tracks become unusable.

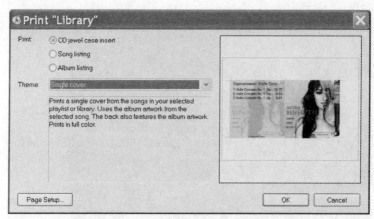

Fig.4.24 The artwork can be printed as a jewel case insert

This way of doing things has its advantages and drawbacks. The main advantage is that you have instant access to a huge library of music that would cost a fortune to buy. There is no need to spend substantial sums of money over a period time as you build up a library of CDs. The obvious drawback is that you are effectively left with nothing if you let the subscription lapse. You only have a huge library of music while you keep paying the monthly fee.

This is fine provided the subscription is set at a reasonable price. You could otherwise be left in the position where the money spent over a period of years would have been sufficient to build up a massive library of CDs. The CDs would then represent a much better deal in the long term. In order to be worthwhile this type of service must also provide the vast majority of the music you require. It would be a bit pointless if you end up going to other providers for many of the tracks you need.

The fact that there are a number of companies providing different types of music download service makes things a bit confusing, but it does mean that there is a good chance of finding at least one that is well suited to your requirements. However, it might take a fair amount of searching, reading of "fine print", and experimenting with some downloaded files to check their suitability. Probably the best advice is not to reach for the credit card at the first download service you find. Look carefully at a range of services and if possible try them out before you actually pay for anything.

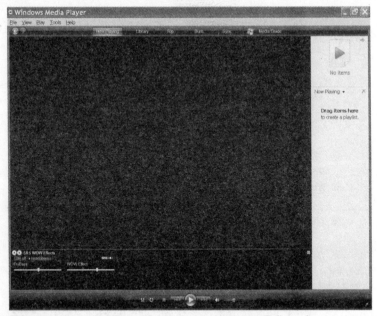

Fig.4.25 Windows Media Player 11 running in the Full mode

Internet radio

There are now a great many Internet radio stations operating around the world. These range from small scale operations that are sometimes almost literally "one man bands" through to mainstream broadcasters. These days it is quite normal for normal radio stations to make their programmes available on the Internet. This is usually in the form of a "live" audio stream, but there is sometimes a facility that enables a selection of recent programmes to be heard via an on-demand facility. Some Internet radio stations are strictly that, with the Internet being used as their only means of distributing their programs.

In the UK the radio section of the BBC has an extensive online presence. All the main BBC stations, their digital stations, and a wide range of local stations are available online. Many programmes are available for about seven days after their broadcast date by way of the Listen Again feature. The Listen Again feature clearly has big advantages for the listeners, since it provides an opportunity to catch up on episodes of the Archers

Fig.4.26 The Radio section of the Windows Media Player

that were missed, to hear the end of the "who dun it" where the telephone had to be answered at just the wrong time, and so on.

In fact it goes beyond this in that you are no longer tied to the broadcaster's schedule. You can listen to any programme whenever you like within the seven day period that it is available, and you can listen to it several times should you wish to do so. In this respect the Internet is having a big impact on the ways in which we use radio and television stations. You can view and listen to programmes when it suits you rather than when it suits the broadcaster.

Radio Tuner

The BBC clearly has a huge Internet radio service, but there are many more radio stations available on the Internet, including the main UK stations such as Talk Sport and Classic FM. It is not difficult to track them down using an ordinary search engine such as Google, and most stations give their web address quite frequently during their broadcasts.

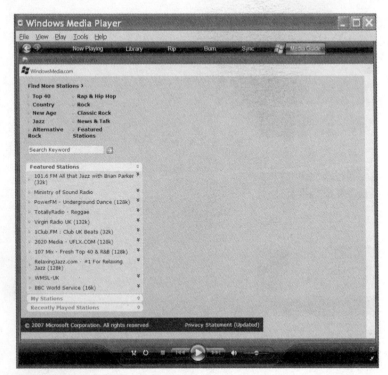

Fig.4.27 This is the Radio Tuner section of the player

Finding the web presence of any large UK broadcaster should not be a problem.

An alternative approach is to use the Radio Tuner function of the Windows Media Player, and this can turn up interesting stations that you might otherwise overlook. Either launch the player by double-clicking its icon on the desktop, or go to the Run menu, select programs, and then search for its entry in the list. Left-click the player's entry to launch the program. The appearance of the player will depend on the version you are using and its operating mode. Figure 4.25 shows version eleven running in the normal mode. If the player is running in Compact or Skin mode it will be necessary to operate the button in the bottom right-hand corner in order to place it in Full mode.

Next operate the Media Center button in the bar just below the ordinary menu bar. This section of the player requires an active Internet

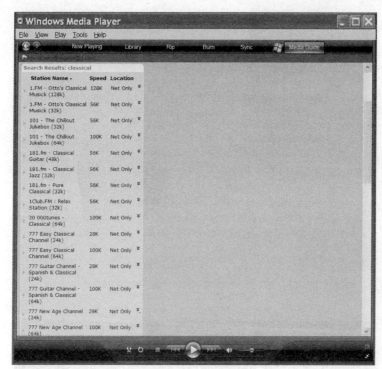

Fig.4.28 A list of results from the search facility

connection, but this obviously this should not be a problem for a broadband user. Operating the Radio tab at the top of the main panel will change the player so that it looks something like Figure 4.26. The main panel provides some suggested radio stations for you to try, but you can go in search of others if none of these are suitable.

One way of doing this is to operate the Radio Tuner link in the right-hand section of the main panel, and the player then changes to look like Figure 4.27. The upper part of the main panel includes a Search facility that can be used to look for stations of the required type. For this example I used "classical" as the search term, which produced a list of matching stations (Figure 4.28). Left-clicking an entry has the effect of expanding it to show more details (Figure 4.29). In this example there is a Play link, and operating this link results in the station being played using the Windows Media Player program.

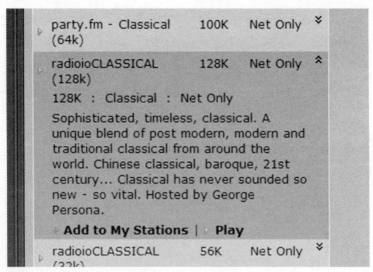

Fig.4.29 A section can be expanded to show more details

In other cases there is a link to the home page of the station, where there should be full instructions for listening to it. Not all stations can be accessed using the Windows Media Player, so it might be necessary to switch to an alternative such as the Real Player, or there might be special software for the station that you have to download. This software is often based on Real Player or another popular media player program, but it is customised to show advertisements.

Peer-to-peer

Downloading music files and playing them on a computer is something that first became popular when peer-to-peer (P2P) networks such as the original Napster became available. The original Napster is no longer in existence, and some other peer-to-peer systems have disappeared. They did not disappear due to a lack of popularity, and in most cases they were extremely popular. It was more a matter of the legalities of the file swapping. Many users were illegally swapping files in which they did not hold the copyright. Anyway, peer-to-peer systems still exist in various forms, and this subject was covered in the previous chapter. Consequently, it will not be covered again here.

Points to remember

Lossless compression is where an audio file is reduced in size without incurring any loss of sound quality. Unfortunately, the reduction in file size provided by this type of compression is relatively small. The MP3, OGG, and AAC formats can use small, large, or intermediate amounts of compression. Very small file sizes can be achieved by using massive amounts of compression, but at the expense of audio quality. At most, a reduction of 90 percent or so can be achieved while still retaining acceptable sound quality.

In an ideal world there would be a single format for audio files, and every hardware or software player would be able to handle that format. In the real world there are a number of formats in everyday use, and many files are unplayable using a given player. It is important to be familiar with the main formats, and methods of converting music from one format to another.

Even where a file is in the correct format it might not be compatible with all players which support that format. Some audio formats can operate with different bit rates, and possibly with other variations. Not all players can handle high bit rates or variable bit rates.

There are programs specifically designed to convert music files from one format to another. It is worth buying a good conversion program if you will need to process a large number of files in order to produce files of a format that is compatible with your hardware players. A program that is properly matched to your requirements will rapidly convert files direct to your desired audio format.

Most conversion programs are also capable of converting files to the same format, but with a change of some kind such as a different bit rate. Many hardware players can not handle high or variable bit rates. Also high bit rates equate to large file sizes, which in turn limits the amount of music that can be stored on a portable player. Converting high or variable bit rate files to a lower and constant bit rate makes them more usable with most portable players.

If you would prefer not to buy an audio file conversion program, it might be possible to obtain the required change using free software. The Apple iTunes program can convert files between a few formats, including WAV, MP3, and AAC. There are free utilities that enable formats such as APE and FLAC to be converted to WAV files, and from there they can be converted to MP3 or AAC format using iTunes. Where files can be legally burned to an audio CD, they can then be ripped to MP3 or AAC files using iTunes. WMP 10 and WMP 11 can be used to rip tracks to the WMA and MP3 formats.

The music files sold by most legal download sites are protected by some form of DRM (digital rights management) system. One consequence of the DRM is that it is impossible to convert the protected files to an alternative format, or even to convert them to the same format but with (say) a lower bit rate. The only form of conversion permitted by most protection systems is to burn the files to an ordinary audio CD.

Assuming your PC is connected to a suitable printer, it is possible to print CD case inserts for music downloaded from the iTunes store. It is possible to produce inserts for other tracks provided you can load suitable artwork into the iTunes program.

Blogging

Zero to hero

Blogging is the latest Internet driven phenomena, and the rise of this activity has been spectacular even by Internet standards. It has achieved mass popularity so rapidly that words such as "blog" and "blogging" are not included in the standard dictionary of my fairly up-to-date word processor. The online spelling checker helpfully offers alternatives such as "bog" and "bogging"! The number of blogs currently online and the range of subjects covered are now so vast that you can easily find yourself reading a blog without realising it. Use a search engine to research practically any subject under the sun and you are quite likely to find that a number of blogs are featured in the results.

Blogging's increase in popularity has no doubt been greatly aided by the attention it has received in the popular media. Blogging seems to pop up fairly regularly on the main television channels. Experts appear on talk and magazine shows to explain just what a blog actually is, and news programs report on personal blogs that provide the inside stories from trouble-spots around the world.

Publicity from the mass media has certainly helped to raise the profile of blogs and increase the number of people who read and write them. On the other hand, a burst of publicity alone is not going to produce the vast number of blogs that are currently available online, or the even greater number of accesses to these blogs. It would certainly not maintain this high level of activity, which if anything is still growing rather than falling in popularity. It is clearly not just a passing fad, and it seems likely that in the coming years many millions of people will regularly write or read blogs.

What is a blog?

There are several types of blog, but by far the most common type at present is the personal blog. The term "blog" is a contraction of "web log", and it is a sort of personal diary. However, it is not the type that you write in a small notebook, hide away in a drawer, and probably show to no one. Just the opposite in fact, with a blog being placed online, and in most cases made available to anyone that would like to read it. In fact things generally go a stage further than this, with most bloggers actively trying to get people to visit their site and read their pieces.

While blogging is a long way from the traditional secret diary approach, and it is a very public affair, you do not necessarily have to be put off by the lack of privacy. Most blogs are written under some form of assumed name. Therefore, although people reading your blog might be reading your personal or even intimate thoughts, they will not know who you are. Clearly it is essential to be careful what you say in your blogs if you wish to retain anonymity. It could be something of a giveaway if too much information is provided about place names, your job, your day-to-day activities, and so on. This information is unlikely to identify you to someone in another country or even in another county, but it would probably make your identity fairly obvious to anyone living in your area. Others such as colleagues at work might also be able to work out that you are the writer of the blog.

Content

What type of information do people include in their personal blogs? Obviously it is necessary to stay within the usual laws that apply to published material, but apart from that you can talk about anything you like. People can write about virtually anything in their blogs, and they certainly do so. I suppose that the great diversity of the content is one of the big attractions of blogs for those that like to read them. Practically everything is probably discussed in a blog somewhere. You can find out about practically any subject, lifestyle, or whatever. In most cases you will be learning from people with first-hand experience of the subject, who have "been there – done that".

In general, blogs have a theme of some kind rather than just rambling and containing what most readers would probably perceive as random thoughts and ideas. On the other hand, most people would not restrict themselves to the point that they would never discuss anything that was off-topic. If you feel strongly about something, then it is appropriate to write about it in your personal blog. However, it is probably best to avoid going away from the main theme of the blog too often and for too long. You might otherwise find that your readers go away from your blog too often and for too long!

The main them of most personal blogs is the day-to-day life of the writer, but the more successful blogs tend to concentrate on one particular aspect of the writer's life. This will usually be the writer's job or hobby, but it could be something else such as the day-to-day happenings in the place where they live. As a couple of examples, a vet might write about the animals they have treated, and someone having photography as a hobby could write about their experiences when taking photographs. In both cases there would presumably be plenty of opportunities to expand the blog into other areas from time to time, if the writer wished to do so.

When writing any blog it is important to bear in mind that the idea of producing it is to communicate with others, which means that you must attract people to your blog. Having managed to get them to start reading it, you need to get them to come back again and again. Successful blogs normally achieve that success by having a high level of repeat custom rather than by getting large numbers of people to pay one-off visits to their site.

Making a blog so interesting that thousands of people keep coming back for more is easier said than done. It clearly helps if the theme of your blog is something that is intrinsically interesting. The previous example of a vet producing a blog is one that falls into this category. Large numbers of people are interest in pets and animals in general, and with the exploits of a vet there is likely to be a "fife and death" aspect to things that provide plenty of drama. It is the type of thing that could easily be made very interesting to a wide audience.

Some blogs are highly specialised and often quite technical in nature, and a vet's blog could be of this type. It could discuss the latest treatments and methods used in the veterinary world, plus any other hot topics in this field. While this type of thing would probably have limited appeal to the world in general, in would probably have a strong following amongst vets around the world. This is the blogging version of niche marketing.

Of course, it is not essential to have something that is innately interesting to write about. The mundane can be very interesting if you write about it in the right way, and there are plenty of blogs that are successful without containing much in the way of "life and death" drama. You have to be realistic about things though, and making the mundane interesting and entertaining requires writing skills that relatively few people possess. Writing about something that is intrinsically exciting does not guarantee that your blog will also be exciting. On the other hand, exciting and interesting subject matter makes it much easier to produce a blog that will attract readers and keep them coming back for more.

Frequency

The main difference between a blog and a normal web site is that a blog is updated much more frequently than most ordinary web sites. Also, existing pages are normally left in place so that a blog gradually builds up into a sort of online book having hundreds or even thousands of pages. While it is not essential to update a blog regularly, most bloggers choose to do so.

I suppose that there is no point in updating a blog regularly and with high frequency if the subject matter only requires the occasional comment. Keeping a regular readership is clearly going to be much easier if there is something new for them to read on a regular basis. People will get used to going to your blog and reading it at a certain time of every day, and it will become part of their daily routine.

A blog will not become part of a reader's routine if it is only updated every few weeks with varying amounts of time between each update. It becomes easy for the reader to forget all about your blog, which in due course they probably will. For this type of thing an ordinary web site is probably a better choice than a blog.

Many blogs are updated on a daily basis, but it is not essential to update one this frequently. Where appropriate, it is probably better to settle for less frequent updating rather than producing a new page every day whether or not you have anything to say. A blog is unlikely to be successful if it has a good page every third or fourth day and a lot of boring padding on the days in between.

In order to keep a loyal readership it is important to have the updates added regularly. If your blog will be updated on something less than a daily basis, endeavour to have updates carried out according to a simple timetable. For example, add the new material every other day, on certain days of every week, or something of this type. The idea is to make it easy for your readers to know when new material will be available. Although your blog will not be part of their daily routines, it at least makes it easy for them to fit visits to your blog into some sort of routine.

Having made it clear to readers of your blog that they can find new material at specified times, it is import to adhere to your schedule as far as possible. If you have ever used any form of web site where new information is supposed to be provided at certain times, you will probably know how frustrating it is when the new material is not available on time. At one time it seemed as though even the biggest of web sites suffered from this problem in large measures. It is a problem that is still around today, but to a lesser degree due to many of the offending web sites having gone out of business!

There is a lesson here for bloggers. Expect your readership to gradually desert your blog if you keep posting excuses or nothing rather than good quality updates. If it is really impossible to update your blog on time, it is a good idea to add a quick note explaining that the update will be delayed or omitted, and why. It is probably better to completely suspend the blog for a while if you are having real problems that are making it impossible to add more than the odd update. Better still, update it regularly but at a much lower rate, or at the usual rate but with much shorter pieces that briefly cover any important points.

Length

What is the best length for posts on blogs? This is almost literally a "how long is a piece of string" question. If you were to ask ten different experts this question you would probably get ten different answers. The general consensus of opinion is that it is generally better to opt for fairly short pieces of text on web sites. People are prepared to read reams and reams of text in books, magazines, and newspapers, but it seems to be different with written material on web sites. In general, people are in a hurry when using the Internet, and are not prepared to spend large amounts of time reading text on a monitor. They could print out the text and read it at their leisure, but in practice few people actually bother to do this.

Although you need to avoid excessively verbose pieces, a blog is unlikely to be taken very seriously if the pages are very short. A reasonable minimum length for blog pages is a matter of opinion, but something in the region of 250 to 300 words probably represents a realistic minimum. If you can say something worthwhile in fewer words, then by all means do so. Most of us though, require something in that region in order to make a few simple and worthwhile points.

A reasonable upper limit is somewhere in the region of 900 to 1000 words. It is necessary to use some common sense here, and with some types of subject matter 1000 words is quite a lot, while with other types it will barely be sufficient to get you started. When you are discussing complex matters it could be difficult to get everything covered properly in less than 1000 words. However, unless there is a good reason for going beyond this limit it is best not to do so. If anything, aim to keep your pieces comfortably within it.

Being realistic about matters, will you have time to regularly write pieces that are much longer than 1000 words? Will you even be able to handle a regular piece of about this length? Writing 1000 words per day for a year produces a blog that is roughly equal in length to a few small/medium sized novels. The amount of material you can produce depends on how quickly you can think up the words, and on the speed with which you can enter them into the computer.

1000 words will probably not present too much of a problem for those who can come up with the words quite easily and are proficient typists. It could be very difficult when the words do not come easily and (or) you are a slow one-finger typist. Those who are not reasonably fast at typing should consider using a voice recognition program. Not everyone finds these easy to use, but a lack of typing skills becomes irrelevant if you can master one of these programs. 1000 words can be entered in the time it takes to say the words, which should be no more than a few minutes. Some additional time will be needed to check through the text and do some final polishing, but the whole process should still be quite quick.

Is it for me?

Large numbers of people produce personal blogs, but millions more do not. As will probably have become apparent by now, producing a regular blog involves a fair amount of effort. It also involves a certain amount of skill. Making a really good job of it involves a substantial amount of effort and skill. Actually getting a blog uploaded and online is not really that difficult, but producing good quality material for your blog can be quite difficult. Producing a personal blog is certainly not for everyone.

Unless you can find sufficient time to produce a personal blog there is little point in getting started. The time taken to upload new material is not usually that great, and setting up a blog in the first place can be extremely quick. The time spent producing a blog is largely the time taken to produce the words. If you can do this reasonably quickly, or you have plenty of time on your hands, there should be no problem.

Things are likely to be more difficult if you are a busy professional or a housewife with several children to look after. It might still be possible to produce a short piece for your blog each day, but it is something that will only fit into a busy lifestyle if it is something you would really like to do. It will otherwise be too easy to find excuses for not producing today's blog, and tomorrow's, and so on.

Blog alternatives

Bear in mind that the Internet offers alternatives to blogging, such as online forums or your own web site. It is well worth considering these alternative methods of getting your pieces online if it is unlikely that you will be able to keep up a regular blog. With an online forum for example, you are not committed to making regular posts. You are free to do so if you wish, but you can contribute as much or as little as you wish. Things are unlikely to grind to a halt if you do not contribute for a while, because there will be plenty of other contributors while you are absent from the site.

Other blogs

A personal blog is the most popular type, but there are other kinds of blog. Some of these probably have less appeal for most people than personal blogs, but they have their uses. Many of the alternative types of blog are still very much in the personal blog category, but they are not personal diaries. We will consider these alternative forms of personal blog first.

Information blog

With this type of blog you simply provide information about any topic that interests you, and where you have gained sufficient expertise to be able to write with authority on the subject. A typical blog of this type would give information about travelling in some of the more out of the way parts of the world. The idea would be to provide truthful background information in the "Rough Guide" style, rather than just giving the type of information found in the glossy brochures.

Review blog

If you are interested in something like films, electronic gadgets, the latest pop music, or anything that can be reviewed, why not produce a review blog covering that particular topic. With this type of thing it is usual to give your honest opinion of something and then ask for comments from your readers. This helps to give the readership a more balanced view of the things being reviewed.

An advantage of a review blog is that the word "review" is one of the most popular search terms when people use search engines to seek information on the Internet. This can be helpful in getting people to your blog site. There is also a slight downside in that review and blog sites are very common on the Internet. With such a large number of alternative sites available there is a risk that your site will be so low down in the search engine results that it will not get noticed. A review site covering something out of the ordinary might actually be more successful than one that covers a mass market product of some kind. A review blog that covers a niche market will have less competition.

Problem blog

A problem blog is one you produce because you have a problem of some kind. Typically, it will be a problem with a product or service of some kind. The idea is to give others the benefit of your experience, and perhaps get feedback from others that you will find will be helpful. For example, suppose you spend 100,000 pounds on a new luxury car but never manage to get more than five miles from home before it breaks down. You could use a blog to let others know of your experiences, and to discover whether others have been having similar difficulties.

With this type of thing it is important to adhere to the facts and avoid the temptation to exaggerate. Only set up this type of blog if you are genuinely having real problems with a product or service, and not because you have encountered a few minor problems and feel like "having a go". If others are having similar problems it is likely that they will find your blog. The word "problem" is another common search term when people use search engines! Before setting up a blog of this type it would be prudent to do a little searching on the Internet yourself. There is little point in starting a new blog that simply duplicates one or two existing and well-established blogs.

Interview blog

If you are good at getting other people to talk, then an interview blog is definitely something that you should consider. Being realistic about things, you are unlikely to get a regular series of interviews with the rich and famous. In fact you are unlikely to get even one interview with someone who is a "household name".

On the other hand, it is not essential to have interviews with famous people in order to produce an interesting blog that will attract a reasonable readership. Ordinary people talking about just about anything with enthusiasm and passion will keep your readership interested. After all, the general public talking about all sorts of things is the staple diet of most local radio stations and one or two national ones as well.

This type of blog normally covers a specific subject, but you do not have to be highly specific. Subjects such as wildlife, the past, sport, gardening, etc., give the blog focus but still leave sufficient scope for you to avoid too much repetition. If you can make it work, there is no reason why you should not have a general interview blog.

So far we have only considered blogs that consist of pages of text. As with any web site, a blog site can also have audio, video, and pictorial content. With an interview site it might be better to have a short written introduction to each interview, which could then be an audio recording or and audio/visual presentation. The audio or video approach avoids the need to transcribe the interview, but it obviously requires extra equipment and skills. It is probably not beyond the abilities of the average PC user though, so it is well worth considering. The alternative of transcribing every interview could be very time consuming even if you edit each one down to a more manageable length.

Rant blog

This is probably a type of blog that is better if it does not quite live up to its name! Rather than genuinely ranting, it is probably best to settle for writing passionately and not shying away from controversial topics and views. On the other hand, you do have to make sure that you stay within the law, and within the bounds of reason.

Providing the blogger with a personal "soap box" for their views is not usually the idea behind this type of blog. It is more a matter of getting readers to contribute and produce a heated discussion. Be warned though, this type of thing can easily get very childish and abusive. If you have ever used any of the online bulletin boards you will probably know exactly what I mean.

Debate blog

This type of blog is similar in principle to the rant variety, but the intention is to have a less heated and more intellectual argument on some less controversial topics. Whether things remain less heated and more intellectual is another matter. It is up to the blogger to use his or her skills to prevent things from getting out of hand.

Profile blogs

A profile blog provides information about a famous person, and in most cases it will cover someone who is still alive. However, this type of blog need not be restricted to living persons such as the latest pop stars, footballers, and so on. It could cover (say) a famous artist or classical composer, with details of their lives, plus more up-to-date information such as dates and venues for forthcoming exhibitions/concerts.

There are plenty of readers interested in famous people, so there is a large potential audience for this type of thing. On the other hand, you will almost certainly find yourself competing with numerous sites about the same person. In the case of a living person there will certainly be an official web site that attracts large numbers of people. As always when putting anything onto the Internet, make sure that you do not infringe the copyright of anyone else. "Borrowing" a photograph of a personality from a web site is outside the rules and inviting trouble.

Political comment blog

While the general level of interest in politics is perhaps not all it used to be, there are still plenty of people interested in reading about politics and giving their own opinions. You can use a blog to give your opinions of the latest happenings in the world of politics, and there will probably be plenty of people willing to agree or take issue with what you have to say.

Satirical blog

This is a form of political comment blog, but one that uses satire and takes "pot shots" at politicians and the political establishment. It is obviously necessary to have a fair amount of talent in order to do this type of thing successfully. Failed attempts at satire tend to be pretty dire and will soon have readers moving on to another site. Get it right most of the time and your blog will probably be extremely popular, and will remain so.

Cartoon blog

If you have an artistic bent, why not try your hand at a cartoon blog? Typically this is a pictorial version of a satirical blog, but I suppose there is no need for the cartoons to be political in nature. You could simply add (say) a new cartoon each week, with a non-political theme to the cartoons, or no theme at all. The only thing they need to have in common is that they make people laugh. There are a number of top quality cartoon blogs on the Internet already, and it is worth taking a look at some of these even if you are not thinking about producing your own. The "Back to the Drawing Board" blog of Royston Robertson is worth investigating (Figure 5.1). It is at this web address:

http://roystonrobertson.blogspot.com/

Fig.5.1 "Back to the drawing board" is a well-known cartoon blog

Prediction blog

I would guess that people have been trying to predict or forecast the future for as long as there have been people on planet earth. In a prediction blog you simply give your idea of what is going to happen in some particular aspect of life, or in the world in general. Other people can be invited to give the predictions or forecasts.

Review blog

This is the opposite of a prediction blog, where you look back at some aspect of life or the world in general. For example, you could review the previous week's events in the world of politics, football, cricket, or whatever.

Link blog

A link blog is one that adheres to the principle that there is no point in reinventing the wheel. Why produce a blog covering a particular topic when there are already a number of blogs and web sites that give in-depth coverage of the subject. A link blog takes the alternative approach of providing links to sites that provide good quality information on a particular subject.

The usual reason for producing a link blog is that you have spent a large amount of time searching the Internet for information on a certain topic. Having found a number of sites that proved to be very helpful to you, it makes sense to put details of those sites on the Internet so that others can go straight to them and avoid the hours of searching that you had to put in.

With this type of thing it is not just a matter of giving a list of links with no explanation. Start by detailing the type of information that you were looking for, and perhaps the reason you needed it. Provide at least a brief description of each site, perhaps detailing its strengths and weaknesses.

Project blog

Many people start a blog when they undertake a major project of some kind. A typical example would be when doing a major renovation of something like an old boat or house. A project blog often accompanies some sort of unusual undertaking or journey that is intended to raise money for a charity. We have all seen this type of thing on television, where someone spends a week in a bath full of baked beans or crosses the Sahara Desert on stilts of unequal length!

One reason for doing a blog of this type is that it might help others who are undertaking something similar. Another reason is that it might result in some helpful information being received from others who have relevant experience that could be useful to you. In the case of a project that is intended to raise money for charity, there is often the intention of attracting some sponsorship.

Instruction blog

An instruction blog simply provides information about undertaking some task or other. This could be something as mundane as fixing a leaking tap, or something more ambitious such as building your own sailing boat. Rather than step-by-step instructions, a blog could simply provide some useful tips that make certain tasks easier, or help to provide professional results. It helps with any form of instruction blog if you can talk with authority and with the benefit of first hand experience. The

Internet contains vast amounts of information, and a fair amount of it is either a bit misleading or downright wrong. Try to avoid adding to the mountain of Internet misinformation.

Critique

As the name suggests, this is a blog in which you give critiques of something. Do not misunderstand the word "critique" though. It does not simply mean criticising something. A dictionary definition of the word is something along the lines "a detailed analysis and assessment". In order to produce proper critiques you need to be knowledgeable about the subject being analysed. You also have to provide a fair and detailed analysis.

Your own thing

This list is by no means complete, and there are no doubt many other types of personal blog. If you surf the Internet and look at a range of web sites, it is likely that it would be possible to produce a blog version of practically any of them. When you produce a personal blog, the form it takes is up to you. It needs to be in a form that will interest other people and attract them to your blog site, but it does not have to conform to any standard format.

Audio blog

It is possible to add audio, pictures, or even video to most blogs, but if the main content is in the form of text, a blog remains an ordinary blog. However, you can simply do away with the text and have the entire content of the blog in the form of audio files. You then have an audio blog rather than the standard variety. There are web sites that are aimed specifically at those who would like to produce an audio blog.

One of the biggest audio blog sites is Audioblogger (Figure 5.2), which is free, but is probably not a practical proposition at present unless you live in the USA. It enables the audio to be placed on your site by phoning the Audioblogger number, and then recording your latest piece. Unfortunately, at the time of writing there is no UK number available for this service.

The alternative method of placing your audio onto the blog site is to record it using a microphone and your computer's soundcard, and then

Fig.5.2 Audioblogger is one of the biggest hosts for audio blogs

upload it to the blog site as a standard audio file such as an MP3 type. In order to use this method it will probably be necessary to buy a microphone, or a headset that incorporates one, but no other additional hardware should be required.

A slight problem with audio blogs is that they require far more storage space than the normal text-based type. If you produce a million words over a period of time, the amount of storage space needed on a server will be quite low. In fact it typically takes about 6 to 7 megabytes to store a million words, and even less space is required if file compression is used.   A million words stored in low quality audio files, with file compression being used, would probably require at least a few gigabytes of storage space. It is probably for this reason that there are relatively few sites that offer free hosting for audio blogs. You might need to hire some web space in order to produce a regular audio blog.

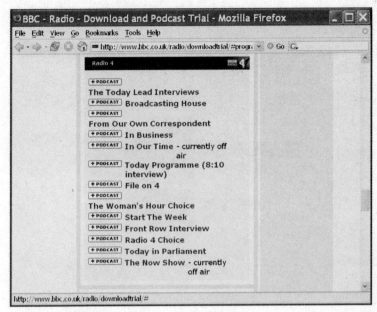

Fig.5.3 The BBC is experimenting with podcasts

Podcasts

Podcasts are an even newer phenomenon than blogging. It is giving the online spelling checker of my word processor the same problem as the word "blog". "Podcast" is too recent to be included in the spelling checker's dictionary, so it helpfully suggests that I might mean "pod cast". Although podcasts are quite new, they have already become very popular.

A podcast is similar to, but not the same as an audio blog. The idea of an audio blog is that people go to the blog site and listen to streamed audio. In other words, when you visit one of these sites the audio data from the site is downloaded to your PC and played through the computer's sound system. There will probably be no facility for playing the audio in any other way, and it will not necessarily be in one of the popular audio formats such as MP3 or AAC.

The idea of a podcast is that you can download the audio in a standard file format that can be played on a computer using a media player such

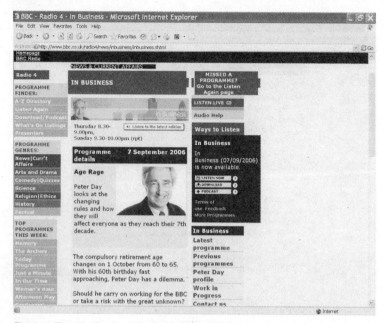

Fig.5.4 The "In Business" podcast web page

as the Windows Media Player program. The most common file format for podcasts is MP3, but other types of audio file are used as well. Because a podcast file is normally a MP3 type, it can be uploaded to an iPod or MP3 player and played just about anywhere, and at any time.

There is nothing to stop you from producing your own podcasts and placing them on the Internet, and there are numerous podcasts produced by private individuals that have proved to be very popular. Some of these regular podcasts have a huge and loyal following. However, you need to be aware that many podcasts are now produced by large media companies, and they provide stiff competition for those producing personal podcasts. Some of the commercial offerings are actually radio broadcasts that are also offered in the form of podcasts. A podcast is effectively an on-demand radio show, and it seems likely that there will be a continuing trend towards radio shows being made available in this form.

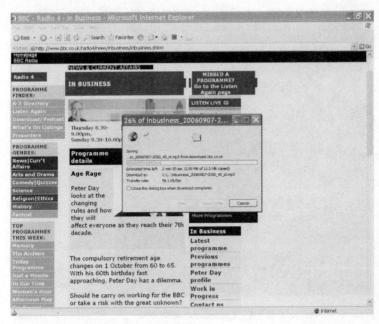

Fig.5.5 The download is under way

Downloading

One way of obtaining a podcast is to go to the appropriate podcast site and download it. For some time now the BBC has made many of its radio broadcasts available online for about a week after they were first broadcast, but these are available as streamed audio. In other words, they are not intended to be used as downloaded files that can be played on an iPod or MP3 player. You have to listen to them using your PC, while it is receiving the stream of audio data.

As an experiment, at the time of writing this the BBC is making a few programmes available as podcasts (Figure 5.3). Operating a link for a programme takes you to its web page (Figure 5.4) where there is a button that enables you to listen to the programme in streamed form using the BBC Radio Player. Another button enables the podcast to be downloaded, and it is then saved to the desired location. The usual bargraph shows how the download is progressing (Figure 5.5). Once downloaded, the file can be played in a suitable media player such as Windows Media Player (Figure 5.6), or uploaded to an iPod or MP3 player.

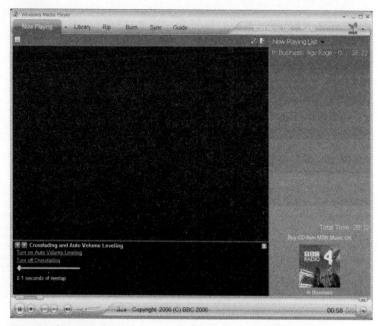

Fig.5.6 The podcast being played in the Windows Media Player

Subscribing

An alternative approach with podcasts is to subscribe to them. In some cases this means paying a subscription fee, much like paying for a magazine subscription. In other cases the podcasts are free, and the term "subscribe" is not entirely apt. The basic idea of subscribing to a podcast is that you can obtain each new podcast automatically, as it becomes available.

It is only possible to subscribe to podcasts if your PC is equipped with suitable software. Most podcast subscriptions can be handled by free programs, and Apple's iTunes is probably the most popular program for this application. On the BBC site you can obtain a Help page (Figure 5.7) by operating the Podcast button, and many sites include a similar facility that explains how to use iTunes with their podcasts. In some cases there will also be instructions for alternative programs such as Juice and Doppler.

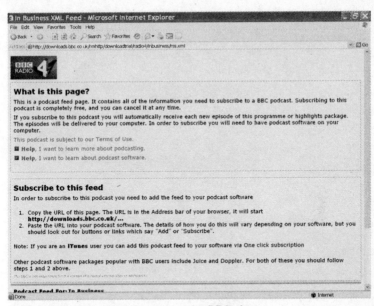

Fig.5.7 The podcast Help page on the BBC site

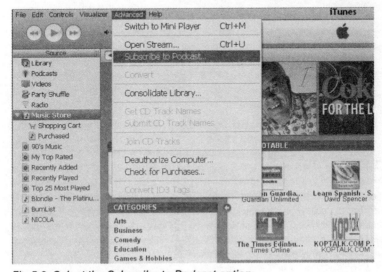

Fig.5.8 Select the Subscribe to Podcast option

Fig.5.9 The URL is Pasted into the textbox

Subscribing is usually just a matter of copying the appropriate URL (web address) into the player program. In the case of the BBC site it is just a matter of left-clicking the address bar to select the address text, and then selecting Copy from the Edit menu. Alternatively, hold down the Control key and then operate the C key. Either way, the address is copied to the Windows clipboard.

In order to subscribe to the podcasts via iTunes it is then a matter of running the program and selecting Subscribe to Podcast from the Advanced menu (Figure 5.8). This produces a small pop-up window where the URL can be Pasted into the textbox (Figure 5.9) by holding down the Control key and pressing the V key. Then operate the OK button to close the window. Next iTunes will automatically switch to the Podcast section, and it will start downloading the latest podcast from the site to which you have just subscribed (Figure 5.10). Once it has been downloaded it can be played in the usual way (Figure 5.11), or uploaded to an iPod and played like any other MP3 file.

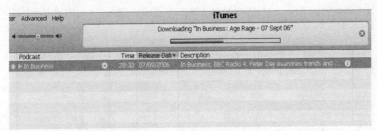

Fig.5.10 iTunes is automatically downloading the latest podcast

Music Store

The Music Store section of iTunes provides an easy way of downloading and subscribing to a wide range of podcasts. It is selected using the Music Store link in the left-hand column of the program's window. Most of the material on offer in the Music Store is, as one would probably expect, music, but there is a podcast section. This is selected via the Podcast link near the top left-hand corner of the Music Store window.

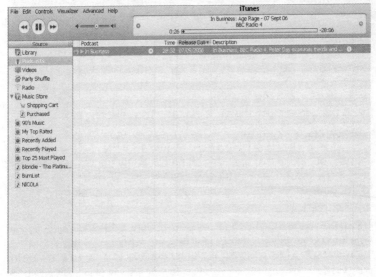

Fig.5.11 The podcast can be played in iTunes

Fig.5.12 The podcast section of the Music Store

Once the program has switched to the Podcast section you are provided with a selection of podcasts (Figure 5.12). Further selections are available via the menu in the left-hand column of the Music Store window, which lists various categories such as comedy, arts, and education. In fact things operate in much the same way as when selecting music.

Selecting one of the podcasts results in the Music Store window changing to give further details of the podcast (Figure 5.13). Not all the podcasts are free, but those that are free can be played by double-clicking their entry in the lower section of the Music Store window. You can subscribe to the podcast by operating the Subscribe button in the main Music Store window.

This produces a small pop-up window (Figure 5.14) that gives you a chance to change your mind, but this is not really necessary if you are subscribing to a free podcast. It is only needed if you are subscribing to one that involves a subscription fee. Operate the Cancel button if you hit the subscribe button by accident or you have changed your mind. The

Fig.5.13 You can obtain more details of a podcast

Fig.5.14 You are given a chance to cancel

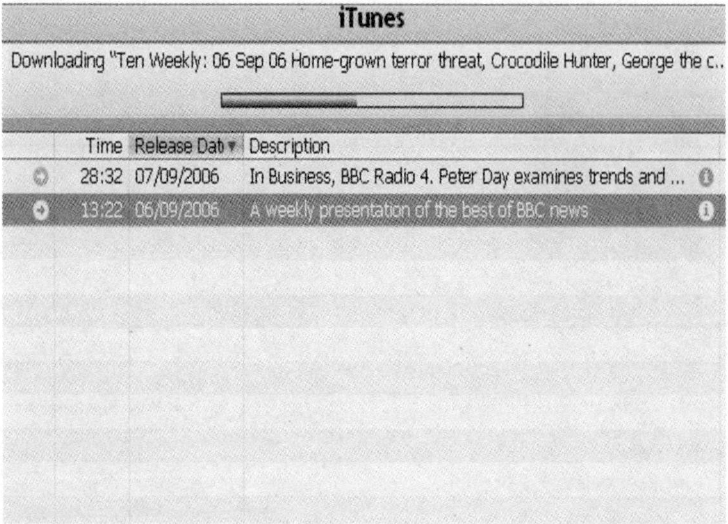

Fig.5.15 The podcast starts to download

latest podcast then starts to download (Figure 5.15), and it can be played or uploaded once the download process has been completed.

Video

While most podcasts are of the audio variety, some are video files. These can be played in most media players such as iTunes or the Windows Media Player, and they can even be uploaded and played on some iPods. The podcast downloaded in the previous example is a weekly roundup of the news from the BBC television news room, and when played it is a video type (Figure 5.16).

Producing your own audio podcasts is not too difficult, requiring minimal amounts of additional equipment and relatively little skill. Doing it really well is perhaps a bit more difficult, but most computer users are probably capable of producing audio podcasts of very acceptable quality. Producing your own video podcasts is another matter, and some reasonably good quality video equipment is needed in order to make a good job of it. The degree of expertise required is much higher, and you

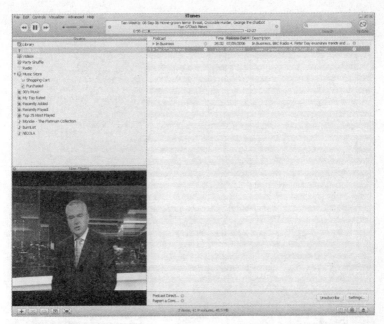

Fig.5.16 This podcast is a video type

really need to become reasonably proficient at making videos before giving serious thought to producing regular video podcasts.

Another point to bear in mind is that the size of a video podcast file will be much greater than that of an audio podcast file of similar duration. Obviously it is not necessary for the pictures to be of particularly high definition. Even so, the amount of data generated when producing low resolution videos is still far greater than the amount of data generated when making an audio file of comparable duration. The amount of storage space required to host video podcasts is therefore quite large, and it could be relatively expensive.

Blog anatomy

At its most basic, a blog could consist of a page of text on a web site, with that text being updated every day, week, or whatever. There is an old saying that goes something along the lines of "you can not judge a book by its cover". A very basic blog that has interesting content and is well written should be successful. In the real world though, something

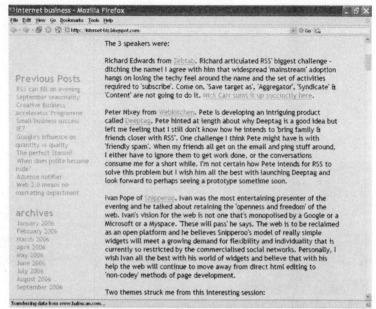

Fig.5.17 Monthly archives can be accessed via the links in the bottom left-hand corner of the window

as featureless as a basic page of text would probably have most visitors exiting the site without bothering to read any of the content.

Another problem with this very simplistic approach is that it only allows visitors to the site to read the current page of the blog. The previous article is overwritten when a new page is uploaded to the site. It would clearly be better if some of the earlier articles were available, and ideally it would be possible for visitors to access all the earlier material.

A "proper" blog site is therefore a bit more complex than a single page of text. As with any web page, it is advisable not to err too far in the opposite direction and produce a page layout that is so complex that it is difficult for users to find the things that they require. An overly fussy web page is just as likely to make users exit your site as one which is too bland.

A basic real-world blog will therefore consist of the current article that is attractively laid out on the page, plus some sort of archive of previous articles. It would probably not be too difficult to produce a basic blog site of this type using standard web site creation software. In fact

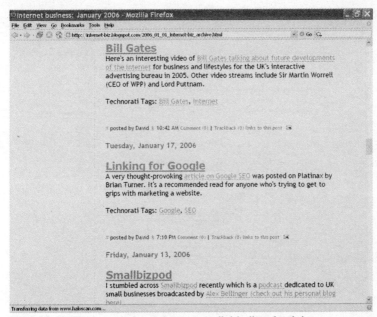

Fig.5.18 Operating a link produces a srollable list of articles

programs of this type are starting to introduce facilities for producing blog sites. There are programs that are designed specifically for setting up and maintaining blog sites. However, initially it is more likely that you will use a blog host that provides facilities for producing attractive and functional blog sites.

Archive

The archive of previous articles is an extremely important part of most blogs. Any software or other facility for producing blog sites should make it easy to gradually build up a large archive. Of at least equal importance, it should produce a site that makes it easy for users to find the particular article that they require. The archive is usually organised using backward chronology. In other words, your latest article appears first, then its predecessor, then the one prior to that, and so on.

This might not seem to be very logical, since anyone working their way through the articles in the order provided by the archive will be working

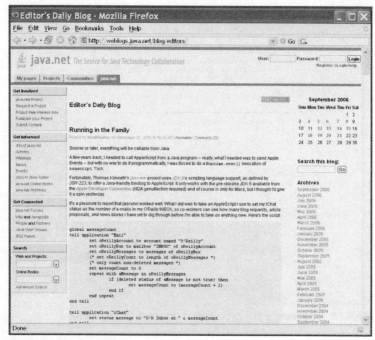

Fig.5.19 Previous blogs can be accessed via the calendar

their way through them in reverse order. On the other hand, it is logical in that the articles are archived in the order in which they were written. A real world blog site usually has facilities that make it easy to jump to a given page of a blog, so you do not have to work your way through the archive in reverse order.

The current page usually has links to the most recent articles, with the title and perhaps a short description of each article being provided as well. The number of articles soon starts to mount up when a blog is updated on a daily basis. When the number of articles gets into the hundreds it is necessary to organise the archive in sections, with a separate section for each month or year.

In the example of Figure 5.17 (The Internet Business blog) there is a scrollable list of recent articles in the main panel, complete with some brief information about each one. On the left there is a menu of recent articles, which provides quicker access for those who know what they

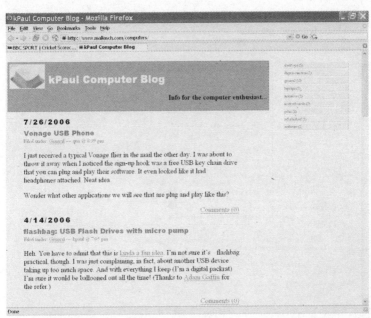

Fig.5.20 Here, previous blogs are grouped by subject (top right)

are looking for. Below this there are links for a large archive of articles that is arranged in months. Operating one of these links produces a scrollable list of articles in the main part of the window (Figure 5.18). This is a fairly typical arrangement for a blog site that contains a substantial number of articles.

A popular variation is to have a calendar, with dates highlighted where there are corresponding blog entries. Left-clicking one of these dates produces the appropriate article. This method is used in the Java.net Editor' Daily Blog (Figure 5.19), where there is a calendar for the current month near the top right-hand corner of the window. This operates in conjunction with an archive of articles arranged by month.

A different arrangement is used in the kPaul Computer Blog (Figure 5.20). As before, this has a scrollable list of recent articles in the main panel, together with some brief information about each one. In the top right-hand section of the window there is a menu that has the articles grouped by subject. Left-clicking the Laptop link, for example, produces the window of Figure 5.21, where the relevant articles are listed in the main panel. Again, there is some basic information on each one.

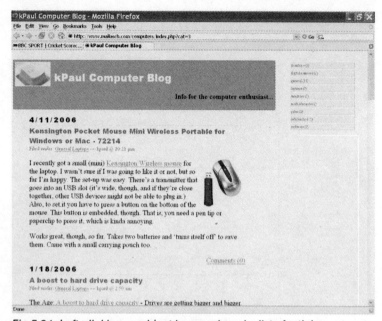

Fig.5.21 Left-clicking a subject has produced a list of articles

Grouping articles by subjects makes it easy for users to find articles that are likely to be of particular interest to them. However, it might not work well with a blog site that contains a huge number of articles. There is no single approach that suits every blog site, and it is important to choose one that will work well with your particular site, and will continue to work well with it.

Search

Some blogs have a search facility so that users can look for articles that contain key words. Whether it is possible to add such a facility to your blog depends on the blog design facility or program in use. With the more simple programs and facilities it will probably not be an option. A search feature is definitely worthwhile with a blog that contains a large number of articles, but it is unlikely to be of great practical value until this stage has been reached.

Other elements

Most blogs have additional elements, with the most obvious being some sort of title bar. This is often augmented by a subtitle or a short piece of text that gives a brief explanation of what the blog is about. With a diary style personal blog, for instance, there is usually a paragraph or two giving some details of the writer such as their gender, age, occupation, and why they decided to create a blog.

Byline

Some blogs have a byline at the start or end of each article. In other words, there is a line showing the name of the person who wrote the piece. This is not really necessary with a personal blog, or any blog that is written by a single person. The writer of each piece will be the same, and will be the creator of the blog. You can still add a byline if you wish, and it is something that is normally included where more than one person contributes to a blog.

Blogroll

Many blogs have a so-called "blogroll", which is typically situated in the left-hand column of every page. It is simply a list of the blog creator's favourite blogs. On the face of it, providing visitors to your blog with a list of good alternative blogs is not a good idea. It would seem to be particularly unwise if any of the recommended blogs cover a similar subject matter to your own. However, this type of thing is not unique to blog sites, and this practice is in fact commonplace on the Internet.

The general idea is to encourage others to reciprocate and list your blog site in their blogrolls. The amount of traffic on your site could increase dramatically if a few popular blogs should reciprocate. Of course, this ploy could easily backfire if your blog is not particularly good. You will simply be directing people away from your site to ones that do a better job. They will be unlikely to return to your blog.

Comments

Many blogs are set up to permit readers to leave comments. Some types of blog site are designed specifically to garner views from readers, while with others it is an important part of the blog's function. In either case it is essential to have this facility enabled. With other types of blog a comments facility is either unimportant, or something that is definitely not required. The web design software used to produce the blog site should enable this facility to be switched off.

Many consider that a blog is not a proper blog unless it has a facility that enables readers to post their views on the site. I certainly disagree with this, and there are numerous blogs that are really good but do not have a comments facility. On the other hand, there are some types of blog where a lack of this feature would greatly limit the effectiveness of the blog. This is something where you have to think it over and come to your own decision.

Bear in mind that permitting readers to leave comments can be problematic. Most people using your blog site will probably be reasonable and behave in a civilised fashion. However, it is likely that there will be at least the occasional problem with troublemakers. There can also be problems with the blog equivalent of spam. You might find that many of the comments are actually advertisements for web sites or products. There are robotic computer systems that search the Internet for opportunities to leave this type of spam, and it is an increasing problem.

Types of host

Having decided to go ahead and start your own blog you are then faced with the problem of finding a suitable host for your site. There are several options available, but it really breaks down into four main choices.

Free blog host

While you might eventually prefer to move to a different type of host, the obvious starting point is to use a specialist blog host. It makes sense to use one of the free blog hosts, as these provide a risk-free opportunity to try blogging. No money will be wasted if you try blogging but decide after a month that it is not for you after all. A huge advantage of using a specialist blog host is that there are usually templates and other tools that make it quick and easy to set up your blog and get started. As demonstrated later in this chapter, you can get your blog "up and running" in a matter of minutes using one of these sites.

There are a few potential problems with any form of free web hosting, where there is an obvious risk of "getting what you pay for". The amount of storage space included as part of a free hosting deal is generally less than that of one where you pay a fee. However, you generally get a fair amount of storage free space these days. There should certainly be enough for many years of blogging provided you do not use large numbers of photographs, audio files, or any other types of file that might give problems.

Another potential problem with free hosting is a lack of bandwidth. There are actually two issues here, one of which is simply a matter of slow access to your site. With your blog on the same server as hundreds or even thousands of other blogs, there will probably be times when large numbers of users try to simultaneously access these blogs. This can result in long delays while people wait for your blog's home page to appear. Since people who surf the Internet are not well known for their patience, it is quite likely that they will not bother.

The second version of the bandwidth problem is not actually anything to do with bandwidth at all, but it often seems to be referred to by this name. It is really a cap on the amount of traffic allowed for your site in a given period of time. This is usually in the form of so many megabytes or gigabytes per month. Depending on the host's terms of business, exceeding the limit results in a charge being made, or users simply find that your site is not accessible until the beginning of the next month.

Again, a cap on the traffic to your site is unlikely to be a problem unless your blog makes extensive use of photographs or other elements that require large amounts of data. I suppose it could be a problem if large numbers of people visit your blog site, but that is a problem most of us would be only too happy to experience. Anyway, it might be worthwhile opting to pay for hosting in cases where a large amount of storage space and (or) a large bandwidth is required.

A final point to bear in mind when using free hosting services is that the company providing the service stays in business by make its money from something other than hosting fees. The usual approach is to place advertisements on the sites that are being hosted. This means that you are likely to find that there is at least one advertisement added to your blog site if you opt for this type of hosting. There should be no problems with wholly inappropriate advertisement appearing on your site provided you use one of the large and well-established hosting companies.

In fact this is unlikely to be a problem when using one of the smaller free-hosting companies. There are supposedly still some examples of people finding their sites have added advertisements for pornographic web sites, etc., but this type of thing seems to be relatively rare these days. In some cases you can express a preference for the type of advertisement that appears on your site, but it is unlikely that the host will guarantee to include only advertisements of this type. By no means all free web hosts actually rely on advertising revenue these days, so there will not necessarily be any advertisements at all added to your blog site.

Paid for blog host

This is essentially the same as using a free blog host, but you pay a fee in order to obtain a higher level of service. Paying for the service should avoid all the potential drawbacks of free services. For example, your site should not have any advertisements added by the host, there should be a massive amount of storage space available, and there should be plenty of bandwidth available. Note though, that there can still be a cap on the maximum amount of traffic to your site each month. The monthly allowance should be a very generous one though.

Your own site 1

If you were provided with some free web space as part of the deal when you signed on with your Internet service provider (ISP) it is likely that this could be used to host your blog. One problem with this method is that a change of ISP will result in your free web space being withdrawn, and your blog being deleted. Of course, your blog can be moved to web space provided by your new ISP, but it will then have a new web address. This might not be a great drawback provided your regular readers are informed of the change well in advance, but changes in web addresses should be avoided if at all possible. Another drawback of this method is that it provides no built-in help. You have to generate the blog site yourself, starting from scratch. There are programs that make this task relatively easy, but producing your own blog site is never going to be as easy as using a specialist blog host.

Your own site 2

This method is essentially the same as the previous one, but you hire web space from a company that specialises in hosting web sites. With this method it is necessary to register a web address for your site, but many web hosts offer packages that include the provision of a web address. A big advantage of this approach is that you own the address, which you can go on using if you move to a new host. Make sure that the web address does become your property and is not owned by the hosting company. If the address is the property of the hosting company you will probably have to buy it from them if you move to another host.

Another advantage of using a normal web host is that the web address you use can be any valid address that is still available. This makes it easy to choose something really appropriate. With other methods of producing a blog site you have to make a few compromises when it comes to selecting the address of the site.

Fig.5.22 The Blogger.com home page

A drawback of using this type of blog site is that you will probably have to produce the site from scratch, with no assistance provided by the hosting company. Another drawback is that it is not free. There is the cost of registering the web address, the ongoing cost of keeping it registered in your name, and the cost of hiring the web space. It is possible to keep the cost within reason, but it is unlikely to be insignificant. Over a period of time the cost will start to build up. This type of blog is likely to prove quite expensive if you opt for an upmarket hosting package.

Quick start

There are plenty of well-known blogging sites that enable users to get their first blog "up and running" in a very short time. Blogger.com is probably the biggest and best known of these sites, and it provides what is probably the easiest introduction to blogging. It has the advantage of being free, and of letting you have as many blogs as you wish. Although it is a free service, it does not place a limit on the number of photographs that you can upload. It is not necessarily the best choice for advanced users, but it is well worth trying as an instruction to blogging.

Fig.5.23 The Create Your Blog link is near the bottom of the page

Figure 5.22 shows the Blogger.com home page, but you have to scroll down to almost the bottom of the page for the "CREATE YOUR BLOG NOW" link (Figure 5.23). This moves things on to the page of Figure 5.24 where you have to enter various pieces of information into the textboxes. The user name is the one that will be used to logon to the Blogger.com site when you need to post a new article or edit something. The name used here is therefore of little importance, but it should obviously be something that you can remember easily.

The same is true of the password, which as part of the usual error checking has to be entered twice. Although some sites require passwords to include at least one or two numbers, this is not the case with Blogger.com. A password that only contains letters is perfectly acceptable.

The display name is the one that will appear on your blog entries. You can use your own name here if you wish, but for security reasons many people prefer not to. An email address must be supplied, but this does not seem to be used to confirm the creation of the new account. It is

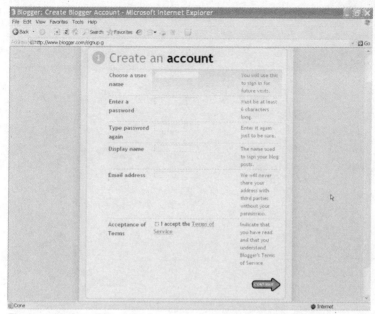

Fig.5.24 Various items of information have to be added here

presumably needed so that Blogger.com can inform you about changes to their service, new services, etc. The Blogger.com terms must be accepted by ticking the checkbox. The new account can not be created unless you do so.

Title

Operating the Continue button moves things on to the page (Figure 5.25), and here a title for the new blog is entered in the textbox near the top of the page. This is the text that will appear on the title bar of your blog, so it has to be chosen carefully, and must be something appropriate to your blog site. Bloggers often use rather ambiguous titles that many would probably consider to be misleading. Often the title is an in-joke, which is fine if the people visiting your site understand it.

A potential advantage of an offbeat title is that it can be very memorable, making it easy for visitors to find your site again. It can also get people talking about your blog, giving it some free publicity in the process. This

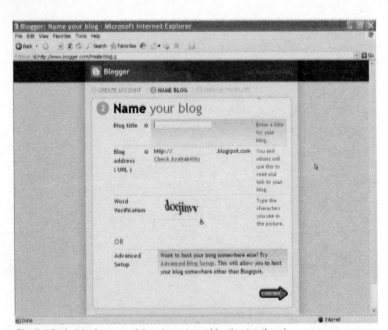

Fig.5.25 A title for your blog is entered in the textbox

is probably the main reason for this kind of title being used so widely. The big drawback is that someone seeing the title will probably obtain little insight into the nature of the site. Although your site might be of great interest to them, they could be misled by the title and pass it by without investigating further.

The middle textbox is used to add the URL (web address) for your new blog site. To be more precise, it is used to add part of the URL for your new blog site. The site will actually be part of the Blogspot.com site, so whatever you add in the textbox will be followed by ".blogspot.com" and preceded by "http://". Note that the usual "www" is not included in the Blogspot.com URLs. As an example, I used "backgardenwildlife" as the name for my demonstration blog, so its URL is:

http://backgardenwildlife.blogspot.com

This is clearly not as good as a similar name but without the ".blogspot" part of the address, but an extension to the URL of your site just has to be accepted as an inevitable drawback of using a free web host. A potential problem when choosing a web address for any new site is that

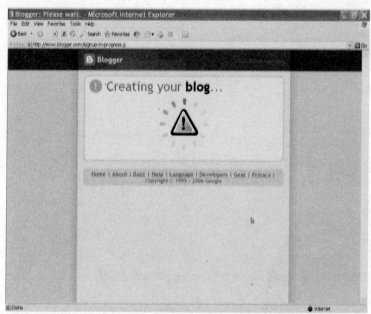

Fig.5.26 There is a short delay while the new blog is created

someone will probably have beaten you to it. Consequently, it might take a few attempts to find an address that is still available. The more unusual your choice, the better your chances of it still being available. A long address is more likely to be available than a short one.

The word verification textbox is used to block automated systems that try to use services such as Blogger.com for placing spam on free Internet sites. You just copy the random text string provided by the system into the textbox beneath. It can sometimes be difficult to decipher the text string correctly, but you will simply have to try again with a new text string if a mistake is made.

The bottom section of the window explains that you can go to an advanced section should you wish to have your site hosted elsewhere. It could be useful to make use of the Blogger.com facilities while having your blog hosted by another site. However, this is not really a method that is suitable for those trying to get a blog "up and running" as quickly as possible. It is not a method that will be considered further here.

Fig.5.27 Confirmation that the new blog has been created

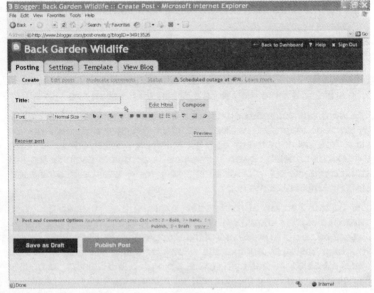

Fig.5.28 This page includes a simple text editor

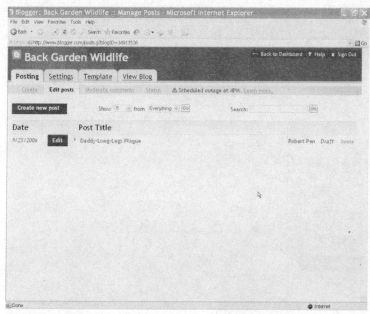

Fig.5.29 The blog has been saved but not yet published

With all the necessary information added it is time to operate the Continue button. A page like the one shown in Figure 5.26 will then appear while your new blog site is generated. This usually takes no more than a few seconds. The page shown in Figure 5.27 then appears, confirming that the new blog site has been created successfully. In order to make an entry to the blog it is then a matter of operating the Start Posting button, which moves things on to the page of Figure 5.28.

Entering text

A simple text editor is included on this page, and you can type in your new blog entry and format it in the usual way. If you have a word processor program installed on your PC it might be better to produce the text on that, making use of its spelling and grammar checking facilities. Having perfected the piece, it can then be transferred to the text editor using the normal Windows Copy and Paste facilities. The text can then be formatted using the facilities of the text editor.

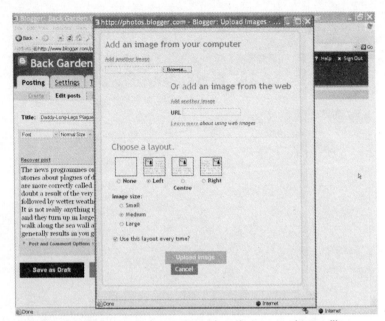

Fig.5.30 This file browser is used to select the correct image file

There is a textbox above the text editor. This is where the title is added, but this is really a sub-title. The main title for the blog is the one that was entered when the site was set up and created. This title appears in large lettering at the top of your blog regardless of which blog entry is being displayed. The title entered in this textbox is the one for the current blog entry, and it will appear in somewhat smaller text at the top of that entry.

With short blog entries you will probably enter the text and then publish it to the Internet straight away. With longer blogs you can save a partially finished blog by operating the Save as Draft button. It is then saved in your posts (Figure 5.29), but the draft version is not published to the Internet.

Photographs

With Blogger.com it is very easy to add photographs to your blogs. The first step is to operate the button that is second from the left end in the text editor's toolbar. This launches a new window (Figure 5.30) where

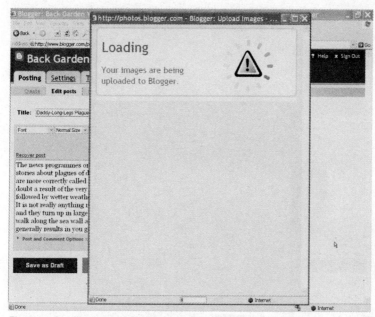

Fig.5.31 It will take a short while for the image to be uploaded

the upper section is a file browser. The image file for the photograph will usually be on your computer, and the browser is then used to locate and select the file in the normal way. Note that the image file must be in one of the standard formats used for web sites, such as JPG or GIF. It is also possible to use an image file stored on the Internet, and it is then a matter of typing the appropriate URL into the textbox provided for this purpose.

The lower section of the window enables one of four preset layouts to be selected, and it also enables the size of the image to be chosen. There are three sizes available, and it is the option selected here that determines the size of the photograph, and not the innate size of the image file. There is no point in uploading large image files, because they will simply be reduced to a size that will fit the page properly.

Having selected an image and set the required size and layout, the Upload Image button is operated. An onscreen message will then appear (Figure 5.31) while the image is uploaded to the server. This will not take long with a small image file and some sort of broadband Internet connection,

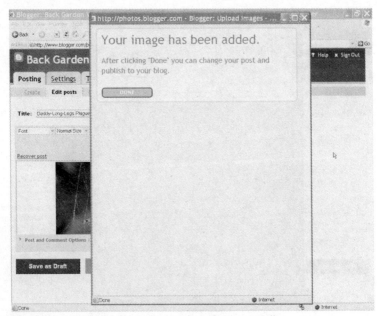

Fig.5.32 The image has been uploaded successfully

but it could take a few minutes when using an ordinary dial-up connection to upload a relatively large image file. Another onscreen message will appear when the file has been uploaded successfully (Figure 5.32).

The image will then appear in the text editor (Figure 5.33), which I suppose is actually a bit more than a text editor since it displays images. It is not quite a full WYSIWYG (what you see is what you get) editor though, and it does not provide the sort of editing facilities found in DTP (desktop publishing) and expensive page make-up programs. You can delete an image if you add it to the page and then change your mind. All you have to do is left-click the image to select it and then operate the Delete key.

Once a blog entry has been completed it is just a matter of operating the Publish Post button. After a short delay an onscreen message (Figure 5.34) will appear on the screen to confirm that the blog has been successfully published on the Internet. If you go to the appropriate web address you should then find your new blog, complete with the text you entered and any images that you uploaded. The example blog was published successfully and the web page looked just as expected (Figure 5.35).

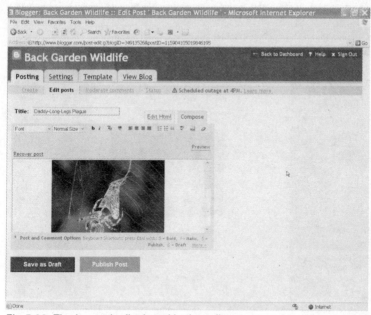

Fig.5.33 The image is displayed in the editor

Fig.5.34 The blog has been published to the Internet

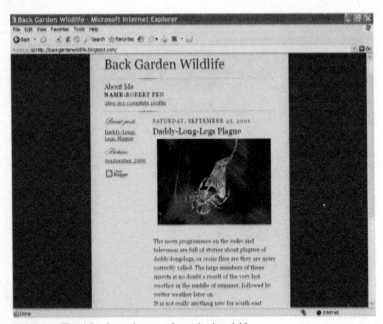

Fig.5.35 The blog's web page is as it should be

Editing and adding

In order to edit existing material or add an entry to your blog, the first step is to go to the Blogger.com home page and operate the Sign in to Blogger link. The page then changes to look like Figure 5.36, where your username and password are entered in the two textboxes. Once signed in, you are presented with the Dashboard (Figure 5.37). At the top of the Dashboard there is a list of blogs, and in this case there is only one, which is the example blog that I produced the previous day.

In order to edit a blog entry it is just a matter of left-clicking its entry in the Dashboard, and then operating the Edit button when the next page appears (Figure 5.38). This takes things back to the text editor, with the appropriate blog loaded into it (Figure 5.39). You then have the normal editing facilities at your disposal so that the necessary changes can be made. It is then a matter of operating the appropriate button to either save the revised version or publish it on the Internet.

Fig.5.36 Your username and password are needed in order to sign in

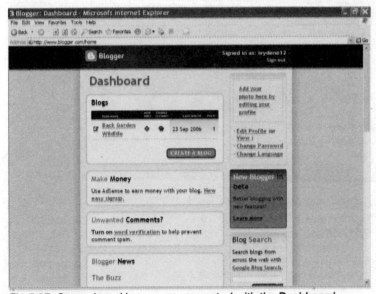

Fig.5.37 Once signed in, you are presented with the Dashboard

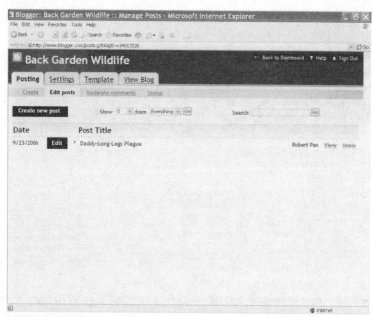

Fig.5.38 Operating the Edit button produces this page

Fig.5.39 The appropriate blog has been loaded

A new entry is added to a blog by first going to the Dashboard, and then operating the New Post button for the appropriate blog. This button is the one marked with a green "+" sign. In the example of Figure 5.40 there is only one blog, so there is just the one New Post button. Do not operate the CREATE A BLOG button, as this will produce a completely new blog rather than adding a new post to an existing one. Operating the New Post button produces a blank version of the text editor, and the new post is produced in the normal fashion.

Fig.5.40 Operate the Create New Post button

In Figure 5.41 I have created a new post for the example blog. It is just a matter of operating the Publish Post button in order to publish it to the blog. Going to the blog's web address confirms that the new post has been added to the blog (Figure 5.42). Recent posts are stacked one above the other on the homepage, so it is possible to scroll down to the first post (Figure 5.43). There is a

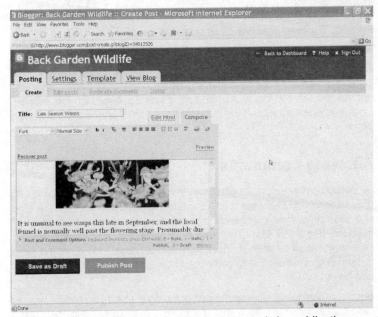

Fig.5.41 A new post has been created and is ready for publication

Fig.5.42 The new post has been added to the blog

link for each post in the right-hand column of the page, and you can jump to an earlier post by activating its link. In Figure 5.44 I have left-clicked the link for the first post, and it has appeared on the screen. However, when accessed in this fashion the earlier post has its own web page.

Allowing comments

By default it is possible for others to leave comments on your blog. All they have to do is activate the Comments link at the bottom of the blog and then type their comments into the textbox of the new page that appears (Figure 5.45). The only requirement is that those posting comments must have an account with Blogger.com. This is not the most demanding of requirements given the ease with which a Blogger account can be set up.

Having others leave comments on your blog is fine if you have a type of blog that will benefit from this feedback. It is something that is not

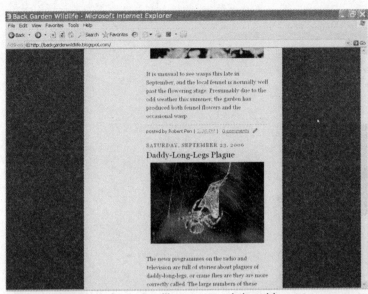

Fig.5.43 The original post is still present and viewable

Fig.5.44 The original post can be viewed in its own page

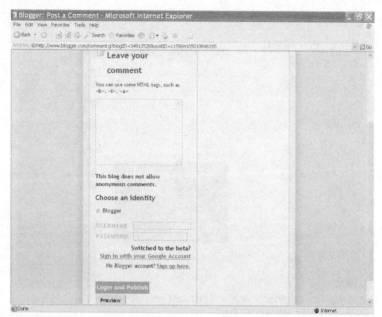

Fig.5.45 Registered Blog.com users can add comments to your blog

appropriate to all types of blog, or you might prefer to block any feedback simply in order to make quite sure that there are no problems with troublemakers trying to disrupt your blog. Comments can be blocked by operating the Post and Comment Options link near the bottom of the text editor. This produces some extra options in the area beneath the editor (Figure 5.46). The only ones of relevance here are the Yes and No radio buttons that enable comments to be allowed (Yes) or blocked (No).

There is a growing problem with automated systems placing spam on blogs and other sites that permit comments to be left. You have to copy some text characters to a textbox when setting up an account with Blogger.com, and this is designed to prevent automated systems from setting up and using large numbers of accounts. The same system can be used to prevent automated systems from using the comments facility to add spam to your blog site. Where a system of this type is available it is definitely a good idea to use it.

Operating the Settings tab produces a page that controls some basic settings (Figure 5.47), but there are various sub-tabs that provide access

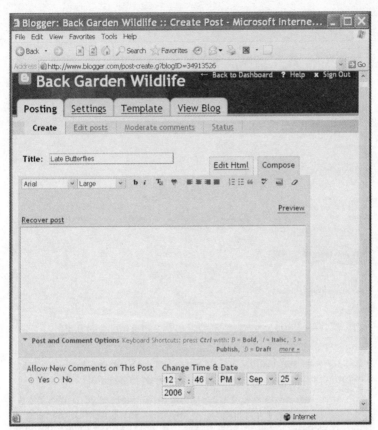

*Fig.5.46 Operate the No radio button near the bottom left-hand corner
of the page if you wish to block comments*

to more pages and settings. In this case it is the Comments section that
is of interest (Figure 5.48). You have to scroll down the page to find the
radio buttons that enable word verification to be switched on and off. It
is worth looking at the other settings to see if there is anything of use to
you.

The default settings could cause a few problems if your blog will be
heavily dependent on comments from readers. As already pointed out,
by default it is only possible for readers to add comments to your blog if
they have an account with Blogger.com. An important point to bear in

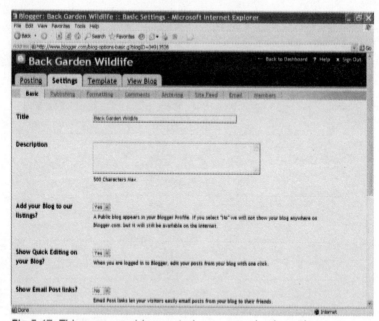

Fig.5.47 This page provides control over some basic settings

mind here is that visitors to your site will not just be fellow users of Blogger.com, but will be users of the Internet in general.

In other words, by default, it is likely that most users of your blog site will not be able to leave comments. They have the option of opening an account with Blogger.com specifically to enable them to leave comments on your blog, but it is unlikely that many people would bother to do this. In fact it is unlikely that anyone would bother to register just so that they could leave comments on your blog.

The top menu on the Comments settings page enables you to opt for comments to be enabled for all visitors to your site. This is the setting that will normally have to be used in order to use comments in a worthwhile fashion. Casual visitors to your blog will then be able to add their contribution to your discussions without having to go through any signing up process.

There is actually a third option, which only permits members of your blog to leave comments. In effect, your blog becomes a club, and only members of the club are allowed to post comments. A blog of this type

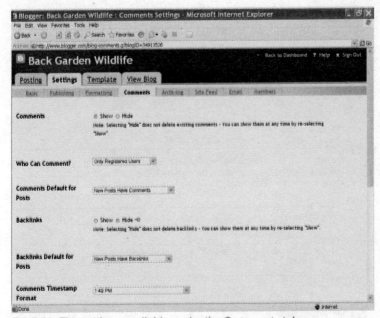

Fig.5.48 The settings available under the Comments tab

is often used where the blog covers the activities of something like a cricket club, art club, etc. It is set up to keep members informed of the latest club news, forthcoming events, and so on. With this type of blog it can be useful to permit members to post comments, but it is probably best to prevent the world at large from doing so.

The default is for comments to be enabled, but they can be disabled by using the extra options available from the text editor. It is important to realise that disabling comments using this method only blocks them for that particular blog entry. This is not a very good way of handling things where comments must be blocked from every blog entry. It would be much better if they could be blocked via a universal setting, and this is possible using the second menu on the Comments settings page.

Setting this to New Posts Do Not Have Comments blocks comments on all further posts. To be more precise, it changes the default from having comments enabled to having them disabled. It is still possible to enable comments for individual posts by activating the extra options in the text editor and operating the Yes button.

Fig.5.49 Some text in block quote form

Text editor

As already pointed out, the text editor used to produce blogs on Blogger.com is actually rather more than a basic text editor. When producing material that will be placed on the Internet it is as well to remember that it will usually end up in the form of HTML (hypertext mark-up language) code. The text editor provided as part of Blogger.com's system is really a simple HTML rather than a text editor.

If you have a word processor installed on your PC, and you use it quite frequently, the best approach is probably to produce the raw text using this word processor. It is the one you are accustomed to using, and with it you should be able to produce polished articles with relative ease. The completed text can then be transferred to the Blogger.com editor and given the required formatting. In general, it does not work properly

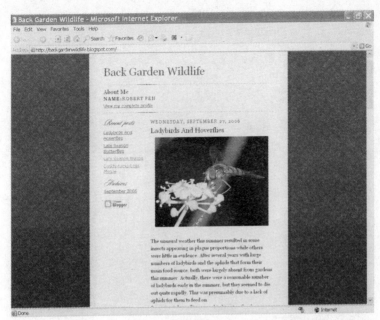

Fig.5.50 A new post has been added to the example blog

if you try formatting text and then transferring it to an editor such as the one used by Blogger.com. The formatting is removed and it is only simple text that appears in the editor.

The reason for this is that, as explained previously, the editor is really an HTML type. Accordingly, it has the limitations imposed by the fact that it is producing HTML pages. Many of the types of formatting provided by modern word processors are either not available at all using HTML, or can only be provided in a somewhat simplified form. If you format the text using a word processor, it is likely that producing an accurate HTML equivalent would not be possible.

It is therefore a matter of transferring the text to the HTML editor and adding the required formatting, or typing the text straight into the editor and then formatting it. Although the formatting available using the editor is a bit limited by the standards of modern word processors and desktop publishing programs, it is more than adequate for producing attractive web pages.

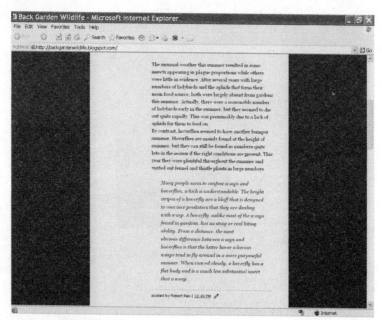

The unusual weather this summer resulted in some insects appearing in plague proportions while others were little in evidence. After several years with large numbers of ladybirds and the aphids that form their main food source, both were largely absent from gardens this summer. Actually, there were a reasonable number of ladybirds early in the summer, but they seemed to die out quite rapidly. This was presumably due to a lack of aphids for them to feed on.

By contrast, hoverflies seemed to have another bumper summer. Hoverflies are mainly found at the height of summer, but they can still be found in numbers quite late in the season if the right conditions are present. This year they were plentiful throughout the summer and visited out fennel and thistle plants in large numbers.

Many people seem to confuse wasps and hoverflies, which is understandable. The bright stripes of a hoverfly are a bluff that is designed to convince predators that they are dealing with wasp. A hoverfly, unlike most of the wasps found in gardens, has no sting or real biting ability. From a distance, the most obvious difference between wasps and hoverflies is that the latter hover whereas wasps tend to fly around in a more purposeful manner. When viewed closely, a hoverfly has a flat body and is a much less substantial insect that a wasp.

posted by Robert Pen | 12:46 PM

Fig.5.51 The page has been scrolled down to show the block quote text

Most of the facilities available from the text editor are the usual formatting tools, such as menus that are used to select the required font and text size. The range of fonts and text sizes is rather limited compared to those available from a word processor or desktop publishing program, but ordinary HTML does not provide the same degree of control that is available using a normal Windows application program. In the case of text sizes, the Blogger.com editor only provides a choice of five. However, this should be sufficient to produce some attractive results.

There is a pop-up palette that provides a useful range of text colours. In general, it is advisable to be fairly conservative with your choice of text colour. Obviously some types of blog are zanier than others, and some blogs might benefit from the use of bright colours. Bear in mind though, that there is no point in producing a bright and eye-catching blog that is very difficult to read due to the choice of text colours. For many types of blog there is no point in using anything other than black, which is the default text colour.

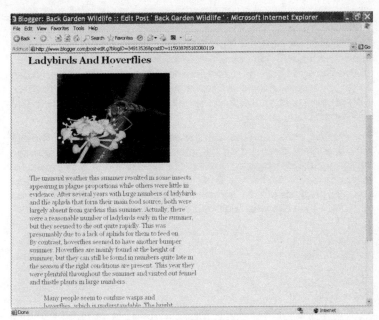

Fig.5.52 The Preview facilty is useful for "fine tuning" your posts

Block quote

The text editor has some useful extras, including a straightforward but effective spelling checker, and a facility that enables the raw HTML code to be edited. There is also a block quote facility. The block quote facility is useful where you wish to have some text that is within but to some extent separate from the main text. Typically, this type of text is used where you are quoting someone, or where you are providing some additional information that does not form part of the main text. In order to place text into block quote form it is just a matter of selecting it and operating the block quote button in the editor's toolbar. The selected text remains unchanged apart from being inset from both the left and right margins.

In Figure 5.49 the text at the bottom of the editor has been placed into block quote form. It has not formatted quite as I would have liked, and a bit of manual editing was required. Figure 5.50 shows the example blog with the fourth instalment added, and in Figure 5.51 the page has been scrolled down to reveal the block quote text.

Preview

The Preview link near the top right-hand corner of the editor is useful when "fine tuning" blog entries. As explained previously, things do not always come out quite as expected when producing web pages. It can be very time consuming if you repeatedly publish a web page, find that it is not quite right, go back to the editor, publish the page again, find another problem, and so on.

The Preview facility enables you to see how the page will be laid out without actually placing it on the Internet and viewing it in a browser. You get a slightly simplified version of the page in the preview mode, with just a plain white background (Figure 5.52), but the layout of the text and any graphics should accurately reflect the layout that would be obtained if the page was published on the Internet.

Points to remember

The word blog is a contraction of "web log". It probably means a sort of online diary to most people, since it is primarily this type of blog that has been reported in the mass media in recent times. However, there are various types of blog, and an online diary is just one of the many possibilities. It is probably the one that most bloggers opt for, but it is worthwhile considering the alternatives.

Other possibilities for blogs include such things as reviews, information on a particular topic, political and satirical blogs, prediction blogs, and so on. In fact it is possible to do a blog equivalent of practically any normal type of web site. If you are not interested in doing a diary blog, there will probably be something else that is more to your liking.

Most blog sites enable photographs, sound clips, and possibly even video clips to be added to blog pages. Things can be taken a stage further, and you can have blogs that mainly use photographs, audio, or video instead of the written word. Of course, a certain amount of additional equipment and skill is required for this type of thing.

A podcast takes the idea of an audio blog a stage further. With most podcasts it is possible for users to listen to streamed audio using their computers, but there is also the option of downloading the podcast as an audio file. This is usually an MP3 type which can then be uploaded to an MP3 player or an iPod. It can then be played in the normal way, just like a music file.

Do not assume that it is just a matter of starting a blog and sitting back while thousands of people flock to read it. There are a huge number of blogs on the Internet, plus the billions of other pages on sites of various types. Getting a reasonable number of people to read your blog will take a certain amount of effort. Placing a blog or other type of web site onto the Internet is usually the easy bit. Getting people to visit it is likely to be the difficult part.

In order to get people to read your blog, and keep reading it, you will have to produce material of a suitably high standard. Also, simply duplicating the type of thing that can be found on thousands of other blogs and web sites is unlikely to attract and keep a large readership. In order to stand out from the crowd it is necessary to cover an interesting subject that does not receive adequate exposure elsewhere. Alternatively, a subject that receives plenty of coverage must be covered in a novel way.

Before deciding to start a blog it is worth considering whether some other form of web presence would be more suitable. For example, a conventional web site might be more suitable, depending on what you are trying to achieve. Other possibilities include bulletin boards and Wikipedia.

If you simply need to produce an online photo album there are web publishing sites specifically for this type of thing. In fact there seems to be an ever growing number of album sites. In most cases the albums can be for your own viewing only, for viewing by selected friends and members of your family, or by the general public.

Instant messaging

Friendly chat

I suppose that instant messaging could be regarded as a more sophisticated version of e-mail. It can be used to communicate with your friends, family, and colleagues in a similar way to an ordinary Email system, but with much faster responses. With an instant messaging system you can see which of your contacts are online, and are therefore able to respond almost instantly to any message you send them. You can "talk" to any of your contacts that are online in much the same way that you would when using a chat-room.

It is not actually essential to have a broadband Internet connection in order to use an instant messaging system, but it obviously works better with an Internet connection that is always active when your computer is switched on. In other words, it works best with some form of broadband connection. The speed of a broadband connection is needed for some of the more advanced facilities available from some instant messaging systems, such as using a webcam.

Drawbacks

Although instant messaging is in many ways a very neat way of communicating with your circle of friends, family, colleagues at work, etc. it does have one major drawback. Unlike voice over Internet telephone systems, there is no significant linking between the various instant messaging systems. With a voice over Internet system it is advantageous if you use the same system as the people you will be talking to, because there is a financial advantage in doing so.

With an instant messaging system it is not so much advantageous as essential. If you wish to communicate with people who are already using

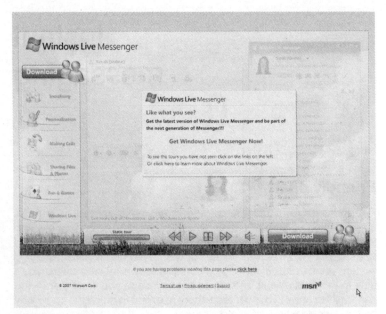

Fig.6.1 Live Messenger can be downloaded from the MSN site

instant messaging, then it is crucial to sign on to whichever system they are already using. Unfortunately, if your family, friends, and work colleagues are using three different systems, it will be necessary for you to use all three systems in order to use instant messaging with all three groups. It is up to you to decide whether this is a practical approach to things.

Of course, you can take the lead in cases where the people you wish to "talk" to via instant messaging are not already using this method of communication. You can use any of the major instant messaging services, and then persuade the others to use the same system. It has to be carefully explained to the other participants that they can only be participants if they sign on to the correct system. Should they choose another system they will be talking to themselves! There are actually programs that attempt to integrate two or more messaging systems, but they mostly offer a rather limited range of features. However, one of these programs might provide a usable solution if you really have no choice but to use more than one system.

Fig.6.2 Once launched, the program has a conventional sign-in screen

Another point to bear in mind as that an instant messaging service has to run as a background task for the whole time that the computer is operating. It would otherwise be impossible for the computer to detect an incoming message and alert you to its presence. You are offline if the computer is switched on, the Internet connection is active, but the instant messaging program is not running.

The additional loading on the computer's resources is not going to be very high when an instant messaging program is launched. The real problem is that modern PCs tend to have more and more of these background services running continuously, and in total they can produce a massive amount of loading on the computer's resources. Even modern computers that have large amounts of memory and fast processors can noticeably slow down under the strain of running numerous background tasks. Older computers, particularly if they are equipped with relatively small amounts of memory, can run very slowly if the number of background tasks is allowed to get out of hand.

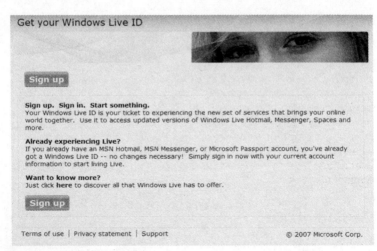

Fig.6.3 If you do not already have a suitable account it will be necessary to create one

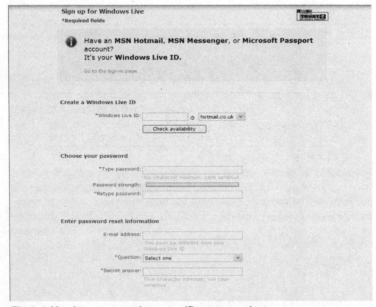

Fig.6.4 You have to supply a user ID, password, etc.

It is a good idea to periodically uninstall any software that has become superfluous, and this is especially important with programs that run background tasks. It might be worthwhile doing some "spring cleaning" before installing an instant messaging program, especially when using a PC that is several years old or has a relatively small amount of memory.

Getting started

There are three main instant messaging services, which are MSN messenger, Yahoo messenger, and AOL messenger. They all operate in essentially the same manner, and at the time of writing this, they are all free services. I will use MSN messenger is the basis of this example. The current trend is to merge various forms of computer messaging into a single "do-it-all" program, and the latest version of the MSN Messenger reflects this trend. The program is called Windows Live Messenger, and it is available as a free download

Fig.6.5 The program has been launched

from the MSN website at www.msn.com (Figure 6.1). Of course, it is not necessary to use the additional features, and it can be used solely as an instant messaging program if that is the only feature you require.

Once installed and launched, the program will present you with a window where you sign on to the system in the normal fashion (Figure 6.2). There is no problem here provided you already have some form of MSN account, such as a Hotmail Email type. If not, it will be necessary to operate the "Sign up for a Windows Live ID" link, which will launch Windows Explorer and take you to the appropriate page of the MSN website (Figure 6.3). Operating the Sign Up button moves things on to

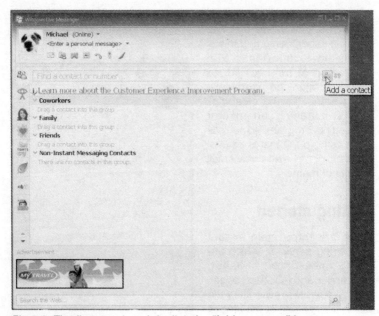

Fig.6.6 The first step is to left-click the "Add a contact" button

the page of Figure 6.4, where a user ID, password, etc., have to be entered in the various textboxes.

When the messenger program is launched for the first time there will be an onscreen message pointing out that the contact list does not have any entries (Figure 6.5). In order to communicate with other users of the system it is necessary to enter their details into your list of contacts. The first step is to left-click the Add a Contact button (Figure 6.6), which launches the new window of Figure 6.7. The only essential information you have to add here is the messaging address of the new contact, and you will need to enter a nickname for them as well. The nickname is the one that will be used to identify them in your contact list.

The menu near the bottom right-hand corner of the window is used to select the appropriate group for the new contact. There are four categories for your contacts, which are co-workers, family, friends, and one for non-instant messaging contacts. There is no problem if you accidentally add a contact to the wrong group or simply change your mind. Entries can be moved from one category to another by simply

Fig.6.7 The messaging address and a nickname must be entered here

dragging them into a different group. Further contacts are added in the same way until all your contacts have been entered.

A new category can be added by right-clicking an existing category and selecting the "Create new group" option from the pop-up menu (Figure 6.9). This produces the new window of Figure 6.10, where a name for the new group is entered in the textbox. Tick the checkboxes for any contacts that you wish to add to the group at this stage. Operating the Save button then results in the new group being added to the main window (Figure 6.11). A group can be deleted by right-clicking its entry and selecting Delete Group from the pop-up menu. Similarly, a contact can be removed by right-clicking the relevant entry in the contact list and choosing Delete Contact from the pop-up menu.

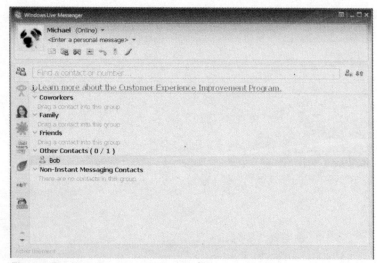

Fig.6.8 The new contact has been added to the list

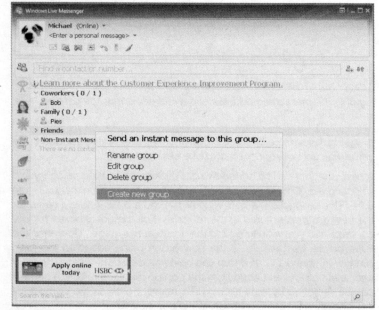

Fig.6.9 A new group is easily added

Joining a group

It is important to realise that the fact you have added someone to your contact list does not mean that you will automatically be allowed to communicate with them via the instant messaging system. This is a fundamental difference between an instant messaging system and using Emails. You can send an Email to any Email address, and it will reach that person or organisation unless there is a fault in the system. The person receiving the Email will probably have a filtering system that enables your Email to

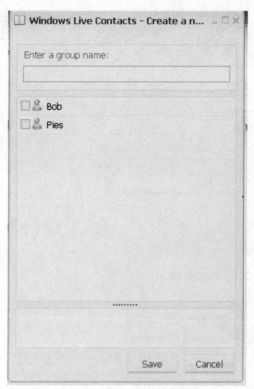

Fig.6.10 Enter a name for the new group in the textbox

be automatically directed to the Trash folder, or something of this type, and can effectively opt out of receiving your Emails. With an instant messaging system you can only send someone a message if they have opted in, and have agreed to communicate with you.

When someone is added to your contact list they receive a message (Figure 6.12) asking if they would like you to be able to see when they are online, and if they wish to receive your messages. You will receive the same message when anyone adds you to their contact list. Operate the upper radio button if you wish to enable contact with them, or the lower radio button if you would prefer to block any contact with them. This will also prevent them from seeing whether you are online. It does not prevent them from including you in their contact list, but it does render

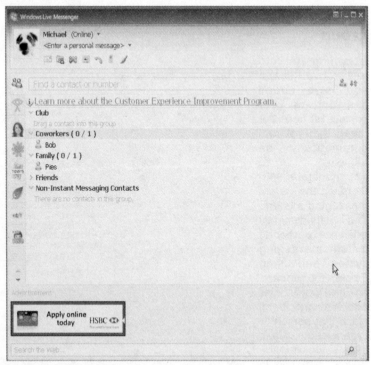

Fig.6.11 The new group has been successfully added to the top of the
         contacts list

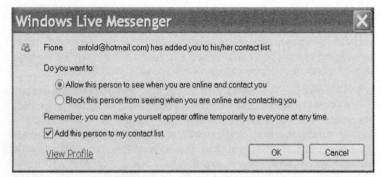

Fig.6.12 A message like this is received by a contact when you try to
         add them to your contact list

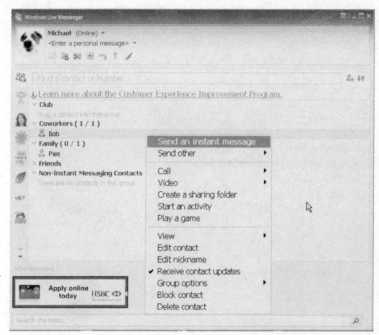

Fig.6.13 Choose the "Send an instant message" menu item

your entry in the list totally unusable. The contact will be automatically added to your contact list if you leave the tick in the checkbox near the bottom of the window.

Spim

It is worth mentioning that, inevitably perhaps, there is an instant messaging equivalent of spam, which is called "spim". The openness of the Email system makes it very vulnerable to problems with spam, whereas the more exclusive nature of most instant messaging systems make it far more difficult to distribute spim. Hence spim is far less of a problem than spam, but it is apparently a growing problem. It should be possible to remain spim free if you do not agree to be on the contact list of anyone that you do not know and trust. You can prevent someone from sending you instant messages by right-clicking their entry in the contact list and selecting Block Contact from the pop-up menu.

6   Instant messaging

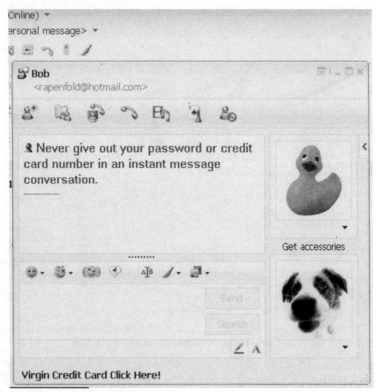

Fig.6.14 This window is used to send and receive messages

Making contact

It is easy to see which of your contacts are online, and can be contacted using instant messaging, because the icon next to a contact's nickname is green if he or she is online. The first step when sending a message is to locate the entry for the recipient. If necessary, you must left-click the entry for the relevant group in order to expand it and display its contents. It is then a matter of right-clicking the recipient's entry and choosing "Send an instant message" from the pop-up menu (Figure 6.13).

This produces a small pop-up window (Figure 6.14), which consists of two main sections. The upper section is used to display any messages that you receive, and initially it just contains a security warning. As with any form of online communication, it is as well to take due care, especially

190

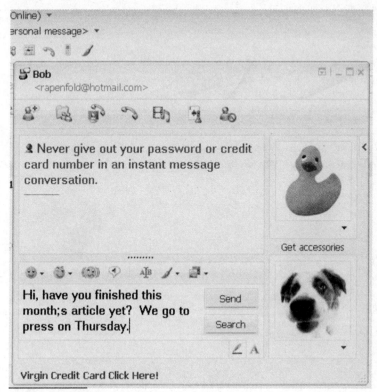

Fig.6.15 Enter your messages in the lower panel

when communicating with someone that you do not know very well. With any system that operates via the Internet you should always be on your guard and should never take anything at face value.

The lower section of the window is where you enter your messages, as in the example of Figure 6.15. Having completed the message, it is then just a matter of operating the Send button, which sends the message to your contact and also moves it to the upper section of the window (Figure 6.16). A small onscreen alert tells your contact that a new message has been received, and on going into Windows Live Messenger they will find your message in the upper part of their message window (Figure 6.17).

If the contact wishes to reply, they enter their message into the bottom section of their message window (Figure 6.18), and then operate the

Fig.6.16 The message has been sent, and it is now in the upper panel

Fig.6.17 The message has arrived at the other end of the system

Fig.6.18 The reply is entered in the lower panel

Fig.6.19 The reply has been sent

Fig.6.20 The reply has been received

Send button. This moves the message to the upper section of their message window (Figure 6.19), and it also appears in the upper section of your message window (Figure 6.20). Messages can be swapped indefinitely, with any message entered at one end of the system appearing in the upper message window at both ends when the Send button is operated.

Offline messaging

It is possible to communicate with contacts who are offline, but the instant aspect of the system is clearly not possible under these conditions. I suppose it is instant in the sense that the message will be sent right away, but obviously it will not be received until the recipient goes online. In order to send a message to someone that is offline it is necessary to

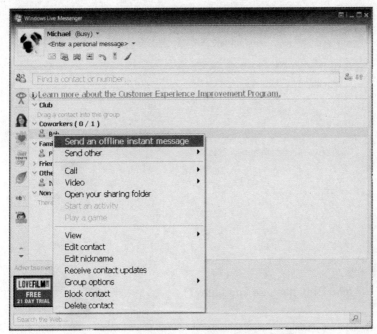

Fig.6.21 A message can be sent to a contact that is offline

right-click their entry in the main window and then select "Send an offline instant message" (Figure 6.21). The warning message of Figure 6.22 will then appear, and this simply points out that the person you are trying

Fig.6.22 You are warned that the contact is offline

Fig.6.23 As usual, your message is typed into the lower panel

to contact is currently offline, and that they will not receive your message until they go online again.

The window that is used to enter your message is much the same as the normal version (Figure 6.23), and as usual, the message is entered into the lower section of the window. The Send button is then operated, the message is sent, and it will be made available to your contact as soon as they sign on to the MSN messaging service. An alternative way of handling things is to activate the "E-mail this" link in the upper panel. Activating this link results in Internet Explorer being launched and you are taken to your Hotmail Email account. The To and From fields are automatically filled in for you, so it is just a matter of adding the subject heading and your message before operating the Send button.

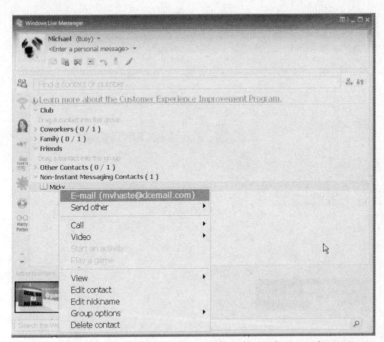

Fig.6.24 It is possible to Email contacts that do not have an instant messaging account

It is possible to include contacts that do not have a MSN instant messaging account, and they are added to the "Non-Instant Messaging Contacts" group in the usual way. Obviously there is no option to send an instant message when one of these contacts is right-clicked and the pop-up menu appears, but there is an option to Email them (Figure 6.24). Operating this link results in Internet Explorer being launched, and you are then signed into your Hotmail Email account. Once again, it is then just a matter of filling in the Subject field, entering your message, and left-clicking the Send button.

It is possible to send an instant message to everyone in a group, and this is basically just a matter of right-clicking the group's entry in the main panel and then selecting "Send an instant message to this group" from the pop-up menu (Figure 6.25). Things then operate much the same as normal, but in chat room fashion rather than on a one-to-one basis.

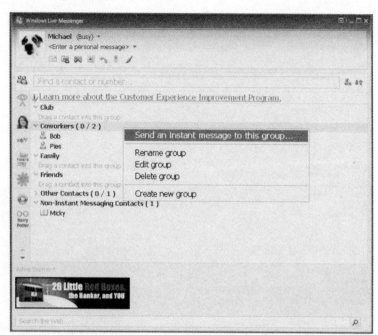

Fig.6.25 It is possible to send an instant message to a group

File sharing

It is possible to share files using the MSN instant messaging system, and this operates in a fashion that is similar to an Email attachment. There is an alternative available from the MSN instant messenger system, and this operates in a fashion that is more like file sharing via a network. In order to use the first method it is just a matter of right-clicking the appropriate entry in the contacts list and then selecting "Send other" from the pop-up menu, followed by "Send a single file" from the submenu (Figure 6.26). This produces the standard Windows file browser which is used to locate and open the file that you wish to send.

Having selected the file, it is shown in the upper section of the message window, but there is a message indicating that the system is waiting for the recipient to accept the file (Figure 6.27). Meanwhile, at the other end of the system the recipient gets a pop-up message indicating that a message has been received, and the message itself indicates that there

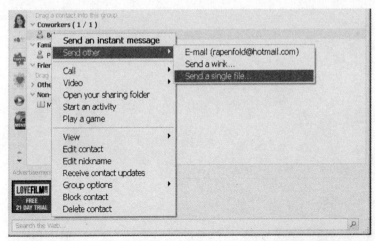

Fig.6.26 A file can be sent via the MSN instant messaging system

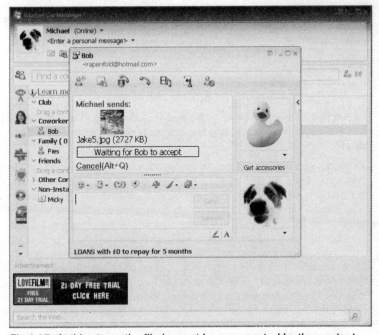

Fig.6.27 At this stage, the file has not been accepted by the contact

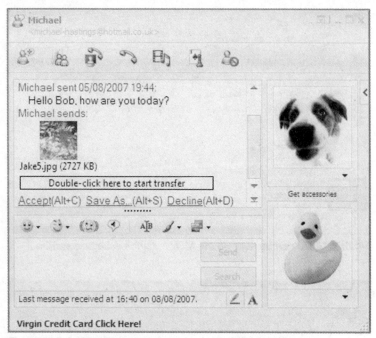

Fig.6.28 Double-clicking the button results in the file being downloaded

is a file that is ready to be downloaded (Figure 6.28). The file can be downloaded by double-clicking the button at the bottom of the upper panel.

Of course, as with Email attachments, you should not download the file unless you are sure that you know what it is, where it has come from, and that it is safe to download and open it. When any file has been downloaded it is a good idea to err on the side of caution and check it using an antivirus program before trying to open it. Once the file has been downloaded, the message in the upper panel will show its location on the hard disc drive (Figure 6.29). Unlike an Email attachment, the file is not uploaded to a server, from where it has to be downloaded to the recipient's computer. The file is copied straight from the sender's computer to the recipient's computer. When the file has been fully transferred, the message at the sender's PC indicates that it has been sent successfully (Figure 6.30).

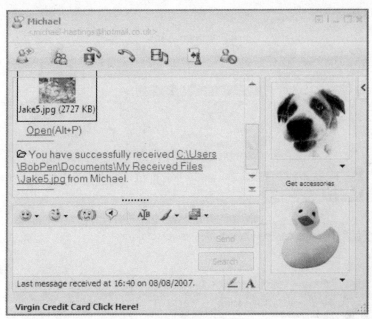

Fig.6.29 The file has been successfully downloaded

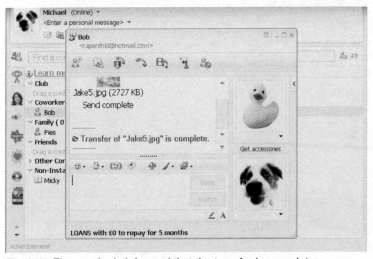

Fig.6.30 The sender is informed that the transfer is complete

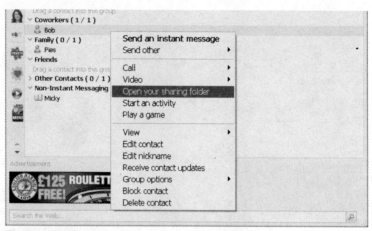

Fig.6.31 Files can be shared via a special folder

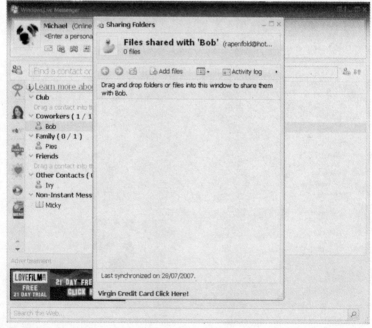

Fig.6.32 The pop-up window represents the shared folder

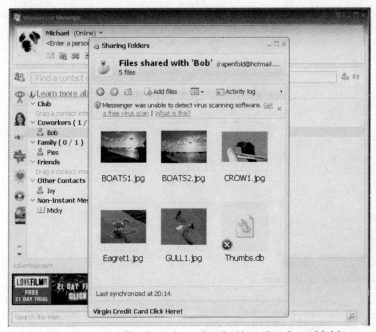

Fig.6.33 Some image files have been loaded into the shared folder

Using a shared folder is equally simple, and the first step is to right-click the appropriate entry in the contacts list and then select either "Create a sharing folder" or "Open your sharing folder" from the pop-up menu (Figure 6.31). This launches a new window (Figure 6.32), and you can either drag files into the main panel, or operate the Add Files button and use the file browser to select and load them. Either way you end up with something like Figure 6.33, after a short delay while the system is synchronised. In other words, there is a short delay while the files are uploaded and made available to the other user.

If the other user goes to your entry in their contacts list and opens the shared folder, they should then find that they also have access to the files. In this example everything worked properly, and the five image files were available to the other user (Figure 6.34). The files in the sharing folder can be used in much the same way as any other files, and right-clicking on one of the icons produces the usual options such as Cut, Copy, Paste, and Open With.

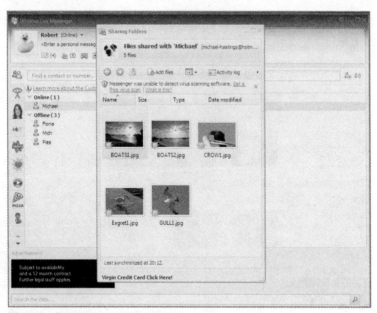

Fig.6.34 The shared folder and its contents can be accessed at the other end of the system

Customising

There are various ways of customising the program, but with anything like this it is best not to get too carried away. The fact that you can add things like fancy animations and backgrounds does not necessarily mean that it would be a good idea to do so. Things like that have to be done skilfully and with restraint or they tend to quickly become distracting and even irritating.

One feature you will probably wish to customise is the small picture that appears in the top left-hand corner of the main window, and effectively forms part of your user ID when sending messages. This can be changed to one of the other images supplied with the software, or to one of your own images. Start by left-clicking the existing image, which will result in a small menu window being launched (Figure 6.35). Select the "Change your display picture" option, which produces the new window of Figure 6.36. Here you can select one of the regular pictures, or use the Browse button to launch the file browser so that you can select one of your own image files. If you use your own image file it must be in one of the standard formats used by Windows, such as Jpg. It is not necessary to have an image of the right size. The display image is tiny, and your image is likely to be massively larger than the required size, but the software will automatically resize it to fit the available space.

The normal menu bar at the top of the main window is not shown by default, but it is easily activated if you would prefer a conventional Windows user interface. It is just a matter of operating the Show Menu button, which is the one at the left end of the row of four buttons in the top right-hand

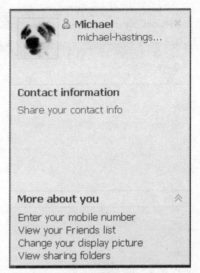

Fig.6.35 Select "Change your display picture"

Fig.6.36 Choose one of the standard images or load your own image

Fig.6.37 If desired, a conventional menu bar can be used

corner of the main window, and then selecting "Show the menu bar" from the pop-up menu. A conventional menu bar and set of three window control buttons then appear (Figure 6.37). The original set of four buttons is reduced to a single button, and left-clicking this button restores the original user interface.

Status

By default, your status will be given as Online when your PC has an active Internet connection and you have the messaging system running. The status will automatically change to Busy when the computer goes into the energy saving Standby mode, or to Offline if you log off or the PC goes into Hibernation mode. When online, you can manually set some other status by operating the name button near the top left-hand

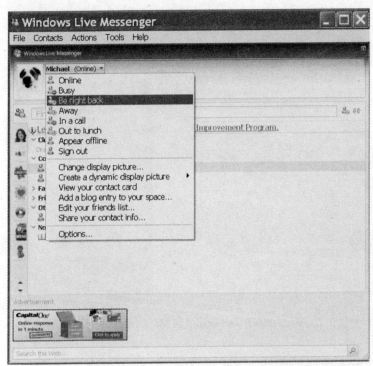

Fig.6.38 A range of status options are available in the upper section of this menu

corner of the main window. A range of options, such as "Be right back" and "Out to lunch" are then available in the upper section of the pop-up menu (Figure 6.38).

Web based version

There is a potential problem when using instant messaging systems when away from home. Everything should be straightforward if you take your portable PC along with you, because it will presumably have the necessary software loaded. Signing on to your instant messaging service in the normal way should present no problems provided an Internet connection can be arranged.

Matters are more complicated if you have to use a computer other than your own portable type, because it is unlikely that the computer will have

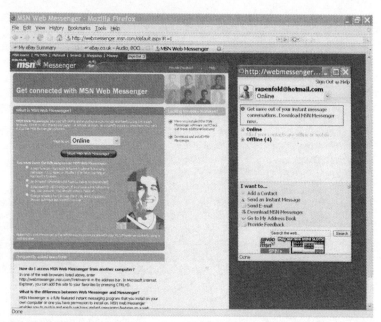

Fig.6.39 The web-based version of the MSN messaging service

the necessary software installed. While it would probably not take too long to get the required software downloaded, installed, and set up correctly, the owner of the computer would probably not agree to you installing any software on in. As a security precaution, most companies have a total ban on this type of thing, and for the same reason, few private individuals are more accommodating.

Most instant messaging services have a way around this problem in the form of so-called web-based messaging systems. Rather than using special software installed on your PC, the web-based approach uses a system that is based on an ordinary web browser such as Internet Explorer. All you have to do is go to the homepage of the web-based service, sign in, and then use the system in much the same way as normal. Figure 6.39 shows the web-based version of the MSN instant messaging service in operation. As one would probably expect, the instant messaging services that are accessed via a browser tend to be somewhat simplified, and lack the "bells and whistles" of the standard services. However, they should include everything you need in order to stay in touch with your contacts.

Points to remember

As with anything that involves sending and receiving information over the Internet, proceed with due care. Do not send personal information, passwords, or anything of this type to anyone unless you are sure that you know who you are dealing with. Ideally, this type of information should never be sent be Email or an instant messaging system, since neither can be regarded as totally secure. Never take things at face value, especially when someone requests personal or otherwise sensitive information.

Unlike voice over Internet telephone systems, there is relatively little connectivity between the various instant messaging services. Consequently, you have to sign up with the same provider as the people you will be contacting. This might not be very practical in cases where you have family members, friends, and colleagues at work, etc., which use different systems.

An instant messaging system has to run as a background task all the time that the computer is booted up and running the operating system. This places demands on the processor and the other resources of the computer, but the extra loading on the system should be quite small. Bear in mind though, that together with antivirus programs and other common background tasks, the total loading can be quite large. Particularly with older PCs, this can result in a noticeable reduction in the speed of the computer.

Instant messaging services are often integrated with other services, such as a voice over Internet telephone system. Having a single program that offers two or more functions can help to minimise loading on the computer, and can also be a more convenient way of handling things. However, it is not necessary to utilize any other services that are available. You can simply use the instant messaging facility and ignore everything else.

Instant messaging services are much like ordinary Email services, but with the ability to get almost instant responses from your contacts. The ability to get rapid responses from your contacts is clearly dependent on them being online at the time, so that they receive an alert saying that your message has been received. They can then respond to you immediately if they wish to do so. You can see at a glance which of your contacts is online, and therefore able to respond at once.

It is only possible to communicate with someone via an instant messaging service if they agree to do so. They can block communication with you, and this also prevents you from seeing whether they are online. Similarly, someone can only communicate with you if you agree to them doing so, and they can not see whether you are online if you block communication with them.

You can send a message to someone that is not online at the time, but obviously they can not receive the message or respond to it until the next time that they go online. With most systems you can have contacts that do not have an instant messaging account with the service that you are using, but once again, messaging will not be of the instant variety. You are just sending them ordinary Emails.

An instant message can be sent to a group of contacts rather than an individual contact, and you then have something very similar to a chat room. However, it is a chat room that can only be used by the people you have placed in your group of contacts. In other words, you can generate your own private chat room.

Internet TV

Changing times

While Internet television is not exactly new, it is only relatively recently that it has "taken off" in a big way. Until quite recently the number of Internet television stations was relatively small, as was the range of programmes available from most stations. Things are now changing, with many of the large broadcasting organisations launching some form of Internet television service. At the moment anyway, this tends to be in the form of an on-demand service rather than live streaming.

One reason for the sudden upsurge in Internet television is certainly the widespread use of broadband Internet connections. There are actually systems that attempt to provide sound and video via an ordinary dial-up connection, but the technical quality of these systems is inevitably very poor. They are suitable for providing a video link with someone using a WebCam, but are not really adequate for watching television programmes.

Even when using one of the slower broadband Internet connections you have to accept something less than true DVD quality, but the picture quality is still sufficient to satisfy most users. However, there is a definite advantage in having a fast broadband connection if you intend to use Internet television services. Some services are only usable if you have a reasonably fast broadband connection, but many offer a lower technical quality in conjunction with a slower connection.

It seems likely that the Internet will change the way that many people use television services, in much the same way that it has changed the way in which many users listen to radio stations. Of course, there is an alternative approach to things that is also becoming quite popular, in the form of gadgets that will record television programmes and store them on a hard disc drive so that you can watch them as and when desired. This method is also possible using a reasonably powerful PC equipped with a suitable television card and software. The Internet approach might be the one that suits you best, but it is obviously worthwhile considering the alternative.

Free **tv**, **Internet TV** Online, watch World **TV** on your PC, totally ...
This site may harm your computer.
free **internet tv**, free satellite **tv**, free **tv**, free web **tv**, **tv** listings, watch **tv** online, watch
TV on your PC, free **tv** online, free **tv** on pc, ...
                                    Similar pages

Fig.7.1 Risky sites are often flagged as such by the search engine

It is only fair to point out that using Internet television does not represent a way of avoiding the need to buy a television licence. The general consensus of opinion seems to be that it does not matter whether television programmes are received via conventional means, satellite, cable, or the Internet, a normal television licence is required in each case. Of course, the situation might be different in countries other than the UK, so readers in other countries should check the situation in their particular part of the world.

Another point worth making is that many Internet television services are not free. This is one respect in which Internet television and radio differ, with paid-for Internet radio services being few and far between. While there are plenty of free Internet television services, you can reasonably be expected to pay for any form of premium content. After all, as far as the commercial broadcasters are concerned the Internet is just another means of distributing their programmes, and premium content has to be paid for in the normal way.

As with Internet radio, Internet television largely ignores the borders between countries, and you are not limited to programmes that originate from your own country. This means that a huge and growing number of foreign stations are available, although it is likely that few if any of these will be of much interest to most people. Anyway, there are numerous stations available from all over the world and it can be interesting to explore some of these.

Equipment

Internet television does not require any special equipment, and practically any reasonably modern PC should be capable of handling this application quite well. Any application that involves video tends to work better using a fairly powerful PC that has a good quality video card. However, there is no need to use an upmarket PC, and practically any reasonably up-to-date PC will do. On the sound side of things, any sound card should suffice. The basic picture resolution is often quite low, so a high resolution

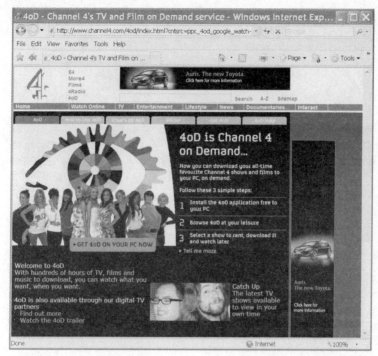

Fig.7.2 The 4oD home page

screen and large monitor are unlikely to be requirements. Although the basic picture resolution is often quite low, most players can artificially boost the number of pixels so that the programmes can be viewed with a relatively large picture size.

The software required to play Internet television stations varies somewhat from one station to another. In some cases the Windows Media Player will suffice, but in other cases it is necessary to use a different program. Although the player will often appear to be one that is unique to the station providing the television service, it is often just an ordinary player such as the Windows Media type, but with a different "skin" added. Where appropriate, the station's website should have a help page giving details of any software required, complete with links to sites where the software can be downloaded.

Before trying to use an Internet television service for the first time it is always a good idea to read through any help or FAQ pages to see if you

Fig.7.3 Instructions are provided for installing the software

can find any useful information. In addition to helping you locate, install, and set up any special software that is needed, there should also be details of any other important requirements. For example, the minimum connection speed needed to view the station properly should be included here.

Warning

As always with the Internet, do not take everything at face value. There are websites that make all sorts of claims about the free Internet television services that they offer, but they actually provide very little if anything. The main aim of these sites is to trick you into installing various types of adware or spyware onto your PC. When they appear in search engine results, many of these sites will actually be flagged as likely to cause damage to your PC (Figure 7.1).

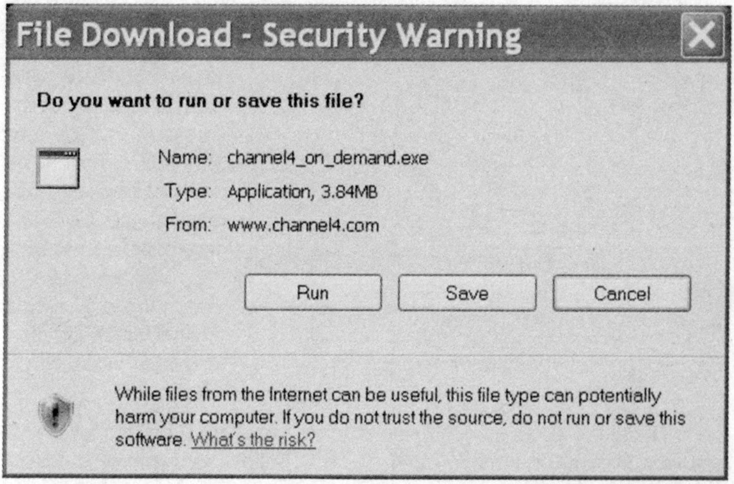

Fig.7.4 Operate the Run button when this pop-up window appears

Never be tempted to visit a site of this type, or to install any software that it offers. If in any doubt about the authenticity of any site that offers Internet television services, close the browser program immediately and do not install any software it offers. The safest approach is to only use the services of the main broadcasting organisations, or smaller ones that do not require any special software to be installed on your PC.

4oD

Most of the UK Internet television services are in the process of being rolled-out at the time of writing this. The one used as an example here is 4oD (Channel 4 on demand), which will no doubt develop over the coming years, but is largely complete as it stands. The home page for this service (Figure 7.2) can be found at the following web address:

http://www.channel4.com/4od/index.html

The 4oD service is fairly typical of one from a commercial broadcaster in that it actually provides what are essentially three different services. The premium content is offered in the form of downloads that can be purchased, or downloads that can be hired. Renting a download is usually about half the price of buying it, but the file is only playable for 48 hours after you start playing it for the first time. There are no time restrictions

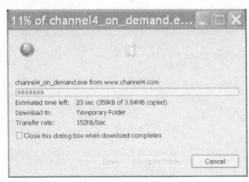

Fig.7.5 The download is under way

on playing a downloaded file that is purchased outright. The third aspect of the service, and the one that will probably be of most interest to the majority of users, is a free download service that can be used to catch up on certain programs transmitted in the previous seven days.

As is usually the case, it is necessary to download and install some software before the service can be used. Following the download link produces a page where download instructions and a further link are provided (Figure 7.3). A small window like the one in Figure 7.4 will appear when you try to start downloading the software. This gives the option of running the software or downloading it to the hard disc drive. If the second option is selected, the software must be run once it has been downloaded. Simply operating the Run button and running the software automatically is the easier option.

Fig.7.6 Operate the Run button when this security warning appears

The small window will then show how the download is progressing (Figure 7.5), and this is

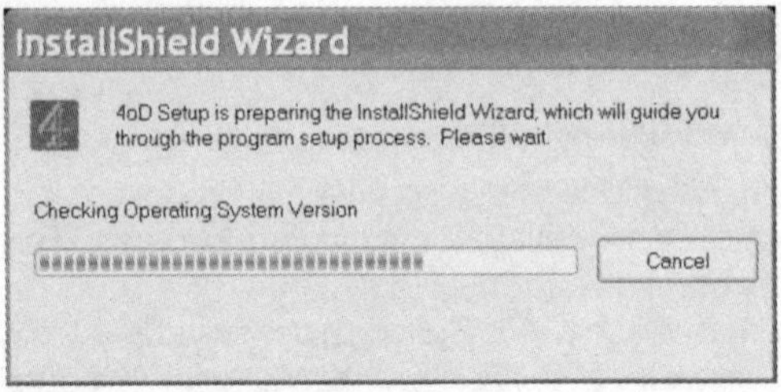

Fig.7.7 Installation has begun

Fig.7.8 The Setup program is installed and ready to proceed

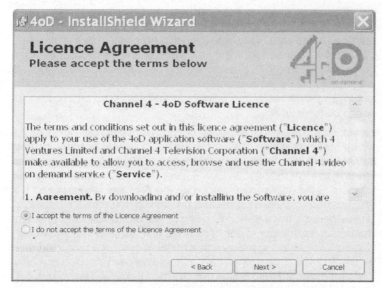

Fig.7.9 It is only possible to proceed if you accept this agreement

Fig.7.10 It is probably best to use the default settings at this screen

followed by a security warning (Figure 7.6) once the download process has been completed. Assuming everything appears to be in order here, operate the Run button. The first stage of the installation will then commence (Figure 7.7), and after a short delay the screen of Figure 7.8 will confirm that the installation was completed successfully and that the Setup program is ready to proceed. A small setting up procedure then has to be completed.

Operating the Next button moves things on to the screen of Figure 7.9 where it is necessary to agree to the inevitable licensing conditions. The software and 4oD service can not be used unless you agree to these terms of use. At the Next window (Figure 7.10) you can elect to have a shortcut to the 4oD service placed on the Windows desktop, and it is also possible to choose the destination folder for the software. However, unless there is a good reason for doing otherwise it is advisable to accept the default installation folder. There will then be a further short delay (Figure 7.11) while the main installation takes place, and the window of Figure 7.12 will appear when the software has been installed correctly. Then left-click the Finish button to close the window and launch the 4oD software.

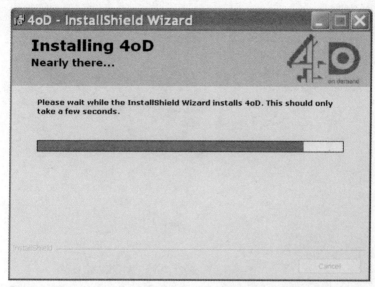

Fig.7.11 There is a delay while the main installation takes place

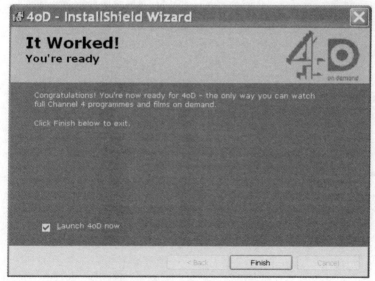

Fig.7.12 The software has been installed correctly

Fig.7.13   The initial screen of the 4oD software

Fig.7.14   The Catch Up section of the 4oD service

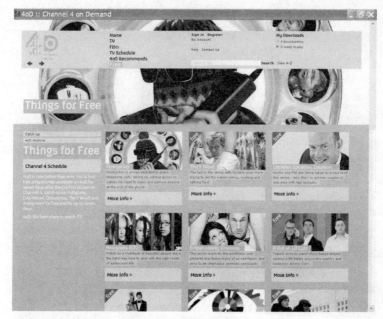

Fig.7.15 The Free section of the 4oD service

Catch up

Once the program is launched it looks something like Figure 7.13, but some of the content is regularly updated, so the appearance varies somewhat from day to day. There are "Catch Up" and "Free" links near the bottom left-hand corner of the window, which produce more information on these two aspects of the 4oD service (Figure 7.14 and 7.15 respectively).

For this example I selected the programme called "Location, Location", and obtained the information screen of Figure 7.16. The previous episode is available for free, and the episode prior to this (the first in the series) is available for rent. Presumably, as the series progresses the previous episode will always be available as a free download, and a growing number of earlier episodes will become available for rent. Anyway, in this case I was only interested in the previous episode, which was offered in streamed form and as a download.

Fig.7.16 The information page for Location, Location

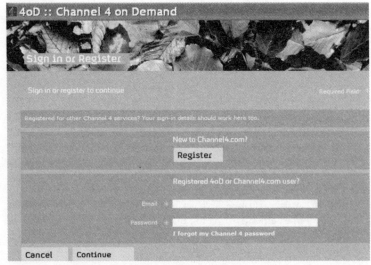

Fig.7.17 Sign on as normal if you already have a Channel 4 account

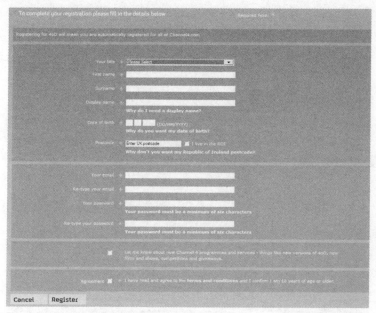

Fig.7.18 It will be necessary to register if you do not already have an account with Channel 4

I opted for the streamed version, but on operating the appropriate link the screen of Figure 7.17 was obtained. It would be an exaggeration to say that it is necessary to register before making use of any download service, but very little seems to be available without going through at least a simple registration procedure. It is just a matter of signing in as normal if you are already registered with one of Channel 4's online services, but it is otherwise necessary to complete a simple registration form (Figure 7.18).

Eventually the preliminaries were completed and the program was played (Figure 7.19). The picture will be quite small when using most monitors, especially where high resolutions are involved. However, there is usually the option of using a larger display area, and there is often a facility for using the full screen area or something close to the full screen. Obviously it is only possible to have true full screen operation when the aspect ratio of the picture matches that of the monitor's screen.

In this case there are two options, one of which gives a slightly increased viewing area and one which runs the player in full screen mode (Figure

Fig.7.19 The streamed version of the program being played. Various screen sizes are available

7.20). Note that most Internet television services operate at quite modest picture resolutions, and that the picture quality in full-screen mode might not be particularly good. However, it is often adequate provided the screen is not viewed at very short distances. The sound quality of Internet television stations is variable, but is generally quite good. In the case of the 4oD service the sound quality is very good and in stereo.

Fig.7.20 The program in full screen-mode

TV download

Streaming a television programme is the easier option, in that it avoids waiting while the file downloads. The download option is better in that the downloaded file can be viewed by other members of the family at a later time. Also, the downloaded version often seems to provide a higher picture quality than the streamed version. With any video download though, the download time can be quite long even when using a fast broadband connection. Practical experience suggests that the download time is typically about equal to the duration of the programme, and in some cases it can be significantly longer.

Selecting the 4oD download option produces the information screen of Figure 7.21. While some free video downloads have "no strings attached", in most cases there will be major limitations on the way in which the file can be used. The free 4oD downloads are effectively rented programmes for which no rental fee is paid. You can use the video file for two days

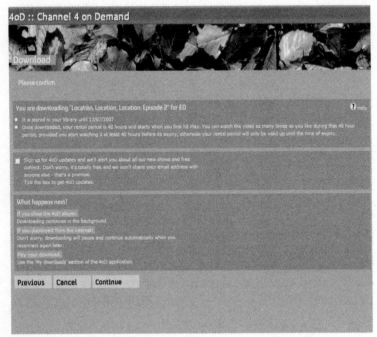

Fig.7.21 Selecting the download option produces this screen

from the moment you first start to play it, but there is a further restriction that only allows it to be used for up to five days after it was downloaded. This is reasonable, given that the idea of this service is to permit viewers to catch up on programmes that they have missed. It is not provided as a means of building up a library of television programmes.

Operating the Continue button on the information screen moves things on to the window of Figure 7.22, where the download will start automatically and the completed file will eventually be added to the list of downloaded files (Figure 7.23). In the meantime the usual bargraph display shows how far the download has progressed. Note that it is not necessary to keep this window open in order to carry out the download. The download process will continue normally if it is minimised, and will even continue in the background if it is closed. The process will obviously come to a halt if the computer is disconnected from the Internet, but it will automatically recommence when the Internet connection is restored.

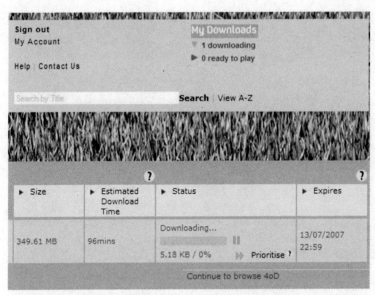

Fig.7.22 The download starts automatically at this screen

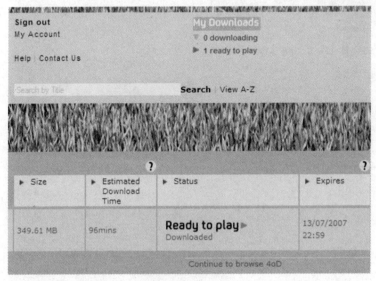

Fig.7.23 The file is now ready to play

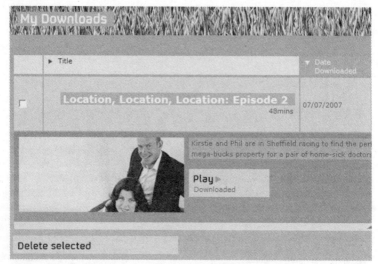

Fig.7.24 Operate the Play button to start the programme

Fig.7.25 The file is playing correctly

Fig.7.26 The home page of the ITV Internet television service

Playing

In order to play a file it is merely necessary to left-click the "Ready to play" section of its entry in the playlist, and then operate the Play button in the expanded version of its entry (Figure 7.24). The player program will then be launched and the file will be played. Figure 7.25 shows the downloaded file being played using the second of the three picture sizes, and it seems to provide noticeably better picture quality than the streamed version.

The downloaded 4oD files can only be played via the My Downloads section of the 4oD software. It is easy to return to this section of the program, since it has a link on the opening screen. Once a file is no longer needed it can be deleted by ticking the checkbox in the leftmost column of its entry in the playlist and operating the "Delete selection" button.

As pointed out previously, it is not only Channel 4 that has an Internet presence, and all the large UK television companies now have some

Fig.7.27 Programmes can be played in full-screen mode

Fig.7.28 A programme in the Best of ITV section being played

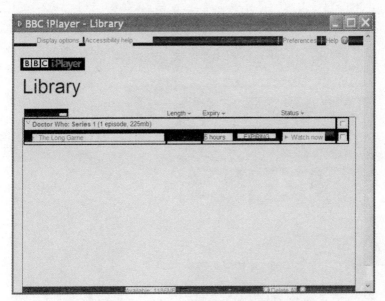

Fig.7.29 The BBC iPlayer library with one programme loaded

form of Internet television service. The ITV service (http://www.itv.com/ Watchnow/default.html) offers the four ITV stations in streamed form (Fig.7.26), but as always with this type of thing, some programs are not available via the Internet for contractual reasons. There is the option of watching programmes in full-screen mode (Figure 7.27), and the quality is surprisingly good. There is a Best of ITV service (Figure 7.28) that enables some programmes from the past to be viewed again, and this should be of great interest to those of us who have long memories.

The BBC's "iPlayer" Internet television service could, in due course, be one of the best available. It enables a range of programmes from the past seven days to be downloaded to a library program (Figure 7.29) where they can be viewed as and when required, within certain limitations. Programmes are stored in the library for up to 30 days, and they are automatically deleted if they have not already been removed when the expiry date is reached. Once you start watching a programme, its file remains usable for up to seven days, with the 30 day limit applying if that is reached first.

The download software utilizes peer-to-peer technology, so your PC will upload as well as download the programmes you choose. Although the

Fig.7.30 The section of WMP 11 that deals with movies

system is still at the beta test stage at the time of writing this, it seems to be well advanced and is working quite well. It seems likely that the final version of the BBC's iPlayer will be very popular.

WMP 11

Windows Media Player 11 has a radio tuner facility that can be used to locate and play Internet radio stations, but there does not seem to be an equivalent function for Internet television. There is a section of the Media Guide that deals with movies (Figure 7.30), and this provides links to many free online videos and video clips, including such things as music types (Figure 7.31) and trailers for the latest movies.

Fig.7.31 A music video playing in WMP 11

Internet TV guides

Finding UK Internet television stations is reasonably easy, and it is basically just a matter of seeking out the web sites of the main UK broadcasting organisations. Any search engine should soon enable you to track them down. As pointed out previously, it is fairly easy to find Internet television stations around the world using a search engine. It can also be worth searching for Internet television guides that list a large number of stations operating in various languages.

Figure 7.32 shows a page from www.beelinetv.com, which lists stations that operate in English and several other languages. Operating one of the links takes you to the website of the relevant station, and from there you can play their streamed content. Many of the links lead to sites that contain a number of video clips rather than material that is streamed "live". The example shown in Figure 7.33 is a short video that is one of many that are available on the NASA website.

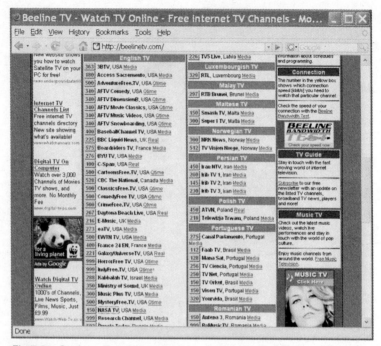

Fig.7.32 Stations from around the world listed on beelinetv.com

One of the most popular Internet television guides can be found at www.wwitv.com (Figure 7.34), and this one is particularly useful if you are mainly interested in "live" streamed television. A number of countries are listed in the left-hand column, and selecting one of these results in the available stations for that country being listed in the main panel. A surprisingly large number of "live" streams are available, including the BBC's News 24 service (Figure 7.35). In general, Internet television is available to every country in the world, so you can view stations that originate on the other side of the world. I had no difficulty in accessing stations based in Australia for example, including a sports station (Figure 7.36). However, in some cases the stations are restricted to people living in a certain country or country. It will not be possible to view the content if you do not live in the area served by a station of this type.

When using Internet television guides it is only realistic to expect a few "dead" links. These are found with practically any type of Internet guide. It is not exactly unusual for web sites to close or move, and with Internet

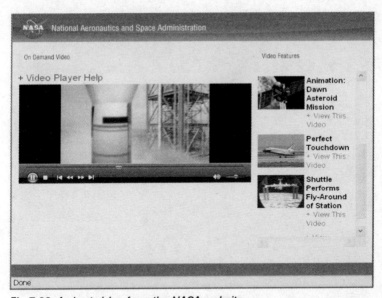

Fig.7.33 A short video from the NASA website

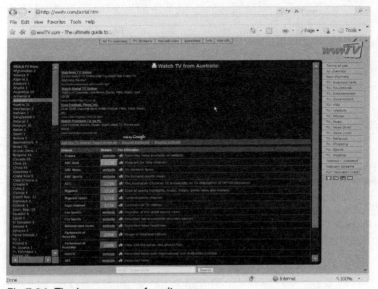

Fig.7.34 The home page of wwitv.com

Fig.7.35 The BBC's online version of the News 24 channel

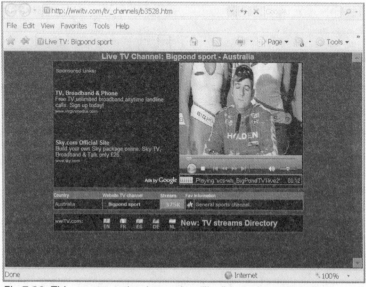

Fig.7.36 This sports station is coming "live" from Australia

Fig.7.37 A video being played on the YouTube website

television stations you have to bear in mind that they will not necessarily operate for 24 hours per day. Although you might be trying to view a station in the middle of the afternoon, it could be the middle of the night in the station's country of origin. Of course, it also works the other way round, which could be useful for insomniacs. In the middle of the night it will be peak viewing time for numerous stations in other parts of the world.

Home video

Uploading and viewing various types of home produced video is an aspect of the Internet that has rapidly grown in popularity in recent years. Probably most users of these sites are only interested in viewing the

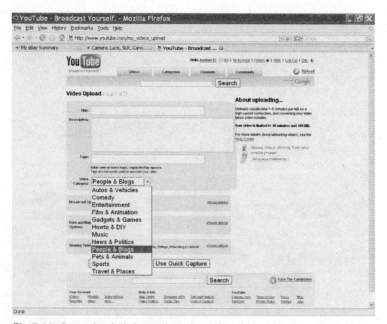

Fig.7.38 Some basic information about the video must be supplied before it is uploaded

videos on offer, and there are a huge number to choose from. With anything like this there is inevitably a huge variation in the technical and artistic quality of the videos. Some are of a high calibre in both respects, but the majority are probably not very good in terms of technical quality or their content. You therefore have to be selective when choosing which ones to view, and there is usually a helpful rating system based on feedback from other users. Alternatively, be prepared to wade through a large number of videos in order to find the really good ones.

By far the biggest and most popular of the home video sites is YouTube (www.youtube.com), which is now part of the Google search engine company. In order to help you find something of interest the videos are grouped under about a dozen categories and there is also a search engine. Videos are watched via the built-in viewer (Figure 7.37), and for most of the content there is no need to register with the site in order to view it.

However, it is necessary to register in order to upload your own videos. This is fairly straightforward, and it is a matter of first entering a title, a

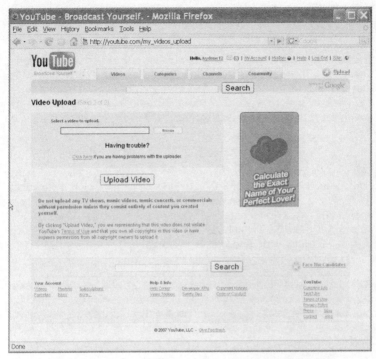

Fig.7.39 Enter the path and filename of the video or use the file browser

description, some tags (keywords for use by the search engine), and choosing the most appropriate category from a drop-down menu (Figure 7.38). Next the "Upload a video" button is operated, and this produces the new page of Figure 7.39 where the name and path for the file is entered in the textbox. Alternatively, the Browse button is operated and then the pop-up file browser is used to locate and open the correct video file.

The recommended file format is Mpeg4 with Mpeg3 audio, but some other formats can be accommodated. The video must last no more than 10 minutes or have a file size of more than one hundred megabytes. Operating the Upload Video button starts the upload process, which typically takes about one minute per megabyte. However, once uploaded it is necessary for the video to be converted into the YouTube format, and at times of high demand it can be a few hours before this processing is completed and the video can be accessed via the YouTube site.

Points to remember

The term "Internet television" covers what are really three different types of service. These are "live" streamed feeds, on-demand programmes that can be downloaded and viewed later, and on-demand programmes that are streamed to your PC. A streamed feed is one that you view as the data is received, rather than storing the data on your PC and viewing it later.

Do not expect DVD quality from an Internet television station. The bit rate used varies widely from one station to another, which means that the technical quality also varies considerably. The higher bit rates enable acceptable results to be obtained together with full screen viewing. The sound quality also varies substantially from one station to another, but it is generally quite good and is often in stereo.

Although UK television stations are starting to provide Internet television services, most of these services are still in their infancy. Some offer premium content that can be purchased or hired, but there is usually a free catch-up service that enables some programmes from the last few days to be viewed.

A large number of stations from all over the world can be viewed via the Internet. Most of these are free, or have some services that can be used free of charge. Some of these stations can only be used by people in certain countries, but most are available to users all over the world.

Windows Media Player has no television equivalent of the Radio Tuner facility. However, the relevant section of the Media Guide can help you to locate a useful range of online videos. There are numerous web sites that provide Internet television guides, and with the aid of these it should not be difficult to locate a number of interesting stations.

In order to view some stations it is necessary to download and install a special player program, or other software. Only install software if you are completely sure that it is being provided by a trustworthy source. Avoid sites that offer massive amounts of premium content at no charge. If it seems too good to be true, it almost certainly is.

VOiP

Talk is cheap

Until not so long ago there was only one way of making phone calls to overseas destinations, and that was via the ordinary telephone system. This tended to be expensive, so telephone calls to family and friends overseas tended to be short and infrequent. These days there are two alternatives to the conventional method of making calls to people abroad, and one of these is to use an instant messaging service. This topic is covered in a separate chapter and will not be considered further here, but it is certainly something to consider if you need to make frequent contacts with people overseas. Refer to chapter 6 for full details about instant messaging.

The second method of making international telephone calls also involves the use of a PC, and also requires a special service such as Skype. Some of the topics covered in this book are also possible using a dial-up Internet connection, but Internet telephone services usually require nothing less than at least a basic broadband connection. Some will actually work using a good quality dial-up connection, but the audio quality is likely to be quite poor, and the normal telephone line will be blocked while calls are being made via the Internet. Internet telephone services have rapidly gained popularity due to the low cost of the calls, which in some circumstances can be free. The cost is usually far lower than when using a conventional telephone system to make overseas calls or calls to mobile telephones.

Services such as Skype are generically known as voice over Internet protocol services, or just VoIP for short. Apart from the cost, there are other potential advantages to using voice over Internet system. One of these is that the audio quality can be much higher than that obtained using an ordinary telephone system. An ordinarily telephone line used in its normal audio mode provides a very limited bandwidth, which is reflected in a lack of high frequencies and a rather "dull" sound quality. A real-world telephone system also tends to provide a fair amount of distortion and general background noise. By contrast, a system implemented via a broadband link can provide true hi-fi quality. Unfortunately, not all voice over Internet systems actually provide top quality audio, and in some cases they seem to fall short of normal landline quality.

Security

There tends to be concerns about security with anything that involves communication via the Internet. In some cases there are good reasons for these worries, and unless encryption is used, Email is not ideal for anything that involves the exchange of sensitive information. There is relatively little to be concerned about with services such as Skype, where the signals are heavily encrypted as standard. While it would probably be foolhardy to claim that any communication system is totally secure, a voice over Internet telephone system is probably as close as you are going to get to a fully secure system. Such systems are probably at least as secure as the ordinary telephone system.

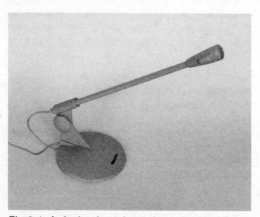

Real world voice over Internet systems often provide additional facilities, and it is as well to remember that some of these may pose a greater security threat than the telephone facility. In particular, any file transfer facility poses the normal threats associated with file transfers. With anything like this it is difficult to be sure that any files that you download are free from viruses, Trojans, or other malicious software. The usual security measures should be taken when using any method of downloading or swapping files.

Fig.8.1 A desk microphone for use with a PC

Equipment

In order to use a voice over Internet system it will probably a necessary to buy some additional equipment, but little is required, and it should cost very little. In fact some computers are supplied with everything that you will need, but in most cases it will be necessary to buy a microphone. Loudspeakers are also required, but are supplied with most desktop PCs, or are built into the laptop computers. Actually, it is probably best not to use the loudspeakers at all, but to instead to purchase a headset that includes a microphone and headphones. Alternatively, there are telephone handsets that are specifically designed for use with a PC and a voice over Internet system.

Any large computer store should have at least one or two microphones that are intended for use with a PC. A typical example is shown in Figure 8.1, and this is a desk microphone. There are also microphone headsets, most of which also include a pair of headphones. The example shown in Figure 8.2 has a single headphone. Desk microphones and headsets are both suitable for PC telephone applications, but there is a potential problem when using either type.

This is simply that there are several types of microphone in common use, and there are also major differences from one PC microphone input to another. You might be in luck and find that the particular microphone you obtain produces perfect results with your PC. On the other hand, if you are out of luck, the maximum audio level from the microphone will be very low, or it will not work at all with your particular PC.

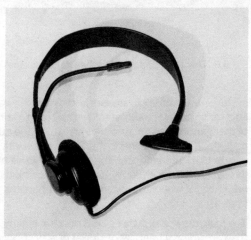

The safe option is to buy a headset that includes a microphone, and which connects to the PC via a USB port rather than using the built-in sound

Fig.8.2 This headset has one earphone and a microphone

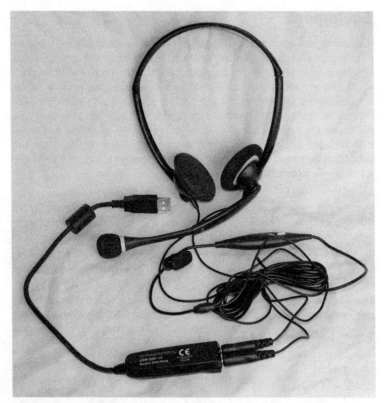

Fig.8.3 This USB headset has headphones and a microphone

system. A typical USB headset is shown in Figure 8.3. These are mainly sold for voice over Internet and voice recognition applications, and any of them should therefore work very well in the current context. The big advantage of a USB headset is that it has a simple sound system built into its USB interface, and the microphone will be perfectly matched to this system. Consequently, it avoids the compatibility problems that can easily occur when connecting a microphone to the PC's built-in sound system.

The main drawback is that a USB headset is significantly more expensive than an ordinary headset of similar quality. However, the cost of a good budget USB headset is not particularly high. Another potential problem is that this type of headset can only be used if there is a spare USB port

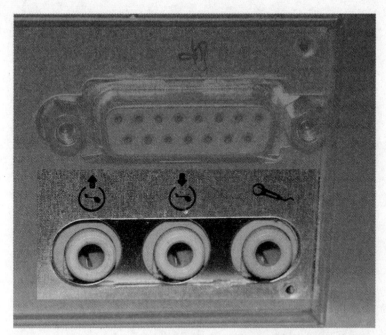

Fig.8.4 A PC usually has at least three audio connectors at the rear

available on your PC, but modern PCs usually have plenty of USB ports fitted as standard. Anyway, where the use of an ordinary microphone proves to be problematic, a USB headset should provide a way around the problem. With the current low cost of USB headsets it is probably better to make this option the first choice rather than the second, and to not bother with a conventional headset. A PC telephone handset will always be of the USB variety, and is therefore installed in the same way as a USB headset.

Making connections

All PCs have a built-in sound system these days, so there will almost certainly be a microphone socket on your PC. There should also be a headphone socket, or another audio output that will work well with most headphones. Sometimes there are audio connectors at the front of a PC, but they are usually concealed behind a panel. If your PC has microphone and headphone sockets at the front, then these will be the easier ones to use than those at the rear.

If there are no audio connectors on the front panel of the case there should be a full set of audio connectors at the rear, and one of these should be a microphone input. Figure 8.4 shows a typical set of audio connectors. There will usually be at least three audio ports, and there can be half a dozen or more if the PC supports some form of surround sound system. The audio ports of any reasonably modern PC are colour coded, which makes it easy to identify the microphone input. The plastic part of the connector will be pink.

Most PCs have a line level output that is primarily designed for use with external loudspeakers that have built-in amplifiers. However, in most cases they are also designed to work reasonably well with most headphones, and will work properly with most PC headsets. The plastic part of the line output socket is lime green. There might be an output that is designed for use with small passive loudspeakers. In other words, the output from this socket is at a relatively high level so that it can drive loudspeakers that do not have built-in amplifiers. Most of these outputs provide only quite low output powers, and will work well enough with many headphones. However, they are less than ideal, and it is necessary to take due care to avoid excessive volume levels. Where fitted, the plastic part of the loudspeaker socket is colour coded brown.

A USB headset can be used with any spare USB port. It does not matter which one is used, but it makes sense to use one at the front of the PC where this facility is available. It is advisable to always use the same port for any USB device. Any inconsistency in this respect can get the operating system confused, with the device being treated as a new device when it is connected to a different USB port. This can result in it being installed into the operating system for a second time, which might cause problems.

A few service providers include the necessary additional hardware as part of their package. This is often in the form of a USB telephone handset. Accordingly, it makes sense to choose your service provider before buying a microphone, headset, or handset. There is otherwise a risk of buying equipment that will ultimately prove to be unnecessary.

Which service

There are several voice over Internet services available to UK users, and asking which is the best one is a very much a "how long is a piece of

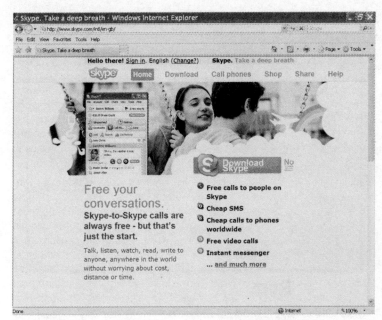

Fig.8.5 The Skype software is available as a free download

string" style question.   Much like mobile telephone service, there are "pay as you go" and subscription services. The "pay as you go" services largely or totally avoid initial set-up charges, and you do not end up paying for unused talk-time, but they are likely to be expensive if used extensively. Subscription services are generally cheaper for people who will use them a great deal, but are unlikely to be economic for occasional users.

Many services offer free calls to people using the same service, so there could be a big advantage in a group of family and friends. Note that you are not usually restricted to communicating with people who have a suitably equipped PC, a broadband Internet connection, and a voice over Internet service. Most systems enable calls to be made to be made to people who only have a conventional or mobile telephone. However, where appropriate you need to make sure that the service you choose supports this method and that the cost is low enough to make its use worthwhile.

If you intend to use voice over Internet as your only type of telephone service, which few people actually do at present, it is essential to choose

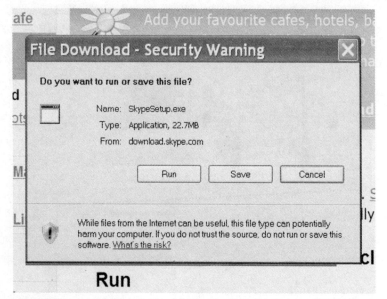

Fig.8.6 Opt to run the program when the security warning appears

one that has the necessary facilities. In particular, you will need one that enables telephone calls to be made and received even when your PC is switched off. This is achieved via an adaptor that takes over when the PC is not switched on. A suitable adaptor is included as part of the package with some subscription services. It will be much more expensive than a handset or headset if you have to buy it separately. You also need to ensure that the service is capable of handling calls to the emergency services.

Before signing up to any voice over Internet service it is clearly necessary to do some research, and to carefully select a service that closely matches your requirements. It is also important to consider how you will use the service, and whether it will actually be used enough to save a worthwhile amount of money. If you do decide to go ahead, there are plenty of Internet sites that will help you compare the various services, making it reasonably easy find one that offers the right features at a competitive price.

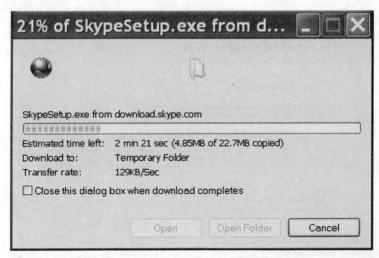

Fig.8.7 A bargraph shows how the download is progressing

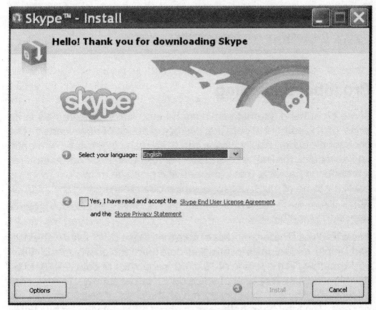

Fig.8.8 The Setup program requires little input from the user

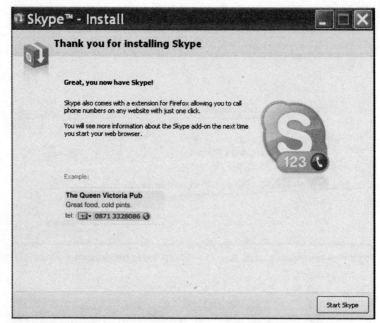

Fig.8.9 The software has been installed correctly

Broadband capping

Some broadband Internet packages have no limits, or extremely large limits, on the amount of data that can be uploaded or downloaded. The cheaper products usually have a cap of so many gigabytes per month, and exceeding the limit results in surcharges being incurred. In general, a broadband package that is capped at a gigabyte or two per month is not likely to be of much use for anything other than surfing the Internet. Applications such as downloading music or audio are likely to rapidly use up the monthly limit.

Audio involves smaller amounts of data than those associated with video, and simple voice signals involve less data than high quality music. Even so, something in the region of 70 to 80 megabytes of data is likely to be downloaded for every hour of voice over Internet activity. This equates to over a gigabyte of data per month on the basis of one 30 minute call per day. The total per month rises to about 4.5 gigabytes for two hours

Fig.8.10 Your name, a user name, and a password must be supplied

per day. Extensive use of voice over Internet services requires either an uncapped broadband service or one that has a relatively high limit.

Getting started

In order to make calls over the Internet via your PC it is necessary to have suitable software installed. This might be provided on a disc by the service provider, or it might be necessary to download it via the Internet. Skype will be used for this example, and it will be assumed that the software is to be downloaded from the Skype Internet site at www.skype.com (Figure 8.5). Operating the Download button produces a page that has brief download and installation instructions, and the usual security warning will appear on the screen (Figure 8.6). Opt to run the program, which will then start to download (Figure 8.7).

The Setup program will be launched (Figure 8.8) as soon as the downloading has been completed, but little input from the user is required.

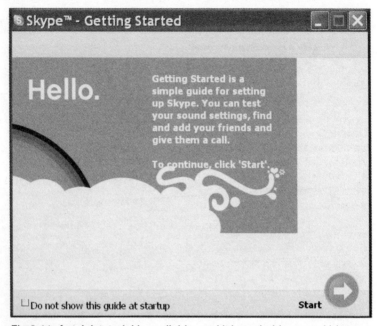

Fig.8.11 A quick tutorial is available, and it is probably a good idea to view it

It is just a matter of selecting the correct installation language from the drop-down menu, and accepting the licence conditions. After a short delay while the program is installed and set up correctly, the window of Figure 8.9 will appear to confirm that the software has been installed correctly. The program can then be run for the first time.

There is still some work to do before the program is ready for use, and the first task is to set up an account. As usual with this type of thing, you must provide your name, a user name, and a password that is entered twice (Figure 8.10). It is also necessary to agree to the relevant set of licence conditions. You then have the option of going through a series of Getting Started help pages, the first of which is shown in Figure 8.11. Those who are new to Skype would be well advised to at least have a quick look at the help system, which does not take very long.

A window like the one shown in Figure 8.12 is obtained once the main program is launched. The two large buttons at the bottom of the window are used for starting a call (left) and ending a call (right). In the main panel the Contacts tab will probably be selected by default. Like an instant messaging system, the list of contacts is crucial, since you need to add the relevant details of people here before you can call them.

Operating the Add a Contact button produces the pop-up window of Figure 8.13, where you enter their Email address, Skype name, or full name in the textbox. Next the Find button is operated, and this usually produces one or more matches for your search term (Figure 8.14). Assuming one of the results is the correct one, it is then just a matter of selecting it and operating the Add Skype Contact button.

Note that this contact system operates in a similar way to the instant messaging variety. You send a message asking whether the contact

Fig.8.12 The main Skype program window

wishes to swap details and be included in your contact list. They do, of course, have the option of declining, but they will appear in your contact list if they accept the offer. You will receive a message whenever someone tries to add your name to their contact list, and you can decline the offer should you not like the idea of being added to their list. It is best not to accept an offer unless you are sure that you know the person trying to

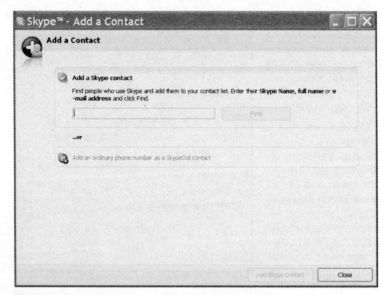

Fig.8.13 This windowis used to add a Skype contact

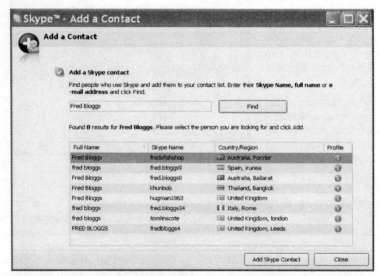

Fig.8.14 The search has produced a number of possible matches

Fig.8.15 The main program window when using the SkypeOut facility. The keypad is used to enter the telephone number, complete with area code

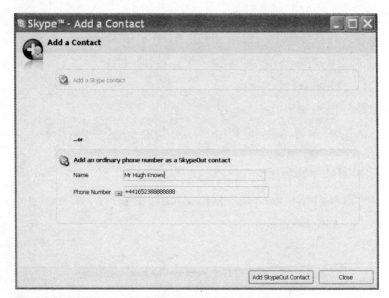

Fig.8.16 This window is used to add a SkypeOut contact

add your details to their contact list. Fortunately, it is possible to edit your contacts list, and it is possible to block a contact that has been accepted previously.

SkypeOut

You are not restricted to contacting other Skype users, and one of the main uses of voice over Internet telephone systems is to enable you to talk to anyone with a telephone, even if they do not have a computer. With the Skype system you can contact non-Skype users using SkypeOut. This is accessed by operating the Call Phones tab, which changes the main panel to look like Figure 8.15. The telephone number you wish to call, complete with area code, is entered into the textbox. It can be added to your SkypeOut contact list by operating the Add SkypeOut Contact button and adding the contact's name in the pop-up window that appears (Figure 8.16).

Of course, the SkypeOut service, in common with similar services, is not free. In order to use it you must first go to the Skype website and purchase some credits. It obviously makes sense to, as far as possible, have your contacts join the same voice over Internet telephone service that you use, so that they can be contacted free via that system. This will probably not be possible in all cases, since some of your contacts will not be interested in joining the particular service you use, and some might not even own a computer. Also, from time to time you will probably wish to contact people via their mobile phones even if they are on the right voice over Internet telephone service. In order to buy Skype credits it is a matter of going to the Account menu, selecting Buy Skype Credit, and then following the wizard-style onscreen instructions.

Making a call

In order to make a call, once the number has been entered, you operate the large green button near the bottom of the window. Things are then very much like making an ordinary telephone call, with the connection being made, the telephone at the other end of the system ringing, and (with luck) the person at the other end answering. Once you have finished the conversation it is just a matter of operating the large red button near the bottom of the window so that the call is terminated. Skype has extra facilities for such things as sending photographs and other files, but these extra facilities will obviously not be available when making calls to an ordinary telephone.

Receiving a call is equally straightforward, and the Skype icon in the right-hand section of the taskbar will flash when someone is calling you. There will also be a "ringing" sound of some kind from the computer's audio system, so it is important that the audio system is left running under standby conditions. Launch the Skype software in the normal way, and you will then be able to see who is calling. You then have the option of receiving the call or leaving it unanswered.

Points to remember

Using a voice over Internet telephone service it is possible to send and receive telephone calls to mobile and fixed telephones around the world. It is also possible to send and receive text messages. The software required is usually supplied free of charge by the service provider.

Making voice over Internet telephone calls will probably require a small amount of additional hardware, although some PCs are now supplied with the necessary equipment. A headset that includes a microphone together with the usual headphones is the minimum requirement, but there are also USB telephone handsets that specifically designed for this application.

Most voice over Internet telephone systems do not charge for calls to other users of that particular service. There is a charge for making calls outside the system, but the costs are usually very competitive when calling mobile telephones and telephones connected to a landline.

Most of these systems operate in a fashion that is very similar to an instant messaging system. Inevitably, the distinction between the two types of service have become blurred, with instant messaging services providing a facility to talk to other users of the system, or even offering telephone calls over the Internet. The Internet telephone services often provide what is effectively a messaging service that can be used to contact other users of the system.

If your computer is equipped with a webcam, it will probably be possible to use your computer as a videophone. Some instant messaging services also have a facility that enable users to communicate using a video/audio link.

Photo albums

Photo albums

In the early days of the Internet there were numerous companies offering free web space, but this type of business went into steep decline when the dotcom bubble burst. One exception to this trend is the number of companies offering free web space for storing digital photographs. The massive upsurge in demand for digital cameras has been matched by an ever increasing number of companies offering online photo album facilities. Any Internet search engine should be able to produce a large list of sites that provide this service.

It is easy to see why this type of facility has become so popular. An online photo album is an excellent means of sharing photographs with your family and friends. They are also a really good way for those having a common interest to share photographs. Online photo albums can be used for enthusiasts to share wildlife pictures, photographs of steam railways, and so on. Many clubs have an online album, or a web site that includes a similar facility.

Free online photo albums are sometimes provided by photo processing companies. This may seem to be exceptionally generous of them, but the idea is that users of the album can order prints that are paid for online and delivered by post. The provider of the service is hoping to make a profit on the service by way of increased print sales. However, there is usually no obligation to buy a certain number of prints in a given period. Also, it is normally possible to download images, making the service suitable for file swapping.

Of course, before signing up to any service it is important to read the "small print" to make sure that there are no hidden surprises, and that it does actually meet your requirements. Obviously there will be a limit on the amount of storage space provided, but there could also be a limit on the size of each file. This could make it impossible to transfer high resolution images via the album. Note that the majority of free web space is supported via advertising, so your online photo album is likely to have a few banner or pop-up advertisements. Companies operating in this

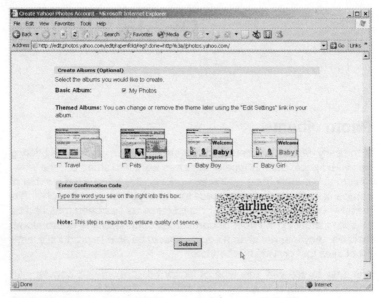

Fig.9.1 Templates for various types of album are available

field are sometimes short-lived, so it is probably best to use a well-established service.

Making an album

Yahoo! has a photo album facility that offers a very reasonable limit of 90 photographs and 30 megabytes. In order to make use of the Yahoo! photo album facility it is necessary to register with Yahoo! if you are not already a Yahoo! or Geocities member. The online album facility can be accessed via the Photos link in the Organise section of the www.yahoo.com homepage. During the initial stages of setting up the album you may be offered the choice of producing special types of album (Figure 9.1), but here we will produce the standard type.

You will probably have to type the "hidden" word into the textbox in order to continue with the process. This is rapidly becoming a standard feature when obtaining any form of free web space. It is designed to stop automated systems from setting up numerous false accounts for use by those looking for free storage space for their porno sites, pirated software,

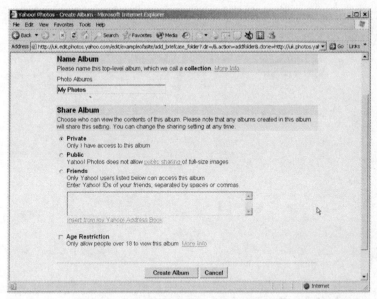

Fig.9.2 From this page the album is named and access is controlled

etc. You should be able to decipher the word quite easily, but it is very difficult for automated systems to do so.

The first task when you start creating the album is to name the album and choose the amount of access there will be to the site (Figure 9.2). In the case of the Yahoo! album facility you can have the site for your own use only, for use by the listed Yahoo! members, or there can be general access. With general access the photographs might not be available at full resolution. This is presumably done to deter illegitimate use of the photo album facility. There is also a facility to block those under 18 years of age from viewing the album.

At the next page your new album is displayed, but obviously it is empty at this stage (Figure 9.3). In order to start adding photographs it is merely necessary to left-click the Start Adding Photographs link, which will bring up the page shown in Figure 9.4. Here the filenames of the photographs, complete with the full path, can be added into the textboxes. Alternatively, operate the Browse button and use the file browser to select each image file. The photographs should be in a standard web format, and Jpeg is probably the best option. Scroll down to the bottom of the page and

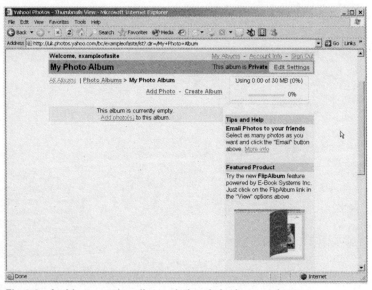

Fig.9.3 At this stage the album obviously lacks any pictures

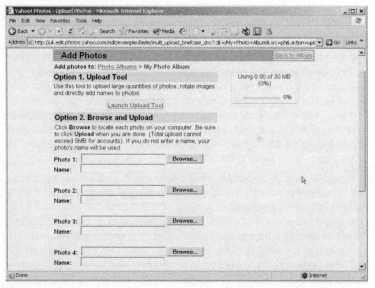

Fig.9.4 This page is used to select and upload the photographs

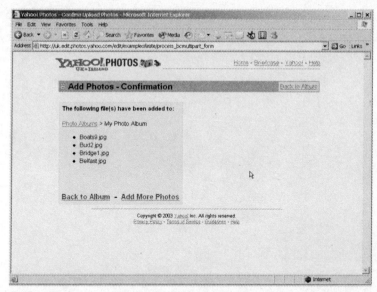

Fig.9.5 This screen lists the photographs that have been uploaded

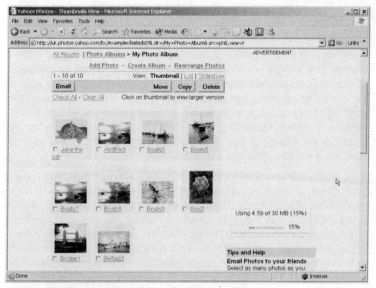

Fig.9.6 The album with ten photographs uploaded

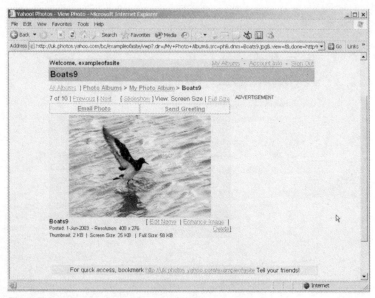

Fig.9.7 Larger versions of a picture can be viewed

operate the Upload button to go ahead and upload the images, or operate the Cancel button if you wish to abort the operation.

If all goes well a confirmation screen like the one shown in Figure 9.5 will appear. This lists the photographs that have been successfully uploaded. By operating the appropriate link it is possible add more photographs to the album or return to the album page. Figure 9.6 shows the album page with some more pictures added. In order to view one of the pictures larger it is merely necessary to left-click on its thumbnail view on the album page (Figure 9.7). With high resolution pictures this will not produce a full-size view of the image.

A low resolution thumbnail image is automatically generated when each photograph is uploaded, and so is a medium resolution version. It is the medium resolution image that is displayed when the thumbnail version is left-clicked. This has a much smaller image file that will download much more quickly than the full-size version. The image can be viewed at maximum resolution by left-clicking the Full Size link that is above and to the right of the medium resolution version. Note though, that a high resolution image will be too large to fit the screen even if a fairly high screen resolution is used (Figure 9.8). The entire image is still accessible,

Fig.9.8 Scrolling might be necessary to view all of a large image

but only with the aid of the scrollbars. Of course, there will only be a higher resolution version if the resolution of the original image was high enough to make this possible.

There are various facilities available from the album page and when an individual image is viewed. The Rename facility enables the name of the image to be changed, but it also permits a short description to be added (Figures 9.9 and 9.10). The Enhance Image facility produces a window that provides some basic image editing facilities (Figure 9.11). It is better to undertake this type of thing using image editing software prior to uploading images, but this method is worth a try if you do not have access to suitable software.

Image hosting

Sometimes it is necessary to have images stored online so that they can be used on a website of some kind. If you have your own website it is likely that there will be no problem in storing the images on the server for your site along with the other files needed for the web pages. It is also

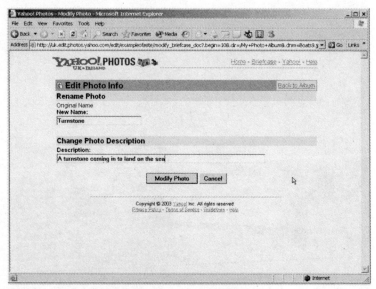

Fig.9.9 A short description can be added to a picture

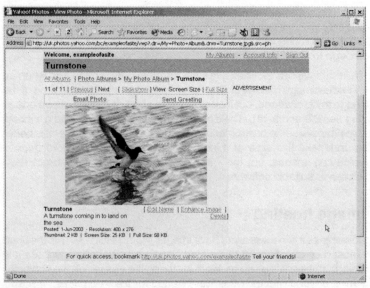

Fig.9.10 One of the pictures with a description added

Fig.9.11 Some basic image editing facilities are available

possible to upload your images directly to some blog sites, bulletin boards, etc. This is not always possible though, and some of these sites do not permit images or any other types of file to be uploaded. They only permit the use of HTML code and text.

This is not to say that it is never possible to use images, sound clips, and so on with these sites. Some sites might have specific rules that ban the use of anything other than text and some HTML formatting, but in most cases it is possible to use image files in a roundabout fashion. Images are used by uploading them to another site and then using a link to that site. By doing things this way you are only storing HTML code and text on the blog site, bulletin board site, auction site or whatever. The images or other linked files are stored elsewhere.

There are a number of options available when choosing a host for files that will be used on another website or websites. Many broadband packages come complete with a substantial amount of web space that in most cases can be used for storing your image files, sound clips, etc. It might be necessary to resort to a normal commercial host if a large amount of storage space is required, and these days the cost of a few megabytes of storage can be quite low.

Fig.9.12 It is necessary to register before uploading any images

Free hosting

Probably the most popular approach these days is to use the free web hosts that specialise in this type of storage. On the face of it, any site that enables you to produce an online picture gallery could be used in this application. In practice it might not be as simple as that, because photo-gallery sites do not always permit direct links to the images stored on their site. In order to view and access the images it might be necessary to go though the normal route, including signing in to your account, and so on. In the present application it is essential to use a host that permits direct links to the images, and there are plenty of free hosts that provide this type of service.

Photobucket (www.photobucket.com) is a popular image hosting site that allows images of up to 1024 by 768 pixels or a maximum file size of

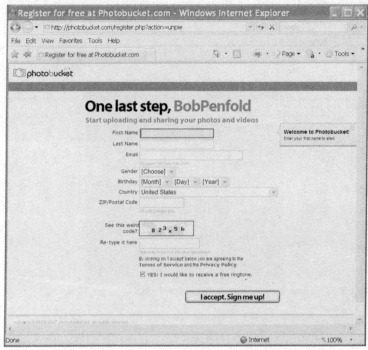

Fig.9.13 A valid Email address is needed when registering

one megabyte to be uploaded when the free service is used. Up to one gigabyte of storage space is available. Larger images can be uploaded if you pay for a premium account, which also raises the limit to five gigabytes of storage space, but for most practical purposes the free service is more than adequate.

The images used on websites are mostly quite small, so the one gigabyte limit is actually sufficient to store about ten thousand typical web images. Note that it is also possible to upload video files to the Photobucket website. This service operates in much the same way as the image version, but it is not something that will be considered further here.

As usual with any service of this type, it is necessary to complete a simple registration process before anything can be uploaded to the Photobucket site. The first step is to provide a username and password (Figure 9.12), and then some further information must be provided, including your name

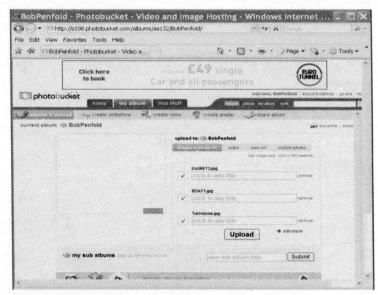

Fig.9.14 Some images can now be uploaded

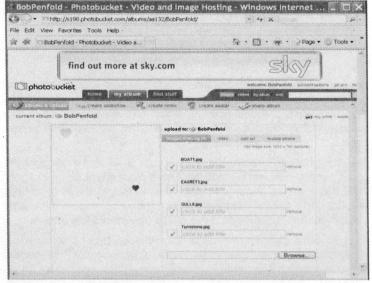

Fig.9.15 More than three images at a time can be uploaded if necessary

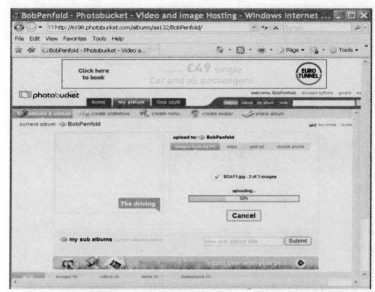

Fig.9.16 The usual bargraph shows how the upload is progressing

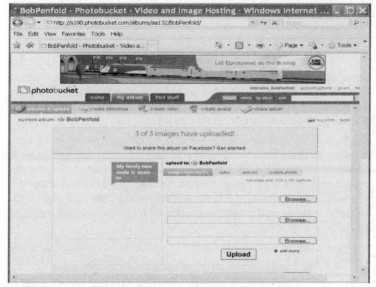

Fig.9.17 The upload has been completed successfully

Fig.9.18 A thumbnail is shown for each image file

and a valid Email address (Figure 9.13). You are then ready to upload some images (Figure 9.14), and up to three images at a time can be uploaded using the default screen. However, this can be increased by operating the Add More button (Figure 9.15).

The Browse buttons are used to launch a file browser that makes it easy to locate and select the required image files. Then the Upload button is operated, and the image files will be uploaded to the server. There is the usual bargraph and status information to keep you informed about the way things are progressing (Figure 9.16). Eventually the upload process will be completed, and a message to that effect will be displayed (Figure 9.17).

It is then a matter of scrolling down to the bottom of the page to check that the images have indeed been uploaded to your album. If all is well, there should be a thumbnail (miniature) version of each image (Figure 9.18). Left-clicking on a thumbnail image results in a larger version being

Fig.9.19 The full-size version of an image can be displayed

displayed. With large images you can display the full-size version (Figure 9.19) by left-clicking the larger view. Just operate the My Album tab near the top of the window if you need to go back to the thumbnail view.

Linking

Beneath each thumbnail image there are three sets of code, and these can be used when linking images to forums, auction sites, etc. Even if you do not understand the codes, it is often possible to successfully link images to other sites, and the Help systems of forums, auction sites, etc., often provide some help in this respect. The image hosting site will often provide some help as well, and fellow users of forums and bulletin boards will usually be very willing to provide detailed help if you run into serious problems. In most cases it just requires a little experimentation to get your images linked successfully to the other website.

Further code can be generated by selecting a thumbnail image (ticking its checkbox) and operating the "Generate HTML and IMG Code" button near the bottom right-hand corner of the window. This produces a new

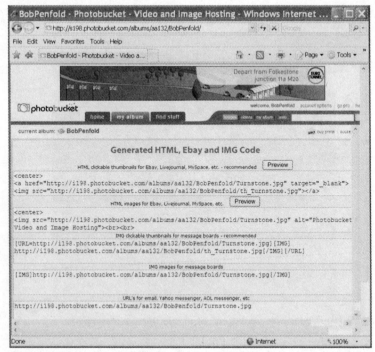

Fig.9.20 Four types of code are provided by default

screen where four types of code are shown (Figure 9.20). The first set of code is HTML that is intended to produce a clickable thumbnail image on the web page. Left-clicking the thumbnail produces a new window that displays the full-size image. This type of thing is used a great deal on auction sites, but could be used to good effect elsewhere.

The code can be checked by operating the appropriate preview button, which should generate a new window, complete with the thumbnail image (Figure 9.21). Left-clicking the thumbnail image should then produce a further window that contains the full-size image (Figure 9.22). Once again, it will probably require a little experimentation in order to get this type of thing working with real web pages, but the modest amount of effort involved should be well rewarded.

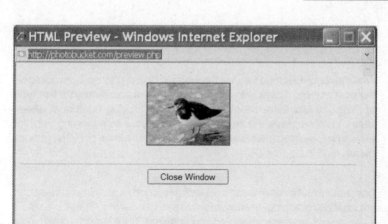

Fig.9.21 The code has successfully produced the thumbnail image

Fig.9.22 Left-clicking the thumbnail produced the full-size image

Points to remember

When swapping image files via the web, an online photo album could be the best choice. There are web publishing sites specifically for this type of thing. In fact there seems to be an ever growing number of album sites. In most cases the albums can be for your own viewing only, for viewing by selected friends and members of your family, or by the general public.

Some album sites have additional facilities, such as simple photo-editing capabilities (cropping, filtering, red-eye reduction, etc.). These are useful if you do not have any image editing software, but it is worth obtaining a good but inexpensive photo-editing program if you produce more than the occasional digital image.

Some bulletin boards, blog sites, etc., allow images to be mixed in with the text, but only if the images are stored on another website. There are several ways of going about this off-site storage problem, but the easiest method is to use one of the free hosting sites that specialise in this type of thing.

Websites that host image files for use on other websites can sometimes generate the code needed to integrate the images with popular auction sites, blog sites, etc. This is a very useful feature, especially for those who are not experienced at writing HTML code. However, it might take a little experimentation in order to get everything working perfectly.

Free image hosting sites often place a limit on the maximum picture size or file size, and a fee has to be paid in order to upload larger images. This is not usually a problem when the images are for use on other websites, since high resolutions are not normally used on web pages.

Wi-fi
networking

Sharing

A huge advantage of using a broadband Internet connection is that it makes it easy to share the connection amongst several PCs. Rather than using a USB modem to connect the main PC to the Internet, it is connected via an Ethernet network port to a combined router and broadband modem. Typically, at least three more PCs can be connected to the router/modem, with each PC effectively having its own Internet connection.

Of course, the bandwidth of the Internet connection is shared between the computers in the system, but the speed of a broadband connection is such that each user can surf the Internet in the normal way, probably noticing no reduction in speed at all. There will only be a noticeable reduction in speed if two or more users indulge in activities that require a high bandwidth. An advantage of this method of sharing is that it enables files and printers to be shared in normal networking fashion via the router section of the modem/router. The main drawback is that getting everything connected together properly can involve the installation of a large amount of wiring. The way around this is to use wireless networking equipment.

Why wi-fi?

Although wireless networking technology has been in existence for some time, it has only gained widespread acceptance quite recently. This rise in popularity has no doubt been triggered by the substantial reductions in the prices of wireless networking equipment, or wi-fi equipment as it has become known. Some generic wi-fi adapters can now be purchased for just a few pounds. This makes wi-fi systems a practical proposition for home and small business users.

Although wireless networking is now reasonably inexpensive, it is still likely to cost somewhat more than an equivalent wired network. Is it worth the extra outlay? The obvious advantage is that it avoids the need to install any wiring. It has to be admitted that for many users this is really the only advantage of the wi-fi approach, but for most users it is a major plus point. A short lead from a computer to a router or other piece of networking equipment is not difficult to implement, particularly if the two pieces of equipment are on the same desk. No do-it-yourself skills are likely to be required.

The situation is very different when the items to be linked are on opposite sides of the room. An "off the shelf" lead is all that is needed to connect the two pieces of equipment, but keeping the lead tucked away discretely out of sight is more difficult. This is not just a matter of making things look pretty, and there is the safety aspect to consider. A lead placed where people keep tripping over is obviously unsafe, although in practice it is probably the networking equipment that is most likely to suffer. It becomes increasing difficult to keep things neat and safe as more equipment is added to the network. A certain amount of do-it-yourself ability is needed in order to install the wiring properly, but it is not too difficult to make a good job of it.

Installing the wiring becomes much more difficult when leads have to be run from one room to another. This type of thing is still within the abilities of the average handyman with an electric drill, but it is not everyone's "cup of tea". Also, it is not a practical proposition unless you are prepared to have holes for the cables drilled in the walls, floors, and ceilings. Apart from aesthetic considerations, having a house entwined with various networking cables could adversely affect its resale value. In the case of a listed building, it is unlikely that permission to install the wiring would be obtained.

It is usually possible to use ready-made cables, but this could mean having to use some standard lengths that are substantially longer than you require. You then have to hide a few metres of cable safely out of the way where no one will trip over it. The bits and pieces needed to make your own custom cables are readily available, but this is a more difficult approach. Surprisingly perhaps, making your own cables can be relatively expensive when all the costs are taken into account.

Drawbacks

Having the longer links in a network provided by wi-fi equipment has a huge advantage for most network users. Even with short links, such as from a desktop PC to a laptop or notebook PC, not having to bother with connecting cables is a major advantage. However, there are a few disadvantages to take into account when considering the wi-fi option. The obvious one is the higher cost mentioned previously, although as technology becomes cheaper this becomes a less significant drawback. At the time of writing this book the additional cost is still significant, although for slower wi-fi equipment it is becoming much less of an issue.

With any relatively new and more expensive technology it is a matter of pricing the various options and making your own subjective assessment with the prices prevailing at the time. With a typical home or small business network there will often be just one or two links that could really benefit from a wireless connection, which should help to keep the additional cost well within reason. Most laptop and notebook PCs, even at the budget end of the market, now come with a wi-fi adaptor already fitted. Again, this helps to minimise the additional costs.

The relatively slow speed of wireless systems is another potential drawback. Although a wired network has a notional speed of 10 or 100 megabits per second, in the real world any equipment you use will support the higher rate. A modern Ethernet system therefore works at 100 megabits per second and you can forget the lower rate. You will never use it. Wi-fi systems normally operate at 11 or 54 megabits per second.

In practice, even a transfer rate of 11 megabits per second could be perfectly adequate. For many users, the main point of networking a system is to share a broadband Internet connection. A standard ADSL connection operates with a download rate of 512 kilobits (0.512 megabits) per second, with an upload rate of just half that figure. Most users now have somewhat faster connections, of up to about eight megabits per second. Even allowing for inefficiencies in the systems, both types of wi-fi link can easily handle the sharing of an ADSL broadband Internet connection.

Wi-fi connections are also perfectly adequate for some types of file sharing. It is popular to use a home network to permit music files stored on one computer to be played on another PC in the system. Music files generally operate at about 64 to 256 kilobits per second, with a few operating at up to about 512k per second. This is again well within the capabilities of a wi-fi connection. Many of the videos played on PCs use a similar bit rate, but high quality video requires higher rates that could stretch a wi-fi system. This is not of significance to most home and small business users though.

The speed of a wi-fi system is likely to be sluggish when transferring large files or large numbers of files from one PC to another. In theory it is possible for a system operating at 11 megabits per second to transfer more than one megabyte of data a second, but in practice the transfer rate could be little more than half this rate. To transfer 500 megabytes of data would therefore take at least eight minutes, and could well take closer to 15 minutes. For this type of thing transfers at 54 megabits per second are preferable, enabling 500 megabytes of data to be transferred in around one and a half to three minutes. A wired network would complete the task in little more than half the time, but would still be something less than instant.

Real speeds

Although, on the face of it, a wi-fi link is more than adequate for most users, there is a "fly in the ointment" that should not be overlooked. The quoted speeds for wi-fi equipment are the highest that can be achieved, and they require quite strong signal levels. Do not be misled by the ranges quoted for wi-fi equipment, which are often something like 100 metres, and in some cases much higher figures are quoted. A usable signal may be obtained at a range as large as 100 metres, but only with clear air between the aerials. Where longer ranges are quoted, these are usually for operation at speeds well below the maximum transfer rate.

When using a wi-fi link from one room to another there will inevitably be walls, floors, ceilings, and all-manner of obstructions between the aerials. How much (or little) effect these have on the signal strength is not totally predictable, and the only way to find out is to use a "suck it and see" approach. Buildings that have large amounts of metal in their structure can be problematic, but a reasonable operating range should otherwise be obtained. A range of 10 or 20 metres is usually possible, but at longer ranges the transfer rate is likely to be significantly less than notional 11 or 54 megabits per second.

When reduced speed is obtained, results should still be adequate for sharing a broadband Internet connection, audio files, etc., but a wired network would probably be a better choice for transferring large amounts of data. An unfortunate truism is that wi-fi equipment performs the worst in situations where it would be by far the most convenient solution. With a large distance plus walls and floors between the two units to be linked, using a connecting cable is very difficult. In this situation a wi-fi link is a much easier option that avoids the awkward wiring, but getting a strong signal is likely to prove difficult. In practice it is likely that many users will be prepared to put up with reduced speed in order to avoid the inconveniences of installing wiring.

Security

Computer security has become a major issue in recent years. There seems to be a significant number of criminals continually thinking up new scams or finding ways of reworking old ones. The early viruses were produced by individuals who were really just showing off, and trying to show how clever they were. It has now become rather more sinister, with people trying to find ways of extracting money from companies or private individuals using what we now know as cyber crime. All Internet users now have to take security very seriously, but it is particularly important to the growing band of users that have a broadband connection.

You do not have to be a computer genius to see that using wi-fi links has the potential to let hackers "eavesdrop" on your network or even gain access to it. At the most basic level, anyone operating a wi-fi equipped PC within the range of your system could have free Internet access by way of your network and Internet connection. This would probably not matter a great deal if you have an uncapped broadband connection. The unwanted guest would effectively reduce the bandwidth of the Internet connection, but probably not to a significant degree.

Someone using your Internet connection could prove costly if you have capped access, where extra has to be paid if more than a certain amount is downloaded each month. Either way, are you really unconcerned about others gaining access to your network for a bit of freeloading? Most of us value our privacy and would prefer to keep the network totally closed to outsiders, even if they have no really sinister intent.

Of course, some hackers trying to enter the network might have a sinister motive. With no security measures in use, someone could potentially hack into your network and gain personal information stored on the system, or even steal passwords or other sensitive information. Unless the network is used for purely unimportant applications such as games or entertainment, it is essential to take steps to keep it secure. Even if the system is only used for trivia, you would presumably still prefer not to have strangers using your Internet connection and accessing your PC.

In some cases wi-fi equipment can be installed with no setup information at all being provided by the user. However, equipment of this type is usually installed without any of the built-in security measures being implemented. There is a temptation to simply "let well alone", and not bother with implementing the security measures. With the network working well, why risk messing up the installation? Taking this attitude is definitely a mistake though, and it is a good idea to read the instruction manuals and get everything set up properly as soon as possible. Setting up a network to make it secure is quite simple and does not take long.

Interference

The range of frequencies available for use with wi-fi networks is quite narrow, but the allocation is broad enough to permit a number of channels to be accommodated. As will be explained later, there are actually two bands available for this type of equipment, and these are at frequencies near 2.4GHz and 5GHz. At present the vast majority of wi-fi devices operate in the 2.4GHz band, and it is primarily this type of wi-fi equipment that will be covered here.

Even though there are several channels, congestion is still a potential problem. This depends on where you live, and to some extent it is a matter of luck. I live in a part of the country that has quite a high population density, but for some time my home wi-fi network failed to detect any other wi-fi networks in the vicinity. These days there are three or four other networks that can be received at good strength. Although the short range of this equipment is normally considered to be a drawback, in this context it is definitely an advantage. In fact a range of a few miles would render wi-fi networks unusable as in many areas interference from other networks would render most systems unusable.

The short operating range largely avoids this problem in most suburban and rural areas, but if you operate a wi-fi network in a town it is quite likely that you will find that you are far from alone. Switching away from the default channel should avoid any major problems with interference from other systems. As wi-fi becomes more popular it could be difficult to find a totally clear channel in heavily built-up areas, giving a more limited operating range. Also, bear in mind that having several systems nearby could reduce the range somewhat even if they are not operating on the same channel as your system.

Many wi-fi users are probably under the impression that a band has been set aside specifically for wireless networking. Unfortunately, this is not the case, and wi-fi shares the 2.4GHz band with several other types of equipment. These include such things as some cordless phone systems, baby monitors, Bluetooth devices, video senders, cordless headphones, and even microwave ovens. These devices all add to the congestion, and can potentially block some channels completely. They also add to the general noise on the band and tend to limit the maximum operating range. Again, in suburban and rural areas any problems should be minimal, but performance could be seriously compromised in some parts of towns.

Standards

Computer standards have tended to be something of a joke in the past. Standards have not only been a problem in the world of computing. The electronics industry in general has experienced problems with competing standards, which inevitably results in many people buying gadgets that soon become obsolete. In fact competing standards can ultimately kill the product, producing a situation where there are no winners and plenty of losers.

An additional problem with computer standards is that manufacturers have tended to "do their own thing" rather than rigidly adhering to agreed standards. It is difficult to understand why a manufacturer would release a product that does not strictly adhere to the rules, but this was quite common in the past. Possibly it was the result of cost cutting, or perhaps it was just poor design work that was to blame. Anyway, even something as basic as trying to get a printer to work properly with a serial or parallel port used to be very difficult. Although "off the shelf" leads were usually available, these ready-made leads often proved to be inadequate.

Fortunately, the situation has improved somewhat over the years, and wi-fi is certainly free from many of the problems associated with wired interfaces. Inevitably though, there is more than one standard to contend with. The wireless networking equipment in common use conforms to the standards laid down by the Institute of Electrical and Electronics Engineers, or the IEEE as it is more commonly called. All the wi-fi equipment falls within the 802.11 standard, but there are three versions of it in common use (802.11a, 802.11b, and 802.11g). Table 1 summarises the important differences between the three 802.11 standards.

Table 1

Standard	802.11a	802.11b	802.11g
Maximum speed	54Mbits/s	11Mbits/s	54Mbits/s
Real-world speed	20Mbits/s	4.5Mbits/s	20Mbits/s
Range (outdoors)	30 metres	120 metres	50 metres
Range (indoors)	12 metres	60 metres	20 metres
Band	5GHz	2.4GHz	2.4GHz
Users	64	32	32
Total UK channels	8	13	13
Separate channels	8	3	3
Compatibility	-	802.11g	802.11b
Wi-fi certified	Yes	Yes	Yes

The ranges quoted here are theoretical, and would probably not be obtained in practice. These are the maximum ranges at the maximum operating speed, and longer ranges can be achieved at lower speeds. Bear in mind that ranges quoted for operation outdoors assume that there is clear air between the aerials. Walls, fences, and other solid objects between the aerials, particularly if they are made from metal, will substantially reduce the range.

I tried operating a 802.11b link between two systems about 100 metres apart, hoping that there would be a sufficiently strong signal to permit one system to use the broadband Internet connection of the other. In practice the two systems remained oblivious to each other, with neither system picking up a discernible signal from the other. There were a few trees and other obstructions between the two aerials, and that was sufficient to shield each aerial from the other unit's signal. The only way to find the maximum usable operating range is to try it and see, but slightly pessimistic forecasts are usually the most accurate.

As already explained, the maximum range indoors is heavily dependent on the type and number of obstructions between the two aerials. A couple of plasterboard walls are unlikely to have much effect on the range, but a few substantial brick walls could massively reduce it. A large metal radiator in the wrong place could totally block the signal. In difficult surroundings, 802.11b equipment probably offers the greatest chance of providing usable results.

802.11a equipment has the advantage of not operating in the overused 2.4GHz band, and it also permits twice as many users per access point. However, for a home or small business network it is unlike that more than 32 users will need to use an access point. There are some drawbacks to 802.11a equipment, and probably the most important one for most potential users is that the cost is much higher than for equivalent 802.11b and 802.11g equipment.

The economics of networking are at least as capricious as those for other aspects of computing, but at the time of writing this, opting for 802.11a equipment means paying more than twice as much for the privilege. Another important factor to bear in mind is that there is relatively little 802.11a equipment available, although choice and availability should improve in due course. Because 802.11a equipment operates on a different band, it is totally incompatible with the other two standards. 802.11b and 802.11g equipment can be freely mixed, but transfers will obviously be at the lower rate if one unit in a link is of the 802.11b variety.

Note that it is possible to obtain 802.11a equipment that is compatible with the other two standards. However, this compatibility is presumably obtained by combining 802.11a and 802.11g gadgets in a single box. As one would expect, the extra hardware required tends to make these units relatively expensive. They are extremely versatile though.

Channels

On the face of it, the 802.11a standard provides fewer channels than the other two standards. In reality it is actually better, since its eight channels do not overlap, and they are genuine channels. The 13 channels of the other two systems overlap to some extent, so significant interference between units operating on adjacent channels is quite possible. In fact the channel overlap problem is so great that it is only possible to have three totally separate channels. Together with its operation on the 5GHz band, this makes 802.11a equipment a safer choice in areas where there is severe congestion.

Wi-fi Alliance

In theory, equipment manufactured to conform to one of the three IEEE standards should work perfectly with any other equipment designed to meet the same standard (or a compatible one). In reality it is never as simple as this with such complex technology, and there have been incompatibility issues in the past. In some cases the level of performance obtained was below expectations, and in extreme cases no usable link was obtained.

The Wi-fi Alliance was formed in 1999, and its purpose was to certify that wi-fi equipment fully conformed to the appropriate standard and would operate properly with any equipment of the same or a compatible standard. A certified 802.11g access point should therefore operate perfectly with any certified 802.11b or 802.11g wireless adaptor. Wi-fi certified equipment carries the Wi-fi logo, and it should also have a badge of approval (Figure 10.1). The badge shows which standard or standards the equipment is compatible with, and it also indicates whether it has protected access. In other words, it shows whether the equipment has built-in security measures to keep unauthorised users out of the system.

Is it essential to obtain equipment that has wi-fi certification? In theory it is safer to do so, but the fact that a unit lacks certification does not necessarily mean that it lacks full compatibility with the relevant standard. In fact, such equipment is likely to be perfectly usable. The wi-fi badge of approval is not as common as one might expect, and there is plenty of good quality equipment available that does not sport the wi-fi logo. On checking a mixture of "big name" and generic wi-fi units I found that very few had the badge of approval.

The cost of gaining approval has certainly deterred some manufacturers from seeking certification for their products. Added costs are obviously unwelcome when making any products, but they are particularly unhelpful when producing cheap generic devices. There is little chance of obtaining approved products if you take the cheap generic route, and customer support is often poor or nonexistent with these units. On the plus side, generic products are almost certain to be based on exactly the same chips as equivalents from the well-known companies.

For those with limited experience of dealing with computer hardware it is probably better to opt for equipment from one of the well-known manufacturers such as Netgear, Belkin, US Robotics, and 3Com. If the equipment is from a respected company and it also has certification, so much the better. If does not have certification, at least there should be a proper customer support service to get things sorted out, and you are protected by your statutory rights.

Bluetooth

There is a common misconception that Bluetooth and wi-fi equipment are the same, or that they are to some extent compatible. The confusion is perhaps understandable, since Bluetooth equipment uses the same 2.4GHz band as most wireless networking equipment, and its function is much the same. It provides a wireless link between two pieces of electronic equipment. Despite the superficial similarities, the purpose of Bluetooth is very different to that of wi-fi equipment.

Fig.10.1 A typical certification badge

Wi-fi is an extension of the Ethernet networking system, and when using wi-fi equipment you have what is essentially an Ethernet based network. A typical wi-fi network will include some wired connections using standard Ethernet ports and cables. Bluetooth is not intended for networking, although it could probably be used to provide networking. Using Bluetooth equipment in this fashion would be doing things the hard way though, and wi-fi equipment performs this task much more efficiently. Therefore, Bluetooth will not be considered further here.

Getting connected

Any computer that will be connected to a network via a wireless link must be equipped with a wi-fi adaptor of some kind. The available options depend on the type of PC, but for a desktop type the main options are a USB wireless adaptor or a PCI type. Provided a spare USB port is available, the USB option is the easier to install. Some of these units are similar in appearance to the popular USB pen drives that contain flash memory, and a few of these devices do actually combine the two functions of wi-fi adaptor and pen drive. There is normally no outward sign of an aerial with these units, as it is contained within the plastic case.

The adaptor can be plugged straight into a USB port of the PC, or connected via a USB extension lead. Using any unit of this type directly plugged into a USB port is convenient, but it leaves the device vulnerable to damage. The risks are probably greater when the device is used with a heavy desktop PC. If someone should happen to knock against the adaptor it is possible that the PC will remain in place and that the adaptor will give way. This would probably render it unusable, and repairs are usually uneconomic with low-cost units such as these adaptors.

I prefer to use a short extension cable with any small USB gadgets. In the current context this method has the added advantage of permitting the adapter to be moved slightly, which can be useful if a "blind" spot is giving problems with poor performance. Note that it is not a normal A to B USB cable that is required, but an A to A extension lead. This has the larger A type socket at one end and an A type plug at the other.

USB wi-fi adaptors are also available in the form of a small box that sits on top of the PC and connects to the USB port via a short cable. Figure 10.2 shows a neat unit of this type made by Netgear. This type of adapter is connected to the USB port via a standard A to B cable, and the rear of the unit has the smaller B type USB connector. This is the type of cable this is used with scanners, printers, and most other USB gadgets, but a suitable lead is normally supplied with the adaptor.

This style of wireless network adaptor tends to be more expensive than the type that is designed to plug straight into a USB port, but one reason for this is that many of them are 802.11g devices. The cheap "pen drive" adaptors are 802.11b devices. An advantage of the box and lead style adaptors is that, as standard, the box part can be easily repositioned in order to find the position that gives optimum results. This is a definite advantage for an adaptor that will be used with a desktop PC, but the pen drive type units are probably a better choice for use with portable PCs.

Speed

Some 802.11b adaptors have a USB 1.1 port, but they will work perfectly well with USB 2.0 ports. On the face of it, a USB 1.1 port is adequate for an 802.11b adaptor, since it operates at more or less the same maximum speed as the adaptor. In practice it is not quite as simple as that, because USB 1.1 only permits a single device to use half of the available bandwidth. This ensures that one device can not hog all the bandwidth to the detriment of the others. Unfortunately, it also means that USB 1.1 wi-fi adaptors might not operate quite as fast as expected, although any shortfall is likely to be quite small.

There is little point in using USB 1.1 for an 802.11g adaptor, because the speed of the USB port would be far too low to accommodate the transfer

Fig.10.2 This Netgear adaptor connects to the PC using an ordinary (A to B) USB cable

rates possible with the adaptor. It is possible to use an 802.11g adaptor with a USB 1.1 port if that is all that is available, but data transfers will be limited by the relative slowness of the USB port. USB 2.0 can handle bit rates well above the 54Mbits per second of the 802.11g standard. In fact USB 2.0 can handle rates of up to 480Mbits per second. An 802.11g USB adaptor should therefore be capable of operating at full speed with a USB 2.0 port.

Note that it is possible to add USB 2.0 ports to a desktop PC that is only equipped with USB 1.1 ports. It is just a matter of adding a PCI expansion

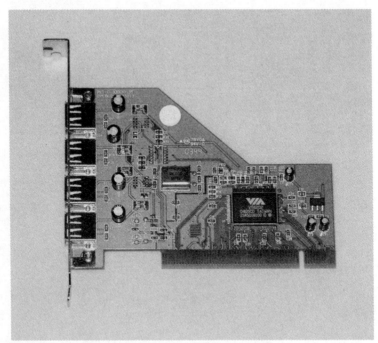

Fig.10.3 This PCI card provides four USB 2.0 ports

card that has what will typically be two or four USB 2.0 ports. The generic card shown in Figure 10.3 has four ports and cost only a few pounds. Of course, the PC must have at least one spare PCI expansion slot, but this will not be a problem with most PCs. Windows XP and Vista are designed to operate with USB 2.0 ports, but Windows ME is not. However, provided you are careful to obtain a card that is supplied with drivers for Windows ME, it should work perfectly well with this operating system.

Note that a USB wi-fi adaptor that is powered from the USB port will probably not work if it is used via a passive hub. This is due to the fact that a passive hub has to share the power from the source USB port between however many USB outputs it provides. This will usually result in too little power being available for a wi-fi adaptor. Connect the adaptor direct to the PC or via a powered USB hub.

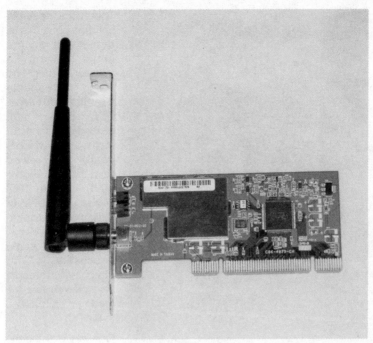

Fig.10.4 A PCI wi-fi adaptor complete with aerial

PCI adaptor

In some ways a wi-fi PCI card (Figure 10.4) is a neater solution than using any form of USB wi-fi adaptor. Apart from the aerial, everything is kept within the main housing of the PC. This avoids having to use a lead or having the adaptor protruding well out from the rear of the PC. These days most PCs have a free PCI expansion slot, but USB ports soon seem to be used up.

There are drawbacks as well though, and one of them is that the aerial is not placed in a favourable position. It is in amongst the leads at the rear of the PC. Even if you can manage to keep most of the leads away from the aerial, it will still be very close to the metal case (Figure 10.5). This situation is considerably less than ideal, and is likely to compromise results. Matters are compounded by the fact that repositioning the aerial to avoid a "blind" spot means moving the entire base unit.

There is a possible solution, but this is dependent on the aerial having a standard fitting and being detachable from the card. Most PCI adaptors do have a standard connector for the aerial, which is easily unscrewed from the card (Figure 10.6). Figure 10.7 shows a close-up of the connectors on the card and the aerial. Note that it is usually necessary to temporarily dismount the aerial so that the card can be installed in the PC.

One way of using the aerial away from the rear of the PC is to use an extension cable.

Fig.10.5 A PCI wi-fi card and a tower case in not a good combination

An alternative is to obtain a new aerial complete with cable. The second method is likely to be much more expensive, but it might be possible to obtain an aerial that has a built-in stand so that it is easily mounted on top of a PC, on a desktop, etc. Unfortunately, aerials and extension cables are less widely available than the wi-fi adaptors themselves, and they seem to be relatively expensive.

The obvious way of adding a wi-fi adaptor is to have a device that connects to a standard Ethernet port. Strangely, I have not encountered a simple adaptor that uses this method, although more complex wi-fi devices do use this method of interfacing. There is a drawback to using an Ethernet port for a wi-fi adaptor, which is that it is not possible to draw power from this type of port. This would make it necessary to have a mains adaptor to power the device, which would be less convenient than drawing power from the PC. Of course, no adaptor is needed for PCI or USB wi-fi adaptors.

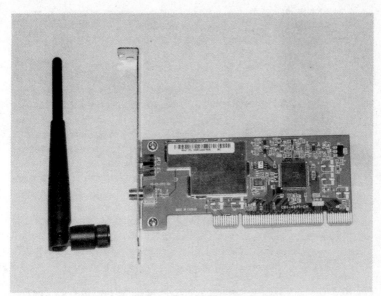

Fig.10.6 The aerial can be unscrewed from the card

Ad hoc

It is not essential to use an access point, and two wi-fi equipped PCs that can receive each other's signals can establish a network in what is called "Ad Hoc mode". This is the wi-fi equivalent of two PCs being connected together using their Ethernet ports and a crossed-over cable. The wi-fi version is actually more versatile in that it enables easy communication between any two PCs that are within range, and no cable swapping is required. However, proper networking effectively provides a simultaneous connection between every unit in the system, and is even more versatile.

Although it is not without attractions, the Ad Hoc method of networking is inferior to using an access point, and is little used in practice. If you really need nothing more than a basic wireless connection between two PCs, then two adaptors and the Ad Hoc mode will certainly do the job. You still have the option of adding an access point at a later date if you should need a more elaborate network.

Note that when installing and setting up a wi-fi adaptor it might be necessary to specify the mode of operation that you wish to use. The adaptor's control software then seeks signals from the appropriate type

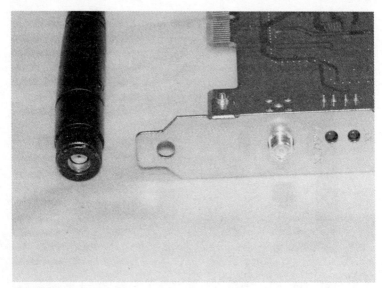

Fig.10.7 Close-up of the connections on the aerial and the PCI card

of wi-fi unit. With Ad Hoc mode selected, the software searches for signals from other wi-fi adaptors, and will only communicate with that type of unit.

The other mode is called Infrastructure mode, and it is used to implement full networking. Infrastructure mode can only be facilitated with the aid of an access point. Some wi-fi adaptors start in what is effectively Ad Hoc mode so that they can search for and list all the available wi-fi signals. By default they will probably connect to and use any access point that is found. As always, it is necessary to read the supplied documentation in order to determine the exact way in which the equipment operates.

As pointed out previously, the main advantage of using Infrastructure mode and an access point is that it enables communications between numerous devices to take place simultaneously. In effect, everything in the network is connected to everything else in the network all the time. In this respect it is the same as a wired network. With Ad Hoc working only two devices can be linked at any one time. Another advantage is that the access point can provide what is termed a "bridge". In other words, it can provide a bridge between wi-fi equipped devices and wired

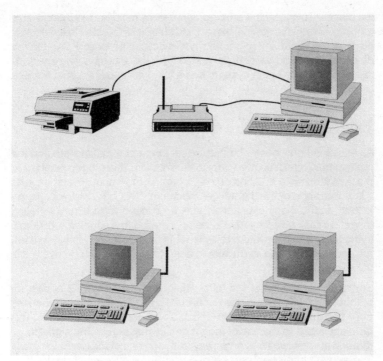

*Fig.10.8 A typical wi-fi network has one PC wired to the access point
and a printer, with the other PCs networked using wi-fi*

network devices. This is an important point, because few practical
networks are purely of the wi-fi variety.

Of course, a wi-fi network can be purely that, with everything in the system
communicating via radio links. No doubt there are many networks that
perform very well using nothing but wi-fi links. In practice though, a
totally wi-fi network is unlikely to be the best solution. With the access
point on the same desk as one of the PCs, there is little point in using a
wi-fi link between the two. A cable will do the job better and at a fraction
of the price.

A typical wi-fi network would therefore use a setup of the type shown in
Figure 10.8, with one PC wired to the access point and a printer, with the
other PCs linked via wi-fi adaptors. Apart from file sharing between the
PCs in the system, it could also be set up to give all three PCs access to

the printer. Obviously this arrangement can be modified to suit individual requirements. For example, there could be other PCs close to the access point, and a wired link might be more practical for these PCs. On the other hand, it could be inconvenient to have the access point very close to any of the PCs in the system, and a fully wi-fi network could then be used.

Extending range

As explained previously, the theoretical range of a wi-fi system and the real-world range are often very different, with the range obtained in practice tending to fall short of the theoretical maximum. In some cases it falls well short of the theoretical maximum. This does not necessarily matter, and in many situations there is no need for a large operating range. Unless a wi-fi system is being installed in a very large building, trying to stretch the system to its limits is unnecessary. However, there are gadgets available if you should need to extend the range of a link in the system.

Some of this equipment is fairly straightforward, such as aerials for outdoor use. Operating from one building to another often produces poor results even though the aerials seem to be within range. This problem is due to the use of indoor aerials that require the signal to go through at least two walls on its way from one end of the link to the other. The signal absorption can be quite high, giving a much lower than expected range.

By having both aerials outside it is often possible to have "clear air" between them, and something in the region of the full 100 metre operating range should be obtained. A significantly longer range is possible if reduced operating speed can be tolerated, but it is probably best not to take some of the claims for these aerials too seriously. For one thing, the greater the operating range, the lower the chance of having a path between the aerials that is totally clear of obstructions.

Directional

The simple aerials normally used with wi-fi networks are omnidirectional, which means that they transmit with equal strength in all directions. When receiving signals, they are equally sensitive in all directions. The omnidirectional term is not strictly accurate, because immediately above and below the aerial (which should be vertical) there are two "blind" spots. With most types of radio communication this is unimportant, but it should be borne in mind when installing a wi-fi network on two or more floors of a building.

In addition to the "blind" spots, signal strengths tend to be reduced when an aerial is higher or lower than the aerial at the access point. The range obtained on floors above and below the access point could therefore be less than the range obtained on the same floor. In fact this is almost certain to occur, because there is the added signal absorption of the floors and ceilings when a link is established between different levels of a building. These factors almost certainly account for the disappointing results that are sometimes obtained when using wi-fi equipment in a multi-storey building.

A directional aerial gives better results in one or possibly two directions. With several pieces of equipment using a wi-fi link to the network, omnidirectional operation is essential for the access point. It has to communicate with various pieces of equipment scattered around the building. It is highly unlikely that they will be conveniently placed so that they are all in more or less the same direction relative to the access point.

The situation is different when there are only two devices to be linked. A directional aerial is then acceptable at both ends of the link. When there are more than two wi-fi units in a network, a directional aerial can normally be used for anything other than the access point. Unless Ad Hoc operation is used, all the other devices in the system communicate via the access point, and do not directly communicate with anything else in the network. They can therefore communicate with the network by way a directional aerial aimed at the access point.

We are all familiar with directional aerials. Ordinary television aerials and satellite dishes are common examples of directional aerials, and for good results they have to be aimed quite accurately at the transmitter or satellite. The point of a directional aerial is that it provides gain. In other words, using a directional aerial produces a stronger signal when transmitting. A stronger transmission in one direction is obtained by having a weaker signal radiated in other directions. Increased sensitivity is obtained when a directional aerial is used for reception, but only in one direction. The sensitivity of the aerial is lower in all other directions. The more highly directional an aerial is made, the greater the gain that can be obtained.

Using a directional aerial can significantly increase the operating range of a wi-fi system, but it also makes it more difficult to get everything set

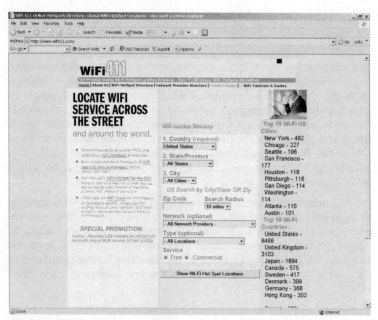

*Fig.10.9 The default is to search the USA, but the site has coverage
          that includes the UK*

up correctly and working well. Also, directional aerials are relatively
difficult to obtain and expensive. It might be necessary to search online
for a specialist supplier of wi-fi equipment in order to find something that
suits your requirements.

Try to organise the network in a way that minimises the risk of range
problems occurring. The access point should be somewhere near the
middle of the building so that it is reasonably close to all the wi-fi enabled
devices. Having the access point at one end of the building maximises
the chances of problems, especially where there will be one of more wi-
fi devices at the other end of the building.

Accelerators

The maximum speed possible using 802.11 wi-fi equipment is the 54
Mbits per second provided by 802.11g equipment, but you might find
equipment advertised as offering something more like 100 or 108Mbits
per second. The increase in speed is obtained by using some form of

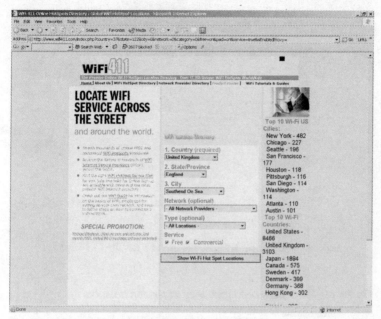

Fig.10.10 I searched for hotspots in the Southend on Sea area

accelerator technology, which seems to mean changes to the way in which the packets of data are encoded and decoded. The radio side of things just uses standard 802.11 technology. Faster versions of 802.11b and 802.11g devices are produced. Note that in order to take advantage of the speed increase it is necessary for all the wi-fi devices in the network to use the same accelerator technology.

Hotspots

If you have a wi-fi enables laptop or notebook PC, it is often possible to access the Internet while on the move using what are called "wireless hotspots". These offer Internet access in numerous locations around the world, with many towns and cities in the UK now having large numbers of these hotspots. A wireless hotspot is a wireless access point that connects to some form of Internet service. This will typically be a high-speed ADSL broadband connection, but it could be some other type of broadband service. It should certainly be something much faster than an ordinary dialup connection, but bear in mind that you might have to

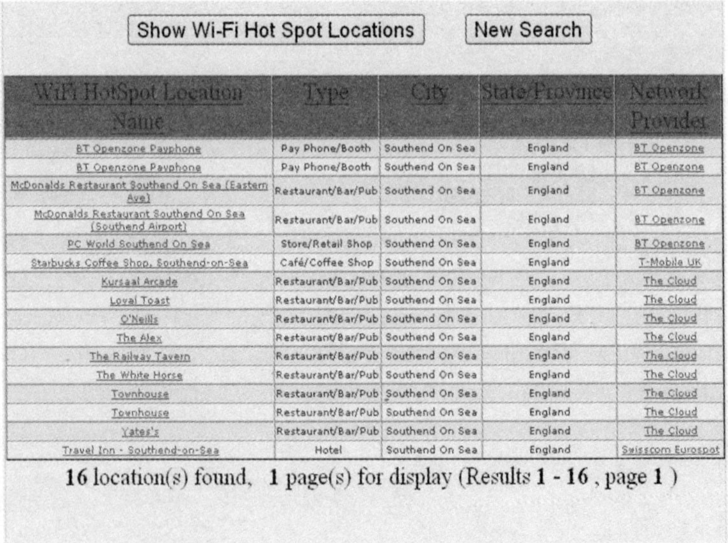

Show Wi-Fi Hot Spot Locations		New Search		

WiFi HotSpot Location Name	Type	City	State/Province	Network Provider
BT Openzone Payphone	Pay Phone/Booth	Southend On Sea	England	BT Openzone
BT Openzone Payphone	Pay Phone/Booth	Southend On Sea	England	BT Openzone
McDonalds Restaurant Southend On Sea (Eastern Ave)	Restaurant/Bar/Pub	Southend On Sea	England	BT Openzone
McDonalds Restaurant Southend On Sea (Southend Airport)	Restaurant/Bar/Pub	Southend On Sea	England	BT Openzone
PC World Southend On Sea	Store/Retail Shop	Southend On Sea	England	BT Openzone
Starbucks Coffee Shop, Southend-on-Sea	Café/Coffee Shop	Southend On Sea	England	T-Mobile UK
Kursaal Arcade	Restaurant/Bar/Pub	Southend On Sea	England	The Cloud
Loyal Toast	Restaurant/Bar/Pub	Southend On Sea	England	The Cloud
O'Neills	Restaurant/Bar/Pub	Southend On Sea	England	The Cloud
The Alex	Restaurant/Bar/Pub	Southend On Sea	England	The Cloud
The Railway Tavern	Restaurant/Bar/Pub	Southend On Sea	England	The Cloud
The White Horse	Restaurant/Bar/Pub	Southend On Sea	England	The Cloud
Townhouse	Restaurant/Bar/Pub	Southend On Sea	England	The Cloud
Townhouse	Restaurant/Bar/Pub	Southend On Sea	England	The Cloud
Yates's	Restaurant/Bar/Pub	Southend On Sea	England	The Cloud
Travel Inn - Southend-on-Sea	Hotel	Southend On Sea	England	Swisscom Eurospot

16 location(s) found, 1 page(s) for display (Results 1 - 16 , page 1)

Fig.10.11 The search produced a list of sixteen hotspots

share the service with other users, which could noticeably slow things down.

The idea is to have hotspots in restaurants, cafes, motorway service stations, hotels, trains, airports, or anywhere convenient for potential users. As one would expect, these services are not usually free, and the hourly connection rates are quite high. Even so, this method can be cost-effective for those requiring Internet access on the move. The speed of the connection is also likely to be much faster than the alternatives, such as using an ordinary telephone socket and the computer's built-in dial-up modem.

There might not always be a hotspot available, but the same is true of the alternatives such as using an ordinary modem and telephone socket. Some hotspots are provided free of charge, so you might get lucky from time to time and obtain free Internet access. Note that simply utilizing any unsecured wireless network that happens to be in range is illegal. You should only use a wireless network if you have the necessary authorisation to do so.

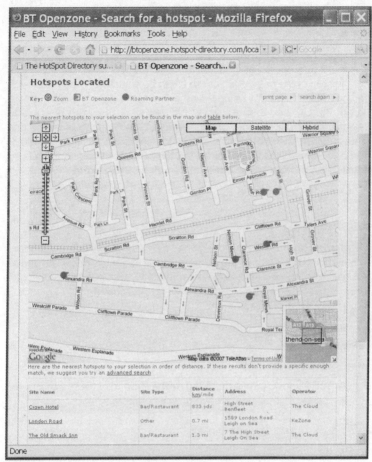

Fig.10.12 A hotspot map provided by Hotspot-hotel.com

Locating hotspots

Hotspots are aptly named, and due to their very limited area of coverage it is important to be in the right place in order to access one. Simply being in the right general area is unlikely to be good enough. The number of hotspots is increasing all the time, and at the time of writing this there a few thousand of them in the London area. Even so, it is a good idea to locate potential hotspots before setting out on a journey. There is a very useful site at this address:

www.wifi411.com

It defaults to a search of the United States (Figure 10.9), but the menu near the top of the page enables the UK to be selected. Then the search can be refined further by using the other menus to select the appropriate part of the UK, and then a town within that area. It is also possible to select a particular network provider and a type of location (hotel, bus station, etc.). The checkboxes enable the search to be limited to either free or commercial access points, but the number of free services is so small that it is probably pointless to search for them alone.

A search for any access points in Southend on Sea (Figure 10.10) produced sixteen results (Figure 10.11), with no fewer than nine being provided by The Cloud, five being part of the BT Openzone network. Most of the sites in the list are cafes or restaurants, but two are at payphones, and one is at a store owned by a well-known computer chain. The train and bus stations are conspicuously absent from the list, and as yet neither of these seem to be used much for wireless hotspots in the UK.

There are other hotspot search engines, and these two are well worth trying:

www.jiwire.com

www.hotspot-hotel.com

Figure 10.12 shows a map provided by the second of these sites, which shows the exact locations of several wi-fi hotspots.

Points to remember

The main advantage of wireless networking is the obvious one of avoiding the need to thread cables around the house or office. This is a huge advantage for a home system where unsightly cables are deemed to be unacceptable, or where adding cables is simply not allowed for some reason.

The ranges quoted for wi-fi systems have to be taken with the proverbial "pinch of salt". The quoted ranges might be achieved in practice, but typical operating ranges seem to be somewhat less than the specifications would suggest. Operation is still possible with low signal strengths, but not at anything like the full quoted transfer rate.

Inefficiencies in the system mean that data can not be transferred at the quoted rates. In practice it is likely that the actual rate will be a little under half the quoted figure. Note also that the rates are in bits per second, not bytes per second. Divide speed figures by eight in order to obtain a transfer rate in bytes per second.

There is only one standard for wi-fi equipment, which is the IEEE 802.11 standard. However, matters are complicated by having three different versions of it (802.11a, 802.11b, and 802.11g). While the 802.11a equipment has potential advantages, it relatively expensive, difficult to obtain, and is incompatible with the other two.

It is 802.11b and 802.11g equipment that are used in most home and small office wi-fi systems. The faster 802.11g equipment is compatible with the 802.11b variety, but when a link uses the two types of equipment it obviously operates at the slower rate.

The short operating range helps to avoid problems with interference due to there being too many wi-fi users in the vicinity, but it is still a potential problem in heavily built-up areas. The problem is worse with 802.11b and 802.11g equipment which has fewer non-overlapping channels, and shares the 2.4GHz band with other types of equipment.

Many wi-fi equipment manufacturers now have their devices approved by the Wi-fi Alliance, but some do not bother. It is obviously reassuring to have approved equipment in your wireless network, but gadgets from any of the large manufacturers should have full compatibility with the relevant standards. As always, cheap generic equipment is a bit more risky and often lacks worthwhile customer support.

Bluetooth is not used for true networking, and is not really an alternative to 802.11 wi-fi equipment. It can be used for something like wireless printer sharing, but in most cases it is only used to provide a link between two devices such as a notebook PC and a mobile phone. It has a relatively low maximum data transfer rate of 1 Mbits per second, but this is adequate for many tasks.

A basic wireless adaptor for a desktop PC can be in the form of a PCI expansion card or an external USB device. USB 2.0 is required in order to make full use of the speed available from an 802.11g adaptor. Most USB wi-fi adaptors will not work in conjunction with a passive USB hub.

A notebook or laptop PC can be interfaced to a basic wi-fi adaptor using a USB port, but a PC card is the more popular choice. Some other portable computing devices can be wi-fi enabled, and a common ploy is to use a special version of a Compact Flash card. Many of these wi-fi gadgets only suit a limited range of devices, so always check compatibility with your particular PDA (or whatever) before buying anything.

Most practical wi-fi networks are based on a device called an access point. This acts as a sort of control centre, with all other devices in the network communicating via the access point rather than directly. The access point often provides other facilities, such as a firewall and bridging to wired network devices. In the current context, it should also include an ADSL broadband modem.

It is possible to network devices without using an access point, and this method relies on using the Ad Hoc mode of operation. This gives only a very simple form of networking, with two devices at a time communicating directly. Although potentially useful, this mode is little used in practice.

A wi-fi equipped laptop or notebook PC can be used to access wireless hotspots at cafes, libraries, computer shops, etc. With a few exceptions, the use of wireless hotspots is not free though. The cost of access can be quite high, but the same is likely to be true of the alternatives. The download speed when using hotspots is usually quite high, and the Internet connection is typically via a high speed ADSL Internet connection.

Index